DÜRER

DÜRER

HIS LIFE AND WORK

BY

MARCEL BRION

TUDOR PUBLISHING COMPANY

NEW YORK

TRANSLATED FROM THE FRENCH
BY JAMES CLEUGH

CONTENTS

NUREMBERG SEEN FROM THE WEST. 1497.
KUNSTHALLE, BREMEN.

PORTRAIT OF A BOY

From the strokes of the silver point, handled boldly yet unsurely by the young apprentice, a strange face emerges. It is that of a boy between twelve and thirteen years old, its expression extraordinarily intent but its attention divided between the sheet of paper on which his sharp and accurate point attempts to create the likeness, a counterfeit, of his living self, and the mirror in which he sees that countenance, at once familiar and unknown to him. For the mirror reflects that self whose true appearance one can only know at chance moments of intuition; and even then one can never be wholly sure that the image is a true one, for a man looking at himself in a glass is apt to compose his features and arrange them becomingly. Thus, before this boy's eyes two separate images, both from the same source, are forming. One is framed in the mirror. The other is gradually taking shape on the paper. It traces the contours of jaw and cheek, sets the ringlets freely flowing, plants the cap firmly on the

7

head, arranges the folds of the wide-sleeved garment and actually presents, by a remarkable feat of the executant's right hand, another right hand, which does not hold a silver point, but points the index finger straight at some object we do not see.

The chief fascination of this portrait of a boy (p. 22) is due to the fact that the boy himself drew it. He may have been impelled to do so both by interest in his own personality and the desire to do something difficult. Few self-portraits had been produced in fifteenth-century Germany. Nor was it very easy to draw while watching oneself in a mirror. To reconcile the two images, both fictional since the reflection had little more reality than the paper copy of it, involved difficult technical and psychological problems. It seemed unlikely that a young jeweller's apprentice would be capable of solving them. The tendency to introspection in a boy of thirteen also appears surprising. At that age the senses and the imagination are attracted by so much in the outside world that there is little time left for observation of oneself. Fantastic dreams of the future, more-over, are so much more common that if a boy turns to the study of something so unresponsive, close at hand and objective as his own individuality, we may well find it astonishing and even somewhat abnormal. At thirteen one is prone to wish oneself a different person; or at any rate one longs, if not to be entirely different, at least to give exuberant and capricious expression to those elements of one's personality, exceptional good looks or an unusual and striking turn of mind, best calculated to flatter vanity and inspire ambition.

There was none of this here. It was no more than a perfectly straightforward and unassuming desire to know the truth which led the boy to sit down at his table, with a drawing-board on his knees and the mirror in front of him, one of those dim metallic surfaces, often of a brownish or greenish tinge, which readily reproduce the colour of grass or water. It now framed and reflected his own image. When the drawing was finished, he signed and dated it, thus con-firming the authentic, autobiographical character of a vision con-veying, he felt, the essential quality of adolescence. He wrote: 'I made this self-portrait from a mirror, in the year 1484, while I was still a child. Albrecht Dürer.' It was his first signed drawing and the

8

first of the many 'counterfeits' of himself he made throughout his life, probably more than any other artist, with the exception of Rembrandt, produced. Rembrandt's curiosity about himself may reflect a preoccupation with the flight of time, charateristic of the baroque period. It impelled the men of that age to respond intensively to transitory impressions but also to give permanent expression to endless changes of time. There seems to have been a definite purpose in the self-portraits of the Amsterdam painter, though he often placed them in a setting of theatrical props and various picturesque fanciful accessories. It is as though each time he began to study his own features in a mirror they appeared unfamiliar, foreign, so that in each case the portrait came to constitute a kind of record of a fugitive self, obstinately unresponsive to interrogation. It would then convey a sense of something unknown, beyond the reach of understanding, a pause in the relentless passage of time.

Dürer had a different outlook. His natural fidelity and honesty caused him to approach reality direct, without hesitation or deviation. Yet he tended, in dealing with his own person, to indulge in an odd vein of ostentation. He had a weakness for outlandish and splendid garments, practically amounting to disguise. He followed up every impulse of his imagination, every visitation of the 'winged spirit', as he called it. Consequently he enjoyed creating almost fictitious versions of himself or at any rate yielding to the temptations of daydreams of a personal beauty, nobility and distinction exceeding those actually possessed by the dreamer. Unable or unwilling to resist the power of his visions, he adopted and expressed those which, by emphasising or toning down certain aspects of his character and physique, transformed his appearance both in his own eyes and those of others. Like an actor, he seems to have wished to play a part, and also to have understood intuitively how studied attitudes and gestures, the whole art of stage presentation, can enhance lifelike portrayal.

But at the time of his *Self-portrait* as a boy, life, which changes one in so many ways, had not yet tempted him with the desire or the idea of himself as another person. He was only interested in his existent self that day when, at the age of thirteen and being

SELF-PORTRAIT. 1493.
LOUVRE, PARIS.

at leisure or weary of the tasks his father had set him, he took up his silver point. He did not mean to draw, this time, the outline of a monstrance or the components of a necklace. He intended to devote an intense, almost painful, effort to the faithful representation of something which had begun to appeal to him as much as or perhaps even more than his immediate surroundings, the landscapes, the items of jewellery and the faces of his studio companions, that he saw every day. That something was himself. It was his indefinable yet ever present associate, one who might prove alternately the most distracting of intruders and the best of friends. The resultant portrait foreshadows the successive generations of 'doubles', so frequent in the later literature and art of Germany, figures evocative of an atmosphere of anxiety, strain, rage and vindictiveness. The drawing, rightly understood, constitutes a landmark, not only in the life of Dürer himself but also in the whole history of German art. It may be regarded, in short, as the symptom of a kind of psychological and aesthetic revolution, illustrative of the Renaissance movement, which reached Germany late and stirred the country to its depths, carrying the seeds of the Reformation. For the ideas and sentiments pushed to their ultimate conclusion by the Reformers had ripened and spread, if they did not actually originate, under Renaissance conditions.

This *Self-portrait*, therefore, is a work of capital importance. The young Dürer, as he cast penetrating glances alternately at the mirror and his drawing-board, was in fact suggesting to German art and thought a method, seldom till then employed by Germans, by which the physical and moral features of the self might be recognised and comprehended and the elusive life of the mind detected beyond the envelope of flesh.

The frankness with which the boy delineated himself is disturbing. In this first portrait it is evident that his youthful curiosity, so ardent, eager and impetuous in every direction, had no expectation of any flattering reflection from the mirror. He was already looking, as he continued to look throughout his life, for no more than the truth. But that truth, he was determined, should be represented with the greatest possible intensity and the keenest possible discernment. His hand was not yet very expert in the rendering of living form. No doubt he had hitherto been concerned mainly with ornaments, drawn in the severe, uncompromising style required by the elder Dürer from his pupils and apprentices. The father was a trainer not of painters, but of jewellers, in other words artists who were still in a sense workmen, ideally as capable of labours on the smallest possible scale as of tasks demanding vigour and energy. Cups, necklaces of precious stones and monstrances were manufactured in the studio. Such decorative objects still retained the vivid animation, the sharply observed detail and the intricacy of the Gothic manner. Thorny stems were entwined round slim columns. Embossed goblets bulged like pumpkins. Monograms were designed for the clasps of bodices and hatpins. Fanciful treatment was encouraged. Animals from the medieval bestiaries gambolled and chased one another amid mazes of leafy boughs. Flowers bloomed in the form of garlands about the rims of chalices. Domestic creatures trotted or reclined in the forests depicted on tablecloths. Mother-of-pearl galleys put to sea on copper waves, lavishly equipped with slender oars, their silvergilt sails bending to a deceptive breeze. Fantastic nuts from distant lands were set in chased gold. The chalky substance of an ostrich egg was netted in strips of precious metal. Sea-shells from southern oceans, in which one could still hear the faint echo of the roar of surf breaking on the reefs, were surmounted by the figure of a lancer or standard-bearer.

Everything in the young Dürer's environment seemed to be alive. One need only study his *Self-portrait* to realise the fact. The objects possessed an independent life of their own, free from human control. The boy would never be one of those who enslaved them, after the brutal and capricious fashion of the majority of mankind. His features, in the drawing, are most attractive: the plump cheeks have a boyish, ingenuous grace. The wide eyes are full of passionate and touching enquiry. They protrude like those of birds of prey, which can look straight into the sun without blinking. The drawing is oddly clumsy, more so than in any other of his works. The silver point, well suited to the meticulous precision required in delineating jewellery, here traces the curve of the eyelids and the highlight of the pupil in a sharp, emphatic line. The resultant gaze has a wild character, almost suggesting hallucination. It may be due simply to the unpractised hand of the young artist. But it is also possible that he already possessed that amazing insight into the depths and peculiarities of his own character which he showed later.

The face is presented in three-quarter profile, thus giving prominence to the tender smoothness of the full cheeks and the brief, aggressive arch of the beak-like nose. Despite the traces that still remain of some softness and even formlessness in the modelling of the flesh, the nose and eyes are so drawn as to indicate a complete maturity in the subject. The boy looks self-confident, already in control of his faculties and his fate. The genius of the young artist is already guiding him, in this drawing, as he explores his own personality, towards his noblest spiritual achievements. By studying his features as if they had a separate existence, detachable, like a mask, from their owner, and by considering them with no particular sympathy or hostility, intent only upon detecting the hidden animation behind the outward forms, he had begun to understand the objectivity of phenomena.

In one of the top corners of the sheet the boy had written, 'I made my self-portrait...' He had taken possession of the image on the paper, recognising it as his property and stating it to be so. For it was his very own face, a gift from its creator, a personal possession of the boy named Albrecht Dürer and received by him for the second time as a creation, not on this occasion by God but by the artist himself. The assertion in this case has a peculiar eloquence. The expression 'I have made this image of myself' meant 'I only know myself to the extent that I personally create myself at each of the moments of my life. I know myself as a physical and moral being, a three-dimensional individual occupying a certain part of the universe, endowed by the senses with power to control the whole of my environment by the use of my hands and the rights which my genius confers. I only know myself to the extent that I see myself. I only possess myself to the extent that I myself enter upon permanent relations, friendly or hostile, uneasy or intimate, with the objects surrounding me. I am both for myself and in myself an

13

object. I am both he who knows and he who is known. I am obviously part of the universe, confined to the range of a child's vision, bounded by these contours marked in silver-point, yet at the same time infinite, stretching to unknown distances in the depths of my being.'

The boy was not studying himself, in this drawing, as one studies a stranger. The hawk's eye, the falcon's beak of a nose, amused him. They attracted the curiosity of the young artist in him. He examined himself coolly, but not without a certain sympathy. He perceived that his outward person corresponded with the traits of his mentality, which his feelings and his intellect helped him to understand. He was already familiar with himself as an individual and not surprised at the peculiarities of the face which he knew conformed with a personality known to himself alone.

Albrecht was the third son of his father. He had been named Albrecht in accordance with a long-standing family tradition, of which he was the third representative so far as has been ascertained. But Albrecht III soon became simply Albrecht Dürer. For posterity took little interest in his older namesakes. The glory that might have been theirs had been appropriated in its entirety by their descendant. His ancestors had been obscure artisans, cattlemen and labourers in Hungary. But he writes his signature, in full, with the assurance of a man of rank. His name, like the outline and modelling of his features, was very much his own. He alone had the duty to render it famous. Dürer's *Self-portraits* are many and diverse. The drawing at Erlangen (p. 29) shows him as a lad, with a nervous, worried expression. In the Lehmann sketch (p. 32) he is a young man tentatively seeking, in hand and face, the proofs of a reconciliation or the admission of an internal conflict. The youth with thistles (p. 10), at the Louvre, has an almost feminine grace. The powerful Teutonic objectivity of the Prado *Self-portrait* (p. 145), as a young man, is touched with Italian melancholy. The bearded figure at Munich (p. 213), with hair falling to the shoulders, looks for the first time straight at the spectator with a weighty and obstinate question in the troubled eyes. The Weimar 'man of sorrows' is represented, like the Bremen portrait, nude and unashamed, in a mood, apparently,

DÜRER'S FATHER. 1490.
UFFIZI, FLORENCE.

of embittered detachment. Probably this portrait was designed for his doctor in the hope of identifying the reason for his endless internal maladies. If all these productions could be placed one above the other in transparent layers, their varied aspects could all be related wihout difficulty to the Albertina *Self-portrait* as as boy, in which the jeweller's apprentice pursued his researches beyond the study of precious metals and accurately proportioned forms into the hidden flux of existence.

The origin of the Dürer family, settled in Nuremberg at this time, can be traced in the Albertina drawing. The exotic type of the eyes, puckered like those of Mongols and approaching the temples, the high cheek-bones characteristic of the Slav and the Magyar, support the statement that the Dürers were of Hungarian extraction. They bore the name, when they reached Germany, of Ajtos, from that of their native village. A restless member of the clan called Anthony had left the farm to seek his fortune in the neighbouring town. His three sons, in their turn, afterwards went abroad. The eldest of them had no taste for manual labour. He entered a seminary, learned Latin and became a priest. The second son, Laszlo, joined a harness-maker's establishment and stayed there for the rest of his life. The youngest, Albrecht, turned jeweller. He had a son, also named Albrecht, who settled at Nuremberg in 1455, after prolonged travels in Europe, to follow the trade he had learnt from his father. He served his apprenticeship in the workshop of Hieronymus Holfer, became a Master Goldsmith and, as often happened in those days, married, in 1467, his master's daughter Barbara, by whom he had eighteen children. He called his third boy, who was not only destined to render his family illustrious but to become the 'father' of German painting, by the traditional family name of Albrecht.

The appellation *ajtos,* which means 'door' in Hungarian, had been changed, during the family's wanderings from Hungary into Germany, to Dürer, the sound of which resembles that of the German word for a door, *Tür.* For this reason the signboard of their workshop represented an open door. Such a door, with its two folding leaves thrown wide, was later introduced by the great Dürer into his armorial bearings.

Holfer's studio, thanks to the talent and industry of his most promising pupil, soon came to be one of the most renowned in Nuremberg. Albrecht the elder was a serious, skilled and hard worker. He was also somewhat taciturn and solemn. His famous son wrote later, in the 'journal' which constitutes a sort of autobiography, 'My father suffered much and toiled painfully all his life, for he had no resources other than the proceeds of his trade from which to support himself and his wife and family. He led an honest, God-fearing life. His character was gentle and patient. He was friendly towards all and full of gratitude to his Maker. He cared little for society and nothing for worldly amusements. A man of very few words and deeply pious, he paid great attention to the religious education of his children. His most earnest hope was that the high principles he instilled into their minds would render them ever more worthy of Divine protection and the sympathy of mankind. He told us every day that we must love God and be honourable in our dealings with our neighbours.'

The elder Dürer, while on his travels in Europe, had worked for a considerable time among the artists of the Netherlands. From Flanders he had returned full of the most devoted attachment to Jan van Eyck and Rogier van der Weyden. He learned some of their technical devices. The fact that his son used a silver point for his *Self-portrait* is significant in this connection. Silver point, as Professor Panofsky very rightly observes, 'requires an exceptional degree of confidence, accuracy and sensitive feeling for its successful handling'. It was in regular use by Netherlands painters at this time, while pen and ink were still being employed for portraits in Franconia (south-western Germany). The young Dürer had been familiarised at an early age, in his father's workshop, with the subtle, delicate style of Flemish art and its subordination of the sense of form to warmth of sentiment. He had been taught to appreciate at the same time the brilliant, glowing colour of the Flanders school, the modesty and reserve with which an intimate atmosphere was conveyed and the discreet, refined treatment accorded to its very realism. By comparison, the German artists seemed crude, heavy-handed, almost coarse.

DÜRER'S FATHER. 1497.
NATIONAL GALLERY, LONDON.

Although he had thus been brought up to admire the Flemings and to adapt, as far as possible, their typical style and sensibility to the technique and aesthetic principles of the jeweller's craft, it was not until the last years of Dürer's life that he visited the country where his father declared that he himself had learned his most useful lessons.

In 1490, only six years after the *Self-portrait* in silver point, executed with such passionate curiosity by Dürer as a boy, he produced a study of his father (p. 15). The features are represented as calm and serious, with a suggestion both of innocence and of disquiet in the eyes, which seem to be confronting remote and mysterious metaphysical problems. The sitter wears his best clothes and is telling the beads of a rosary. He looks more like an ecclesiastic, a man accustomed to meditation and contemplation, than a workman. This portrait, painted by Dürer at the age of eighteen, is evidence of an astonishing depth of psychological insight in the young artist, together with a powerful and disciplined plastic sense and a tender filial affection which invests the solidly moulded countenance of the jeweller with a halo of benevolence and serenity. The design is simple and the treatment broad and fluent. The picture differs strikingly from the father's own *Self-portrait* in silver point (p. 23), formerly attributed to his son, but notably archaic as compared with the young Albrecht's work of the same period. The father's manner is here awkward and strained, the technique of expression clumsy, thoroughly medieval. The elaboration of detail, the statuette of St George held by the artist and still more the meticulous handling of the drapery, the overworked calligraphy of the hair and the ill-adjusted balance of the facial planes are characteristic of an older fashion. By 1486, when this portrait was executed, the son had left such methods far behind him. Even in his *Self-portrait* of 1484 the freedom of the design and its direct expression reveal, by comparison, the frigidity, diffidence and artificiality of the father's work.

The vicissitudes of the old jeweller's career, the difficulties involved in the support and education of his eighteen children, left their mark upon his pacific features. Gradually, as the moment approached when he would meet face to face the God whom he had adored and served throughout his life, a look of anxiety and suffering, of almost tragic distress, came into his eyes. The mouth grew hard and bitter; the shrunken flesh of the neck disclosed the sinews. The years had not been kind to the old craftsman, but he had accumulated enough wealth to occupy a fine house, not far from the ramparts, near the quarter inhabited by the artists, scholars and printers of the city. The Dürers' dwelling belonged to a prominent member of the community, Johann Pirckheimer, whose son was to become the young Albrecht's best friend. The elder Dürer took an interest in literature and science. He frequented learned circles in which the talk was in Latin and also the meetings at which the Mastersingers displayed their talents. He had become friendly, too, with Anthony Koburger, the publisher of prints and books, who employed over a hundred workmen at his forty presses.

Conspicuous as the mild and thoughtful cast of the elder Dürer's features had been at the time of the 1490 portait, the keen eye of his son, seven years later, detected alarming changes in them (p. 18). The aged craftsman had no more than five years to live. The stunned look in his eyes seemed already to foresee his own death. They no longer scrutinised those distant, mystic visions, alternately hiding and manifesting the Divine essence, as when gleams of sunlight appear and vanish among fast-moving, stormy clouds. The impatient, overwrought, almost haggard intensity of the father's questioning gaze was directed upon those about him as if they could solve the urgent problems to which his own set lips had no answer. The wisps of dishevelled hair escaping from the dark cloth of his cap stirred in the tempest of his agitation. The flesh of his cheeks hung in great, flaccid folds. His hands, concealed in the long sleeves of his robe, could not now be thought of as manipulating the implements of his trade or the instruments of prayer. Their inactivity must have been a grief to him. His opinion of his son's art is not known. He may have appreciated the talents of the young man of twenty-five, still spellbound by what he had seen in his first travels and now in possession of a technique far surpassing those of the masters of south-west Germany whose teaching his father had recommended. On the other hand the elder Dürer, who appears, in the portrait painted by his son, to direct an almost hostile glance at the artist, may have simply regretted that the boy had entered upon a restless career, of uncertain prospects, instead of carrying on the family tradition and producing cups, jewels and ornamental weapons for the customers of the studio, among whom the father could point with pride to princes, bishops, abbots and the Emperor Frederick III himself, who had entrusted the establishment with the decoration of his armour.

According to the 'journal', 'In the year 1486 after the birth of Christ, on St Andrew's Day, my father promised to apprentice me to Wolgemut.' The boy was then fourteen. By that time his gifts as a painter were conspicuous enough for the father to keep his word by taking him personally to the master considered best qualified to develop his talents and help him to enlarge his range.

The modern traveller regards Nuremberg as a medieval city. But in point of fact its surviving monuments nearly all belong to the Renaissance period. The German Renaissance, however, retained so many medieval features as to confuse the student who does not realise that each country adapted the characteristics of that movement to its own time-honoured conventions and unalterable national peculiarities, rooted in its own soil and blood. In 1486, the year in which the young Dürer first began the free exercise of his chosen profession, the inhabitants of Nuremberg took pride in the 'modern' aspect of their city. It did not, however, in the least resemble that of contemporary Italian towns, which had already themselves undergone changes consequent upon the Renaissance. When Cardinal Aeneas Sylvius Piccolomini, the future Pius II, emerged from the forests of Franconia and perceived the city of Nuremberg, with its 187 towers, the massive, menacing bulk of its citadel and the gardens below the ramparts, he rhapsodised: 'What a vision! What brilliance, charm and distinction! What a Government! Is there anything lacking to make Nuremberg an ideal city? What majesty and what cheerfulness in its outward aspect! Within, how clean the streets and houses are! Is there anything more splendid than the sanctuary of St Sebald or the church of St Lorenz? Is there any grander or more mighty building than the Citadel?' The catalogue of the wonders of Nuremberg continues in the same high-

SELF-PORTRAIT AT THE AGE OF 13. 1484.
ALBERTINA, VIENNA.

22

DÜRER'S FATHER: A SELF-PORTRAIT. 1486.
ALBERTINA, VIENNA.

23

flown style, surprising in so renowned and enlightened a prelate, who had seen the most beautiful cities of Italy. He even praises the private houses of Nuremberg 'which kings might inhabit. A Scottish king would rejoice to be lodged in such luxury as any ordinary middle-class citizen of Nuremberg can afford.' The cardinal was to express even greater amazement at the splendid tournaments organised in his honour, where the city merchants jousted against one another just like the chivalry of former days. When he enquired the names of those who wore such magnificent suits of armour, he was told that they were members of the Imhoff, Tucher, Tromer, Herdegen and Holzschuher families, all bankers, industrialists or traders.

The city was thoroughly democratic in the sense that each of its occupants possessed the same rights and felt bound to perform the same duties as his neighbour. No ostentatious, arrogant and provocative display of wealth occurred. Though much pomp prevailed in daily life, it was all in good taste. No one thought any the less of a scholar for being a good craftsman. No one considered a labourer presumptuous or fanciful if he wrote poetry.

Yet throughout Germany, as it happened, the fruits of the Renaissance were not all enjoyed in equal measure. Scientific and literary novelties were welcomed and absorbed more rapidly than those in the artistic sphere. There were many humanists at Nuremberg. Schedel collected pictures and drawings, preferably copied from the antique. The poet Conrad Celtis was later crowned by the Emperor, in the same way as Petrarch had been crowned at the Capitol in Rome. Astronomy was represented by Bernhardt Walter, cosmography by Regiomontanus. The navigator Martin Behaim discovered new oceanic routes and mapped previously unknown territories. Pirckheimer, who aspired to the fame of the Medici, collected rarities, including Greek and Roman coins. But while general education and learning achieved almost the same level as in Italy, German art itself still remained Gothic in style.

This situation is easily explained. In Italy the Renaissance was a native phenomenon, with actual roots in Italian tradition and Italian soil. The movement developed, so to speak, biologically, like

A QUARRY.
KUNSTHALLE, BREMEN.

a living growth. In Germany, on the contrary, the new ideas astonished and disturbed the inhabitants, whose thoughts and feelings were deeply Gothic in character. The Germans, therefore, had to make an effort before they could assimilate the concepts and fashions imported from Italy. There they had been the natural and direct consequence of national development. But in Germany they arrived, as it were, by chance, administering a kind of shock introducing something essentially foreign which could only be thoroughly digested slowly and painfully.

The extreme rapidity with which humanism spread was due to its conveyance in books, the diffusion of which was considerably augmented by printing. The literary Renaissance only needed to find a favourable market to ensure its acceptance and adoption. A substantial number of scholars in Germany had some knowledge of ancient authors. But the new art could not be appreciated and taken up without a profound and complete change in the individual's outlook upon and reaction to life. His aesthetic responses, his taste and also his bodily senses were involved in this transformation. In such directions Renaissance art, thought it might appeal to a few connoisseurs, did not correspond at all with the trend of thought on the subject in fifteenth-century Germany. The rays of Italian enlightenment, powerful as they were, were dulled and dispersed on reaching that country, of which medieval art was the complete and exact expression. In Dürer himself a dramatic conflict arose between his sincere love of the new ideas and what almost amounted to a congenital incapacity to introduce them into his work. Until he visited Italy he had never seen a production of the antique world. He only knew such things through drawings and engravings. It was long before Germany as a whole came into direct contact with the art of Antiquity. Consequently, the country could not absorb the Renaissance in the sense of becoming physically and emotionally aware of it. The new movement could only be assimilated through the interpreting medium of the intellect, as an abstract lesson to be learned, as it were, in the classroom, not as a concrete experience to be gained by the exercise of all the faculties of mankind.

At the time when Dürer began his apprenticeship under Wolgemut the 'light of the Renaissance' had not yet penetrated to the studios of Franconia. More exactly, he found there, not the Renaissance style itself, but a species of evolving Gothic art, somewhat restless, and struggling to free itself from the older conventions in order to develop a method of expression related to the new direction being taken by humanist thought. This delayed action of 'plastic' as compared with 'intellectual' response is not confined to the history of the German Renaissance. It was a general feature of the period, more or less common to all the regions of Europe. The tendency accounts for the different rates at which general education and artistic progress move and the resultant lack of coordination between them. While the Italian developed naturally, without effort, into a 'man of the Renaissance', the German 'medieval man' had to make profound and radical modifications in his mentality in order to enter the former category. He never, in fact, reached it. After a brief interval during which Renaissance influence worked upon and expanded medieval practice so as to effect its evolution into the Baroque style, it was the latter alone which brought to full maturity the aesthetic principles, sensibility and technique of the German artist. His Renaissance characteristics had never been anything but superficial and nominal.

DAWN OF THE GERMAN RENAISSANCE

The piety of the masses and the growing prosperity of the middle classes had for some time been increasing the number of large altarpieces presented to parish churches by local merchants and bankers. These pictures were dedicated to the patron saints of the donors, who were proud of having their names associated with the gift. Imposing architectural frames of painted and gilded wood, together with statues and carvings in low relief, accompanied these works, specifically regional in their pregnant and idiosyncratic style. The painters responsible had often been trained in Bohemia, Italy or the Netherlands, where their talents had developed under the influence of foreign techniques and ideas. But the forceful flavour

COVERED BRIDGE AT NUREMBERG.
ALBERTINA, VIENNA.

of their separate personalities, their rude, earthy simplicity, redolent of their native soil, remained unaffected by their schooling. They retained their characteristic medieval severity, stiff and puritanical, fearful of any display of sensuality, awkward in the expression of feeling and ill at ease with the representation of strong emotion.

Their art, essentially religious in both form and content, never shed a type of austerity derived from both monastic and domestic sources. The terms of reference prescribed by the donors left the artist no room for the reflection of his personal ideals, theories or affections. He confined himself to illustrating, with that fidelity to appearances typical of the patience and devotion of a good craftsman, traditional episodes from sacred history and the Golden Legend. Since these stories did not appeal greatly to his imagination, unless they involved a swirling flight of angels or demons, he applied his talents, with relish, to the naturalistic depiction of persons and things. He regarded no object, however common or banal, as unworthy of inclusion or of the pleasure he took in representing it. The tenderness of his mysticism did not recoil from the delineation of ludicrous or hackneyed detail. On the contrary the association of

SELF-PORTRAIT. About 1492.
UNIVERSITY LIBRARY, ERLANGEN.

the supernatural and the familiar in both early painting and the books and conversation of contemporary mystics proves that the eccentric trivialities in these works, as well as their most lofty aspirations and ardent spiritual exaltation, engaged the whole attention of their authors.

The altarpiece was often, in almost the same way as a cathedral, the result of collaboration: the whole staff of a studio, sculptors as well as painters, worked on it. Such productions were, above all, of a thoroughly popular character. For the mobility of their wings ensured their participation in every aspect of civic life, from joyful festivities to sorrowful days of mourning. Each wing was opened on the appropriate occasion, so as to arouse in the congregation the emotions suitable to the date being celebrated. But the full display of all the colourful panels was reserved for the most majestic ecclesiastical ceremonies of the year. The rarity of such opportunities itself lent a certain mystery to the aspect of the winged altarpiece. Its wonders were seldom seen in their entire extent, whereas the whole of an Italian fresco remained permanently on view to any visitor. This reserved, discreet, slightly intimidating character of the triptych is characteristic of the medieval mind; people passed their lives for the most part within their own souls, as well as within their houses.

It was long before German painting freed itself from the influence of illumination and manuscript illustration. Until the fourteenth century the altarpiece was no more than an enlarged example of such work, didactic rather than decorative in intention. The masters of Hamburg and of Soest, the Thuringian and Saxon primitives, the forerunners of Lochner's delicate refinement, retain the stiffness of the earlier manner and a childish diffidence in the expression of form and feeling. The religious impulse which lay at the root of all medieval life still controlled the outlook of these artists upon the world and their methods of representing it. They were the product of centuries of unsophisticated adoration, when men looked heavenwards for glimpses of angelic beauty and longed for the weightless freedom of spirits unencumbered by the dross of matter. The plastic sense, in the circumstances, could not escape from the demands of piety. While the artists continued to delight in their ordinary mundane surroundings, they were at the same time detached from them by attraction towards a world of transparent, ethereal beings, liberated from the tyranny of the flesh by devoting all its mortal ardours to the love of God.

The universe of the fourteenth-century painters thus remained unreal. The evanescent figures they depicted, poised upon jagged peaks, allow only the vaguest suggestion of flesh, light as a breath, to appear through their garments. They move with the brittle grace of marionettes and seem wrought of spun glass. Broad-winged angels traverse, like a flight of swallows in spring, the skies of the Westphalian primitives. Only angels, it seems, could breathe so rarefied an air. The saints who accompany them through these crystalline spaces have left behind for ever the dark and cumbersome appurtenances of the common, sensual earth.

It was a dream-world, evoked in the ecstasy of prayer or the speculations of a leisured hour, devoted to the contemplation of the supernatural. In the works of Meister Francke or Meister Bertram the awkward gestures of childish, diffident little figures against red or blue backgrounds suggest a region beyond that of real life, a realm in which the soul may be mirrored in the illusory prison of the body. Such artists, still in the grip of the rigid Byzantine convention, shrank from investigation of the impassioned and restless convolutions of their actual environment. They were absorbed in their dream-images. The taste for naturalism, arising from sheer delight in the recognition and representation of appearances, only began to be exercised in the productions of the Flemish masters. It gradually undermined the hieratic and supernatural conceptions which had for so long confined German painting to the enchanted, almost impenetrable forest of a Sleeping Beauty. The stylised grandeur and austerity of the Bohemian painters whom the Emperors summoned to their Courts, with its tendency to frigid splendour in decoration and its monumental spirituality, eventually gave place to the realism which invaded the world of German art, as with the shock of a revelation, about the year 1400. A sudden and powerful impulse towards a naturalism simultaneously ardent, tender, delicate,

SELF-PORTRAIT. About 1493.
LEHMANN COLLECTION, NEW YORK.

clumsy and forced, came to characterise contemporary painting in Cologne, Swabia and the Tyrol.

The graceful unreality of the Hanseatic style at Hamburg soon followed the commercial and political importance of the Hanseatic League into obscurity. Conrad de Soest helped to bring about the radical changes in the Westphalian manner which culminated in the work of the Master of Liesborn. The Rhineland painters introduced an attractive and domestic type of religiosity, an atmosphere of contented pacificism, puerile lack of restraint and naive sensuality. The new movement was led in turn by the Swiss, whose uncompromising naturalism did not exclude an emotional element, by the Swabians of Ulm, inspired by Multscher's close observation and rustic vigour of execution, and finally by the Franconian artists. The latter, so long enslaved by the Prague masters, now discovered their true vein and exploited it to the full.

When the young Dürer began his apprenticeship in Michael Wolgemut's studio, Meister Berthold, who was probably responsible for the emancipation of the Franconian school from the influence of Bohemia, already seemed old-fashioned to the new generation. For their own art was more broadly based, more sensual, more dramatic, in a word, more humane. They still produced 'religious' paintings, so far as feeling, subject-matter and destination were concerned. But these works were novel in permitting ordinary natural objects to play their part in conveying deep emotion and creating harmony between the real and imaginary forms represented. There is no doubt that the Nuremberg painters, in touch with those of Venice through the commercial channels which linked the two cities, the Queen of the Adriatic and the 'merchant's wife' of Franconia, underwent North Italian influence at the same time as they absorbed that of Prague. The Venetians were then still confined in the strait-jacket of Eastern stylisation, a sacerdotal framework in which the work of Jacobello del Fiore, for example, remains enclosed like some gorgeous insect in a chrysalis of enamel and gold. But this hieratic tendency ran counter to the instinctive delight felt by the artists of Nuremberg in the aspect of everyday objects. They preferred the Flemish manner, unrivalled in the grace with which it combined naturalistic detail and lofty feeling. Thanks to the example of such work as that of van der Weyden, the younger Nuremberg masters freed themselves from the spell of those unreal and dreamy abstractions which had restricted the visions of their elders to a kind of transparent crystal ball, peopled by the shadowy images of legend.

At last, one day in the year 1457, Hans Pleydenwurff arrived from Bamberg. He was granted citizenship, put up a signboard above his workshop and displayed paintings in its window which immediately amazed and delighted experts. He had brought to perfect fruition tendencies hitherto potential in Franconian painting, thus completing an evolution which Meister Berthold had been unable to carry to its final stage. Pleydenwurff died a year after the younger Albrecht Dürer was born. But his rugged and strenuous genius, austerely tragic in expression, with something of the bear in its ponderous, superhuman strength, was for long the model for his rivals and successors. Pleydenwurff's great altarpieces at Breslau and Cracow, produced during his prolonged visits to Silesia and Poland, were not known to Dürer at this time. But enough of his work remained at Nuremberg to attract a boy so devoted to painting. Albrecht was able to admire in it the old master's characteristic dramatic intensity and lavish colour, the latter inspired by the glowing art of Flanders. His realism in the depiction of human action and emotion arose from qualities which the apprentice recognised as basic to his own gifts, noticing the power with which form and movement were rendered, the noble pathos of an anguish driven in upon itself and thereby deepened, as well as the familiar landscapes, the towers and steeples of Nuremberg, shown in the background of the Crucifixion scenes. Pleydenwurff's masterly representation of tragedy, his dexterity in the reproduction of glistening garments or the dazzling gleam of armour, and his close observation of quiet streets of modest buildings with strollers gazing into the shop-windows, were typical of the lasting impact of his forceful and confident genius upon the whole output of the Franconian school.

The master's most promising pupil, Michael Wolgemut, had been perfected by him in a technique derived from both Flemish practice and the earlier German tradition. Sobriety and a robust sincerity were the keynotes of the methods taught by Pleydenwurff. He made no attempt to force his own aims and ideals upon the style of his disciple, contenting himself with passing on to Wolgemut a first rate instrument, to be used in whatever way the latter's character and ambitions might suggest. Michael grew up in the Bamberg painter's studio and helped in the production of his large altarpieces. When Pleydenwurff, after concluding in exemplary fashion the work for which he had been born, closed in death the eyes which had looked with so much affection upon earthly beauty, his loyal assistant finished the pictures which the master had left incomplete, married his widow and began the artistic education of his son Wilhelm, then not yet ten years old.

The clients of the deceased artist transferred their patronage to Wolgemut, who had inherited his house and his renown as well as his widow. The pupil, though very different from his master, deserved the fame which he now began to acquire and the commissions he consequently received from bishops, merchants and noblemen. No doubt they appreciated in him a degree of freedom from Flemish influence which Pleydenwurff had been unable or unwilling to achieve. Wolgemut retained the attractive chromatic brilliance of Flanders painting. But he resuscitated the severity, with its stress on line, of the earlier Franconian school. He carried Pleydenwurff's attention to naturalistic detail a stage further. Nor did he show any aversion from comic episodes or elaborately depicted anecdotes. In rendering emotion, moreover, he abandoned the gravity of his master's manner, preferring the gestures of common life, with a tendency to caricature and even facial distortion. These grimaces, however, were intended to be significant, to disclose an actual state of mind. Pleydenwurff's aristocratic distinction lost something of its refinement in Wolgemut's ruder style. But the latter had deeper roots in real life. The disciple's poetry had a shorter, more jerky rhythm. Its vigour was often crude. But its impetuous flow of mingled pure and impure, vulgar and sophisticated elements is hard to resist.

It did not occur to the young Dürer to beware of copying his master's faults. He thought only of Wolgemut's merits, and he was quite right to do so. There were few artists in Germany at the time who disposed of so extensive and efficient a technique. Its foreign components were by now fused in a pungent originality which would have strongly attracted painters even more difficult to please than the youthful apprentice who then fixed his prominent eyes, with their eagle-like stare, in a mood of timid, deferential enquiry, upon his teacher. Albrecht was more impressed by Wolgemut's art than by his appearance, striking as that was. He recorded afterwards (p. 52), in particular, its almost comic features, the huge parrot's beak of a nose, big ears, long pointed chin, protuberant underlip, the complexion of parchment, the pendulous folds of the neck. But the eyes were magnificent, their frank and bold gaze conveying both the headstrong and the visionary sides of the man's nature. The towering brow was furrowed by deep vertical wrinkles. Such was Wolgemut when Dürer painted him thirty years later. But at the time of the boy's first arrival at the studio, his new master was in the prime of life, fifty-two years old, impulsive, choleric and tyrannical, conscious of his genius and of his fame in every city where the art of painting was admired. He was also overwhelmed with orders, his work being incessantly in demand by collegiate churches and monasteries. He had several apprentices, including Hans Pleydenwurff's son, working industriously under his directions. Albrecht found himself in a new world. For hitherto he had only entered such places with diffidence, simultaneously attracted and intimidated by their secrets. But now he had become the equal and colleague of the lads who ground the colours, scrubbed the panels and heated, over a slow fire, strange compounds of resins or yolk of egg.

The wings of altarpieces at various stages of execution were scattered about the studio. Wolgemut, wearing a leather apron and a black scarf tied round his high forehead, would be carefully painting, with his great beak almost touching the panel, the abruptly emphasised planes of some bony countenance or a hand gesticulating so convulsively that one could almost hear the finger-joints crack. In his devotion to all the aspects of real life, even the most common-

DÜRER'S MOTHER. 1514.
KUPFERSTICHKABINETT, BERLIN.

place, he was never repelled, as he searched for means of expressing the truth, by the grotesque.

Dürer learned lessons in Wolgemut's studio which the jeweller's workshop could not have taught him. He undoubtedly found it necessary to drop certain habits of hand or mind or eye and forget some of his father's instructions, while remembering those of permanent value and importance for his future work. He was attending a good school. Neither Cologne nor Ulm nor Augsburg could have given him a better teacher. When he compared Wolgemut's pictures with the altarpieces of an earlier day which he had so long admired in the churches of St Lorenz and St Sebald, Dürer understood the great strides which German art had made in the hands of his present master, who had first followed and then outdistanced Pleydenwurff. The paintings in these churches, presented by prominent Nuremberg families such as the Hallers, the Tuchers and the Imhoffs, still showed traces of the mannerisms and blunders of the old school. The most recent of them were contemporary with Wolgemut's first great achievements. The earliest dated back to the first half of the century. But the differences between the styles of the two periods were enormous.

The attempts by such painters as Meister Berchthold and Caspar Hewn to render form and expression in naturalistic terms must have seemed highly novel when they were first exhibited. Yet these experiments, still tentative and awkward, amounted to little more than the muffling of squat human figures in heavy draperies, which veiled almost entirely the composition of the body beneath. For artists were reluctant to work from the nude model, regarded as suspect by the piety of the times. When they did do so, the result was sketchy and fugitive, showing little understanding of human anatomy, with its muscles, bones and joints. Nevertheless, the figures in the old Nuremberg altarpieces, so often studied by Dürer as a boy in the churches of Our Lady, St Sebald and St Lorenz, have a certain appeal. They suggest a timid and hesitant approach to life, like that of buds in spring. The painters who freed themselves from the unreal formalities and mannerisms of the early schools of Cologne, Westphalia, Saxony and Bohemia portrayed clumsy, uncouth and thick-set personages, who still seem ill at ease, as if their bodies had been newly acquired, an unfamiliar framework of twitching nerves and coursing blood. And yet they are obviously alive. They look like people met with every day. They are no longer the phantoms represented by Meister Conrad de Soest, nor the diminutive, crystalline beings evoked by Meister Bertram. They wear their flesh with an awkward air. But the sincerity and ardour of their creators in striving to attain objective truth are most evident.

It was no wonder that Dürer called Wolgemut his 'second father'. For the boy's eyes had been opened by his teacher to all the beauty of the universe. In the workshop of his actual father his horizon had been limited by the metals and ornaments he treated in so dry and meticulous a style, hard materials, to be hammered, chiselled and incised. In Wolgemut's studio he came to delight in the brilliance and tractability of the paint he spread on his palette and in the brushes he loaded with thick, fluid colours. The drawings he had made as an apprentice jeweller, professionally stiff and angular, were replaced by freer designs, suitable to the depiction of soft flesh and the massive, winding folds of drapery.

Wolgemut, though he instantly recognised the boy's intuitive artistic genius, would not at first allow him to paint as he pleased. In the interests of that very genius he subjected Dürer to the same discipline he imposed on his other pupils. They all accepted it without protest, even Wilhelm Pleydenwurff, son of the former head of the establishment. The new apprentice had everything to learn about his future trade. It was necessary for him to acquire the new knowledge slowly, till it became a part of himself, unconsciously assimilated by the creative depths of his being. Consequently, Wolgemut kept the boy busy for a long time on the elementary details with which all technical study begins. A great deal of time had to be spent by Albrecht in the preparation of panels, the smoothing of delicate layers of plaster, the mixing of colours and the cleaning of brushes before he was given permission to start actually painting. He practised the application of pumice and varnishes for months before being allowed to finish the section of a robe or a patch of blue sky. No doubt he sometimes felt impatient. He was in a great hurry to learn

VIRGIN IN MAJESTY. 1485.
KUPFERSTICHKABINETT, BERLIN.

VIEW OF ARCO. 1495.
LOUVRE, PARIS.

the most important secrets of his profession. But the rules of apprenticeship were rigorous and the various stages of progress strictly prescribed. Years passed, occupied with sketching, designing and the labours of an assistant who was little more than an ordinary workman, before Wolgemut considered his pupil proficient enough to help him paint the panel of an altarpiece. Even then he would not at first permit the restive lad to act independently. He continued to impose his own authority and superior skill. But by degrees, corresponding with his judgment of the apprentice's growing capacity and confidence, he allowed his disciple more and more freedom.

Accordingly, all the work in the studio, with its tumultuous crowd of young learners, was carefully regulated. Dürer, both as man and artist, profited greatly from the four years he spent there. The day came at last when Wolgemut only added a few touches, for little more than form's sake, since he already recognised the superiority of the young man's maturing genius to his own, to a picture completed by Albrecht, which the master then praised in the presence of all the students, embracing its author. It was merely in order to maintain the necessary prestige of a teacher that Wolgemut refrained from admitting that he regarded this pupil as a master from whom he himself ought to take lessons. His own conscience informed him that the lad he had trained now outstripped him as far as in his own day he had outstripped Pleydenwurff and the latter had formerly outstripped Meister Berchthold.

Dürer was then released from his apprenticeship, to enjoy the freedom he required for his development. Wolgemut advised him to travel, keeping his eyes open to see what painters were doing in other countries. His former master had nothing more to teach him. In the rest of Germany he would meet other masters, with different methods and different aesthetic principles. He must study their productions, compare them and decide which he preferred. On the basis of this experience he must then evolve his own style, on vigorous and original lines, owing nothing to any of the artists he had seen at work. A comparatively small town like Nuremberg could no longer satisfy the aspiration of youthful talents which had a right to acquaintance with every variety of beauty to be found in the outside world. On his return, enriched by all the knowledge thus absorbed, the narrowness of his native environment would cease to impede his career. For memory would provide him with images of all the landscapes he had contemplated and all the paintings he had studied. His own integration would be the more complete as a result of his digestion of other men's art. Knowledge must precede supreme achievement.

FIRST TRAVELS

The centres of German art at this period were mainly in the south. It was in that direction, accordingly, that the young Dürer proceeded as soon as he left Nuremberg. To go south has always been and always will be the ambition of German artists and poets. The attraction of the mild Mediterranean climate, the full enjoyment of life which can only be experienced in sunny regions, was destined eventually to bring Wolgemut's pupil to Italy. He had heard that country described by the artists and merchants of Franconia as a land of wonders. But limited aims are best to begin with. Dürer had seen few Italian pictures. He knew the works of the Venetian and Florentine masters only through drawings, copies and engravings. Their productions were utterly different from those of the German painters, who were nevertheless fascinated by them. If Dürer were to push on southward, he would reach the Alps, and beyond those snowy peaks, slopes of orange and lemon trees in flower. All Italy, with its sensuous, easy-going charm, its caressing airs and graces, would lie open to him.

The temptation had to be resisted. As an artist, moreover, Dürer was not particulary interested in too early an acquaintance with Italian practice and methods. His nature was not perhaps impetuous enough to welcome, without preliminary study, the revelation of an art so alien from his own. He would need preparation to understand, still more to assimilate, its teaching. Wolgemut had in fact recommended him to become familiar with the ideas and techniques of the various German schools before venturing south of the Alps. As the master had never been to Italy and his temperament and training were always essentially nordic, he may have added that a German painter had nothing to learn from the Italians. Dürer, though he respected the older man's judgment, had his doubts on

THREE LINDEN TREES. About 1494.
KUNSTHALLE BREMEN.

the subject. It seemed to him that an up-to-date style should be so far as possible a synthesis of the characteristics of both German and Italian painting, however antithetical they might appear to some people, especially to Franconian artists. He may even have foreseen that he himself would be privileged to combine the elements in question. For no one else in Germany during the fifteenth and sixteenth centuries possessed talents adaptable, adroit and impressionable enough to make use of all the resources of Italian practice without permitting their influence to undermine a personality strong enough to resist it.

But the time was not yet ripe for him to accomplish this task of unification. His first step was to take both his own parent's and his 'second father's' advice and tour Germany. He resolved to visit Italy at a later date, when he might be able to do so with more profit to his art. For the time being the new scenes and deeply interesting works he encountered put the matter out of his mind. On reaching Nördlingen, for instance, his first important destination, he thought of taking up residence in the city. For he was spellbound by the architecture, sculpture and painting he saw there.

Friedrich Herlin, one of the leaders of the Swabian school which had successfully combined the influence of the Netherlands with its own genuine and profound originality, was then fifty-five. It is true that his excessive devotion to the style of Rogier van der Weyden had prevented him from inaugurating a new era of German painting. But he was an artist of much charm and elegance, blending an acute sense of real life with a feeling for the monumental and a gentle piety, both borrowed from Flanders. But he lacked the dexterity and tact of the Netherlands masters. Consequently, his outlines of the human figure are rather stiff and his colour, though fresh, is somewhat crude and naive. He continued for some time to use the gold backgrounds of the primitive painters. When he substituted landscape, his enthusiasm for this novelty was tempered by timidity and caution. The young Dürer chiefly admired, in Herlin's works, the obstinate originality which preserved him from mere imitation of van der Weyden. The Swabian school was prone to perpetual oscillation between blind submission to Flemish principles and its

Entrance to a Quarry near Nuremberg. 1505.
Musée Bonnet, Bayonne.

THE HOLY FAMILY. About 1493–1494.
KUPFERSTICHKABINETT, BERLIN.

own rugged, graceless and unstudied manner. But Herlin stood for an intelligent attempt to produce a fertile mixture of the two. Dürer was a good enough critic to appreciate the elements of novelty, discretion and circumspection in Herlin's frank, unpretentious style. The latter's work, and probably also his advice, taught the younger man an important lesson. He saw how, in the case of German painting, a strongly marked and vigorous national character, full of rustic vitality, still only half conscious of its rich potentialities, might benefit from foreign importations, provided that they could be adapted, used and finally assimilated without injury to the basic nature of those who received them.

Dürer had not come into direct contact with Flemish art at Nuremberg. Its effect on Pleydenwurff had been diluted and to a great extent abolished in Wolgemut's pictures. But those of Herlin showed the way in which a foreign influence may be immediately digested and transmuted by an artist individual enough to be stimulated rather than harmed by methods borrowed from abroad. Dürer did not forget this discovery when he came to know Italy and the Italian painters. But for the moment he concentrated upon his enjoyment of the splendours of Gothic architecture at Nördlingen, reserving consideration of Herlin's valuable advice for some future time, when his own restless temperament would have suggested that he had absorbed everything Nördlingen had to offer and sent him out once more upon the road.

His stay at Nördlingen could only be in any case a preliminary experience in his investigation of the Swabian school. Herlin, a mere eclectic, had not the capacity to organise an important group of painters. The true centre of Swabian art was to be found at Ulm. In that city Dürer was enraptured by the grace and strength of the cathedral, a five-aisled basilica designed by Ulrich von Eisingen. He also met some of the famous local sculptors whose wooden figures were so lifelike that they might be thought real persons. He arrived in time to be introduced to the most illustrious of these artists, Jörg Syrlin the Elder, recently responsible for carvings of wonderful beauty in the cathedral and for three equestrian statues in the main square, instinct with the dreamy charm of medieval legend.

THE LITTLE PIECE OF TURF. About 1502.
ALBERTINA, VIENNA.

Dürer may have been still at Ulm in 1491, on the day when Jörg Syrlin was laid to his rest. He had been the most venerated of all the artists then in the city. Hans Multscher, the founder of the existing Swabian school of painters, had died more than twenty years previously. The young traveller greatly regretted that he could not profit by the counsels of that ruggedly eccentric personage, whose pictures he excitedly sought out in every church of the town.

Multscher's style and methods were by then outmoded, owing chiefly to his pupils' refinement of his harsh irony, crude humour and simple pathos. The most popular painters at Ulm were Hans

Schüchlin and his comparatively youthful stepson, Bartholomäus Zeitblom. But Multscher was still regarded as having invented and established, by his own efforts, a new movement. Dürer had very little in common with him. But his altarpieces taught Wolgemut's former apprentice a fruitful lesson, learnt from their vigour, their sobriety, their simplicity and their nobility.

All Swabian painting derived from and depended on Multscher. He was respected even by those who insisted on their freedom from his influence, Schüchlin, for instance, or Zeitblom. The latter, already a master at forty, impressed Dürer by his commanding appearance, the clarity of his intelligence, his broad style of execution and his imagination actually foreshadowing that of the Baroque period. There were so many artists in Ulm, attracted by the works in progress at the cathedral, and the commissions to be expected from a wealthy and cultivated middle class, that Dürer could not find time to visit all the churches and studios he heard of. What he most admired among the brilliant young masters and their grave instructors was their loyalty to the deep-rooted peculiarities of their school. They took from the study of Flemish art only what they could best use, its technique. German painters had developed at this period an intense devotion to the unique qualities of the native genius, its characteristic needs, aims and instinctive bias. Their bold refusal to accept artistic dictation from abroad was highly appreciated by Dürer. For it requires a good deal of courage to reject notions considered attractive in themselves and likely to be beneficial. But in the artistic field such renunciations have to be made if originality is to be preserved. German art at the time was longing for freedom from all but national traits, permanently rooted in its own blood and soil. All the schools of the day were making similar efforts, though their success and talents varied, to shake off the burden of tutelage and go their own way, without the officious assistance and oppressive guidance of others.

The Ulm group was perhaps the first to achieve such liberation. Dürer himself felt entirely at ease with Multscher's successors, even when they departed from the young traveller's own principles. He participated with keen enjoyment in the discussions among artists of his own age, in the low-ceilinged taverns, over foaming mugs of beer. These youthful enthusiasts, in common with those of all nations throughout history, were bent on rejuvenation of the art of the world. They were delighted with Dürer's drawings, with his first engravings and the small pictures he had already painted, independently of Wolgemut's directions or opinions. The visitor from Nuremberg was joyfully declared to have joined in the struggle for the emancipation of modern art and to have brought a notable daring and an uncompromising emphasis to the task.

At Constance, where official Councils of the Church were held from 1414 to 1418, German artists had already encountered the painters of Italy who accompanied the luxurious escorts of the cardinals. Dürer found the gleaming lake, in its tranquil and charming setting of green foliage, and the smooth, gracious landscape, insinuating rather than imposing, a great relief after the mountains and forests so often a feature of his journey hitherto. The Council meetings, with their festive bustle, were by then long over. Constance had returned to its status of an ordinary little town. But the citizens still talked of the splendid ceremonies, solemn processions, knightly tournaments and theological debates which had for some time imparted a transitory animation to their peaceful dwellings, which seemed naturally adapted to a life of quiet repose.

Some of the artists, however, who had come to the city with the cardinals and hoped to be given plenty of work there, found the rural environment to their taste and stayed on. Thanks to their activities and the ecclesiastical rivalry responsible for the introduction of a whirl of gaiety, magnificence and beauty into the lives of the inhabitants, the tempo of society had accelerated. People had grown more frivolous and impulsive. Sleepy provincial eyes had opened to the variety of glories presented to them by the outside world. The artificial excitement induced by the Councils had not yet quite died down. More and more patrons of art appeared among the nobility and the merchants. The efforts made to extend a fitting hospitality to illustrious visitors had refined the perceptions and culture of the citizens. Thus stimulated, they now set a higher value on the possession of works of art and their creators. The prolonged

NUREMBERG WITH THE LITTLE CHURCH OF ST JOHN.

52

About 1494. KUNSTHALLE, BREMEN.

presence, moreover, of so many churchmen from Tuscany and Rome had rendered the town largely italianate, affecting both its sentiments and its language. A certain cheerful and tolerant attitude to life, quite unprecedented in Dürer's experience, had, in fact, come into being at Constance.

He always afterwards thought of the city as the threshold of a sort of fairyland, a realm of strange, half-heard, but insistent and deeply seductive music. But its subtle and perilous charm was counteracted, for him, by the rugged and deliberately objective genius of a painter then recently dead. The Councils had attracted him to Constance and he had left there some of his finest productions. Though unassuming and still somewhat archaic in style, their tentative modernity was at the same time so unmistakable and forceful as to strike quite a new note. Lukas Moser, in the episodes from the life of St Mary Magdalen which he depicted for the collegiate church of Tiefenbronn, not only showed the most delicate and tender personal feeling, but also suggested, with exquisite ingenuity, those of the figures portrayed. He was, moreover, one of the first northern artists to give landscape vivid expression for its own sake. He was the first to study and render with consummate skill the aspects of the country with which he was familiar, the trees quivering on a sloping hillside, the distant blue of mountains and the ruffled transparency of the greenish waves lapping the shores of his beloved lake, where he did not hesitate to present Lazarus and his sisters crossing the waters in a boat. Dürer was too committed to the modern style in painting to take Moser, whom he considered over-retentive of old-fashioned methods, as a model. But the young Franconian, in the first flush of his natural impetuosity and impatient creative urge, realised that the most daring innovator of a day so long past had taught him, across fifty years, a lesson of inestimable worth.

The quiet commercial city of Basle, which had formerly prided itself only on its wealth and reputation for honest trading, had the honour of being the scene of a Council sixty years before Dürer's arrival. The celebrations had immediately given it aristocratic status. The citizens adopted the manners, customs and extravagant tastes

54

of the prelates who lodged in their houses. When it was learned that the Emperor Sigismund would himself attend the sittings of the Council, together with representatives of the noblest families in Europe, excitement rose to fever pitch. The merchants of Basle, proud of their ancient city, determined to invest it with splendours calculated to enrapture and amaze the distinguished visitors. Many painters, accordingly, left their native towns and domestic workshops to take up profitable work in Basle. Some began to paint the fronts of the houses with gay frescoes, in the Italian style, to brighten up the streets. Others produced altarpieces and separate panels which it was hoped that the ecclesiastical dignitaries would take away with them when the Council ended. Basle, in these circumstances, began to live a new life. On the conclusion of the religious services and festivals and the departure of the cardinals and counts the citizens did not abandon their newly acquired luxury and refinement. Having once started to take an interest in art, they continued to subsidise painters and adorn the churches and houses of the city.

Dürer thus found a familiar atmosphere in Basle, one he had known at Nuremberg ever since his childhood. Both places were dominated, socially and administratively, by businessmen. But the wealth of the Basle merchants was derived from the trade of the Rhine. They were engaged in agency and transport work rather than in industry, as at Nuremberg, or banking, as at Augsburg. But their enlightened learning and love of the arts rivalled those of the other two cities. Possibly even more engravings were issued at Basle than from the presses of Koberger and his Franconian colleagues. The Basle printers were persons of great importance and the books they published were prized by connoisseurs. The preference of the Italian humanists for parchment and calligraphy instead of the new invention, which enabled copies of a work to be multiplied indefinitely, was of little moment to the men of Basle. The wonders of learning and the glories of poetry could henceforth be brought, in the printed book, to every fireside. The fantastic illustrations of these productions opened up endless possibilities to the armchair traveller. The most modest home might now possess a hand-coloured woodcut of angels or a wild scene of prancing, grimacing demons.

INNSBRUCK AND THE PATSCHERKOFEL. 1494.
ALBERTINA, VIENNA.

Yet it was not only the apparatus of printing at Basle that enthralled Dürer. The Roman cardinals had inspired the citizens with a love of Italian painting. They had begun to buy, like the prelates, pictures by artists renowned at Siena, Florence and Venice. The tender, sensual charm of these works and their frequently dramatic impact appealed strongly to the young visitor, while to some extent disturbing him. The vigour of their beauty, its rhythmic and stirring qualities, deeply intrigued him. Above all, the exuberant technique, the facility of the southern painters in playing off form and colour against each other and the exquisite tact with which they unified realism and a certain dreamy splendour astonished him, arousing his impassioned curiosity, envy and desire to emulate them. They had everything, he thought, which German art, cramped by its traditions and inhibitions, still lacked. When he listened to the Basle children humming the pungent or languishing refrains of Italian ditties, picked up in former days from cardinals' pages, he longed to study not only the art but also the life of Italy. For the latter, too, he could see, had nothing in common with the narrow outlook of middle-class Nuremberg.

Hitherto all the towns he had visited had enabled him to examine closely and at length the work of one of the German masters. At Basle he discovered the remarkably individual style of Swiss painting, quite distinct from that practised on the other side of the Rhine. Conrad Witz, the most attractive and eccentric of the Swiss fifteenth-century masters, had accompanied the delegates of the Church from Constance to Basle, where he took a wife and settled permanently. He depicted there a whole series of thick-set, ironically smiling personages, which ended only with his death of the plague.

The art of this good-natured, wandering man of genius was so far in advance of his time that Dürer's amazement at it may well be imagined. The style was altogether different from anything he had found at Nördlingen, Ulm or Constance. Nor did it bear any resemblance to any of the methods taught by Wolgemut. Witz had contrived, in some extraordinary fashion, with disconcerting ease and delicacy, to upset every supposedly immutable canon of his day. It was clear that he had taken as much as suited him from the school of Flanders. Yet, as soon as he ceased his novitiate, this strange man began to paint in an absolutely unprecedented way, playing with space and light as if the weightiest of problems meant no more to him than a popular ballad. With astounding skill he laid bare the most unexpected aspect and essence of an object. It seemed as though he had listened to the secret music of every variety of life and was thus able to transfer it to his pictures. His vision of and experiments with form were so novel that he might have been using his eyes for the first time. When he set up his easel on the shores of Lake Geneva, the resulting landscape was so naturalistic as to render each detail of a pebble under water, a blade of grass shaken by the wind or the ripple of a wave against rock. But other painters had done as

THE CHILD JESUS HOLDING THE GLOBE. 1493.
ALBERTINA, VIENNA.

much. Lukas Moser, in the first 'marine' of European art, had foreshadowed what Witz was to accomplish in *The Miraculous Draught of Fishes*. But Witz saw landscape as part of human life itself. He did not regard it either as a concept or as a phenomenon which, however attractive to the observer, must remain for ever separate from his own being. On the contrary, he felt that it shared the same substance as humanity, though it was transmuted in his work by some mysterious magic of his art or feeling.

ANGEL WITH A LUTE. 1497.
KUPFERSTICHKABINETT, BERLIN.

59

Witz had the ability, in the highest degree, to portray communion between man and inanimate objects. It is for this reason that the figures he painted are themselves so entertaining in their paradoxical grace and move with so much ease in the depths of space, through a rarefied atmosphere. Dürer in comparing himself with this master, who had died more than fifty years ago, could not believe that his own work would ever be more 'modern'. He himself, for all his intuitive and patient genius, would never know, he thought, the secrets with which Witz had been familiar. He studied in detail the Basle altarpieces and that at Geneva, which he only knew from copies: they were prophetic of the art of several centuries to come. Witz taught him more essential truths about painting than he had been able to learn either at Nuremberg or in the course of his 'German tour'. The master had in fact reached a peak of achievement only accessible to those in whom absolute humility and a deep capacity for affection are united with transcendent genius. It is perhaps still too soon to expect understanding of all the mysteries and revelations contained in Witz's work. In my opinion Dürer himself never learned them all, no doubt because he did not possess all the qualities necessary for adequate and profitable comprehension.

It is highly probable, also, that he realised the impossibility of any degree of imitation of so exceptional an artist, one of those condemned to isolation by their very singularity, their peculiar virtues being the most difficult of all to pass on to others. Thus Dürer is likely to have left Basle without having penetrated the true nature of this master's performance. If Witz had been still alive, he might have been able to expound it to a young man so well fitted by nature to undergo momentous initiations of this kind. But it may well be that such convictions, instinctive rather than explicit, arise from lifelong habits of mind, not susceptible either of verbal definition or posthumous transmission to those best qualified to receive them.

Meanwhile years were passing and it might be prudent to think of returning home. Dürer's sketchbooks were accumulating and he himself, as he turned northward into Alsace, was no longer the innocent apprentice, still somewhat uncouth, who had left Wolgemut's

COURTYARD OF THE HOFBURG AT INNSBRUCK.
ALBERTINA, VIENNA.

61

studio, one fine morning, to see the world. But the young man, with so many drawings in his baggage and so many dazzling memories of the places and pictures he had seen, with so much experience of the world now, especially of the worlds of human nature and of art, had determined to visit, before going back to Franconia, two cities of which he had heard a great deal, Colmar and Strasbourg.

But he did not intend to spend much time there or make any further excursions, for his tour had already lasted too long. He did mean, however, to consult an artist with whose work he was by this time quite familiar, though he knew it rather in the form of drawings and a large number of engravings than through pictures. So far he had only been able to receive enlightenment from the works, not from the lips, of the most important masters in any of the towns he had visited. Multscher, Moser and Witz were already dead. Of the living neither Herlin nor Zeitblom nor Fries – the latter a resident of Basle whom he may have met – had provided him with any of the momentous revelations he had expected. The dead men's paintings were undoubtedly more eloquent than any spoken advice could have been. But Dürer, with his passionate interest in technique, loved to watch artists at work. He wished his teachers to illustrate their theories in practical fashion, palette in hand, on a blank panel.

He regretted not having started his investigations earlier. Death declines to make allowances for human tardiness and indolence. We supinely permit it to deprive us of those who might have been our best friends, our most essential counsellors of heart and brain, before we apply to them for what they could and should have given us. No man ever keeps up with the pace of his own life. When it comes to an end, he inevitably realises how many opportunities offered him by fortune he has lost.

Martin Schongauer died shortly before Dürer reached Colmar. No painter in Germany had been more famous. His renown was due, perhaps, as much to his combination of the tender feeling of the medieval past with Renaissance innovation, as to the brilliance and depth of his colour, the charm and warmth of his personality and the ease and grace with which it was expressed. His Swabian birth had endowed him with a taste for unaffected realism. His early

62

training in the workshop of his father, a jeweller like Dürer's, was responsible for the meticulous precision of his drawing, delicate as if traced with a steel point. He had learnt his trade under the Alsatian Caspar Isenmann, who had retained the tight, uncompromising naturalism of the primitive school. It was a basis on which the somewhat foppish refinement of the Cologne style could not flourish. Schongauer matured, accordingly, under the influence of the low-lying countryside, soothing to both sense and spirit, of Alsace. It encouraged him in a joyous and effortless abundance of creation. To this adopted land, which suited him so well, he owed the simple piety, the intent yet guarded sensuality of his art. He died while still under fifty. His whole production is filled with the light and colour of a favoured and easeful adolescence. His engravings soon became celebrated. They carried his high reputation to the most distant towns of Germany. He never visited Italy. But both his eye and his brush seemed vaguely to forecast the Florentine Madonnas he could not have studied.

Eventually Dürer reached Strasbourg, the last stage of his travels before, turning his back on the rest of the world, he took the road to Nuremberg. The rose-coloured cathedral of Strasbourg, its busy printing-works and the many engravings produced there, sold even at country fairs, had made the city one of the most active and prolific centres of art in Europe. The Swiss artists themselves came to stay there, absorbing the influence of movements converging in the town from both France and Germany.

The vigorous eclecticism of Alsace welcomed foreign currents of thought without modifying in the slightest its own inviolable and ineradicable characteristics. The region thus acted as a kind of cultural turntable in the fifteenth century. The beauty of its rural setting, the cheerful, hearty temper of its inhabitants, fundamentally serious in their union of Teutonic gravity with Latin grace, were extremely attractive to young painters, who benefited greatly from the mingling of artistic tendencies they found at this aesthetic crossroads. The youthful Dürer more than once judged that the whole enchantment of the district, its simultaneously profound and amiable qualities, could be summed up in the fine sculptures by

DÜRER'S TEACHER MICHAEL WOLGEMUT. 1516.
GERMANISCHES MUSEUM, NUREMBERG.

Nicolas Lerch at the Town Hall and the archaic, smiling figures of the Wise and Foolish Virgins adorning the porch of the cathedral. One of the most interesting of the artists whose strong personalities engaged his attention at Strasbourg was the young Hans Baldung, nicknamed 'the Green'. At eighteen he already seemed destined for a glorious future as one of the most powerful, strange and disconcerting exponents of the new art of the north. His tragic sense of life and death, imposing melancholy and the technical dash that led him into such bold tonal experiments, shocking to the traditionally minded, aroused in his Franconian contemporary a keen affection for the Alsatian lad, a colleague whose eccentric imagination and noble talents made him one of the most extraordinary personages Dürer had encountered since he began his travels. At their parting, as they embraced and promised to meet again, each of the two young men saluted the other as 'Master of German Painting'. In fact, both equally deserved the title. When they did meet later on, after each had realised his youthful ambition by producing masterpieces, they recalled with much emotion the stirring days they had passed together, as young men, under the clear, sunny sky of Alsace.

At last Dürer beheld once more the fields and gardens surrounding his native city. He had played in them as a child. They had seen the development of his early ideals. Then he entered the familiar, noisy streets and recognised many a well known face, glimpsed through the open door of a shop. The cobbles provided by a prudent municipality to prevent overflow of the muddy gutters rang to his steady stride. Now his mother, frail and worn as ever, was making a fuss of him. His father appeared, holding his rosary, which he always picked up as soon as he dropped the tools of his trade. Albrecht's boyhood friends, including fat Willibald Pirckheimer, who emerged from a house close by, were already pummelling him and he was hitting them back, just as they did when they were children. He savoured the delights of returning to a stable environment, a permanent possession, not to be relinquished the following day in the mingled excitement and distress of endless departures. He was conscious, too, of how submissive the mind is to such things. One's house, parents, friends and the articles one uses every day are regained. But they in their turn, perhaps even more, regain oneself, in the feeling experienced that the idea of escape is really a delusion and that both the people and objects in question will never let one go again.

They crowded round him to ask questions. They wanted to be told about everything he had seen and discovered. He soon became a prey to the peculiar embarrassment of returning travellers, who find it impossible to put their experiences into words and give a coherent account of the contending chaos of emotions, sensations, ideas and memories by which they are assailed. A chance phrase would set him longing, with bitter regret, to relive his recent adventures. Two personalities difficult to reconcile, the Albrecht who had set out and the Albrecht who had come back, surged within him. The rooms of his father's house seemed smaller and the ceilings lower, though in reality it was a commodious enough residence for an artist.

Worst of all was the despairing and irremediable certainty that he had not found what he had really been looking for, that his journey had been a mere attendance at the threshold of a mansion he had been unable or too timid to enter. He felt that he still lacked the revelation, the indispensable knowledge: he had only glimpsed it from afar. His journey had been too conventionally prudent, limited to Germany; he had not dared to break the circle that ended where it began. He ought to have gone further, beyond the mountains, and reached the sunny valleys sloping towards the sea.

He had certainly been much excited by his four years of wandering from town to town. But he was sure that it had been no more than his duty to undertake that further stage in his education. Something more remained. It would be a pilgrimage embarked upon for private reasons, one not considered essential for young painters in Franconia. Neither his father nor Wolgemut nor Pleydenwurff had made it.

Wolgemut was asked his opinion. Though he had never been beyond the Alps he knew that magnificent work in painting was being done there. He agreed that it would be good for a young artist to continue to enlarge the field of his technical knowledge and the range of his taste. He believed that Albrecht's personality was strong enough to resist the temptation to import nothing more from

DÜRER'S WIFE AGNES. 1494.
ALBERTINA, VIENNA.

Italy than sterile imitations of time-saving devices. He considered
therefore that the youth should be allowed to follow his ambitions,
for travel could only be of advantage to his genius.

ITALY AT LAST

This time the journey could not be leisurely. The period available
was too short to allow him to stay for as long as he pleased at any
town or village that attracted him. The insatiable appetite for every
possible experience which had sent him on his first expedition had
been well indulged during the German tour. In those days, four
years ago, he had been ready for any impression and adventure that
came his way. But now it was only Italy that he wanted to see.

Until he reached Augsburg he scarcely stopped except to eat, sleep
and visit the local church in the hope of finding old or new paintings.
He was enchanted, and tempted to delay, by the beauty of the
regions through which he passed. But he moved on inexorably
towards his goal, that city of luxurious splendour, a vague, glittering
mirage on the far borders of his imagination, of which he had heard
so many wonders. It lay scattered, in his dreams, on the shores of
the green Adriatic, as though set up on its islands by magical or
divine hands. All the same, it would be unpardonable for a young
painter to pass through the Swabian capital without pausing.
Augsburg, in fact, was one of the most celebrated and prolific
centres of German painting. Its artistic renown rivalled that of
Nuremberg, just as its merchants and bankers engaged in the most
embittered and ferocious competition with those of his native city.
But Dürer had often heard the artists of Augsburg praised, both in
his father's workshop and that of Wolgemut. An aristocracy originally of middle-class stock, but wealthy and refined, had given the
town a position in Germany comparable with that of Florence in
Italy. In both places political sovereignty, economic power and
artistic dictatorship were concentrated in the hands of traders and
men of business.

The Augsburg patricians dealt mainly in imports, transit clearance
and loans. Commercial transactions between Italy and the Low
Countries were carried on across the counters of its banks. Matters
not directed personally by the heads of such houses were of
'interest' to them in the sense that they took a percentage of practically all profits. Some of the prosperity thus acquired by the

68

exchange and transport of goods was fortunately passed on to the artists entertained by the rulers of the city, through their indulgence in luxurious tastes, pride or sincere love of beautiful objects. Such a palace as that of the Fugger family, for example, with its opulence and comfort, might almost be thought a royal residence. Its decorative magnificence was maintained by the riches of its proprietors. Its taste had been cultivated by the society of artists and the enlightenment of several generations of merchant princes.

The Fugger fortune, however, happened to be of fairly recent growth. The family carried on negotiations with the Emperor and the Pope. Many impoverished or debt-ridden noblemen depended on its support. But it was not of aristocratic origin. Nevertheless, the Fuggers were sophisticated enough to make no pretensions to gentility. They never denied their peasant ancestry, not even the first of their illustrious name to be recorded in history, the Hans Fugger who found himself too weak for labour in the fields, tried his luck as a weaver, failed to make it pay and flung himself with desperation into the stormy sea of 'business'. His gamble took place towards the end of the fourteenth century. A hundred years later the third generation of his family were communicating with monarchs on equal terms. The name of Fugger was respected in every centre of art and commerce. Fugger bills took precedence in every market. A century had been enough for the Fugger authority and prestige, based on the management of money at a time when its power was beginning to exceed that arising from other sources, to ensure the family princely rank. The energy and intelligence of its members, together with a cupidity which they knew how to combine with generosity and honesty, had made them the richest and consequently the most important men in Europe. A good reputation is proverbially worth more than a belt full of gold. The Fuggers had both. Business men found them severe and unyielding. But they showed sympathy to the poor and hospitality to artists.

They kept open house for painters. Everything was of the best, but without the characteristic ostentation of the nouveaux riches. The Fuggers knew they belonged to an exceptional family. But they did not try to compete with the nobles. The young Dürer recognised

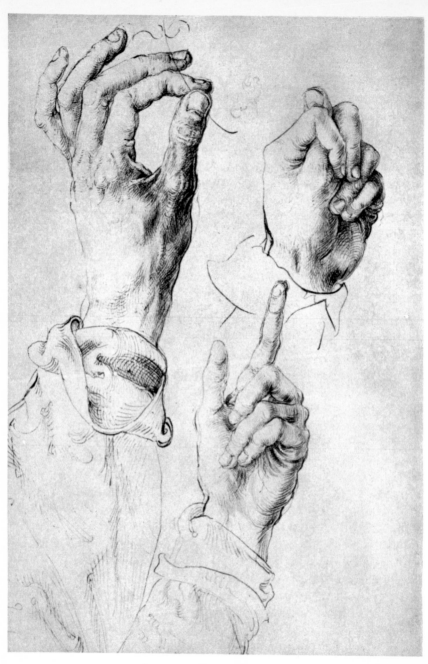

STUDY OF THREE HANDS.
ALBERTINA, VIENNA.

in their hospitality the same sort of solid comfort and splendour, adapted for use rather than ornament, which he had noticed in the households of such Franconian merchant princes as the Imhoffs and the Tuchers. The traveller was politely received and immediately asked to show his engravings and drawings. He was then made free of the society of jewellers, sculptors and painters who worked for the 'House' and attended at the Courtly routine. Old Jakob Fugger, the son of Hans, with his big nose and wary eyes, had been the real architect of the family fortunes. But he had been dead for twenty-five years. Dürer met, instead, two of his sons. Of these Ulrich, a man of distinguished manners, with refined, melancholy features and a thoughtful expression, seemed to care more for art than for business. Jakob II was called Jakob the Rich, to distinguish him from his father, as if the latter's millions could bear no comparison with those amassed by his son. Dürer, though he liked Ulrich better, could not help admiring in Jakob the Rich one of those inspiring persons who excel in all they undertake. He would undoubtedly have made as great a statesman as he was a banker if circumstances had permitted it. With his shrewd, obdurate and ironic glance, his heavy jaw, thin lips and the great nose inherited from his father, together with the latter's commercial genius, Jakob II reigned practically supreme over European trade. When monarchs found themselves short of money, they applied to Jakob. But he never made any loans unless he anticipated a good return. Yet he was generous to a fault in other directions, paying extravagant prices for pictures he liked, subsidising the best of the Augsburg artists and commissioning portraits of himself from foreign painters passing through the town.

Munificent by nature and also perhaps afraid of ignoring a promising talent, he gathered about him a swarm of young artists who had not yet acquired fame. They enjoyed his liberality in common with such celebrities as Hans Holbein and Hans Burgkmair, who held the title of 'Court Painters'. For Albrecht Dürer his acquaintance with the two latter was as important an event as his discoveries of the works of Multscher, Witz and Moser, which he had so much admired during his previous tour. At Nördlingen, Ulm, Constance, Basle and Colmar he had come to know the most vigorous and authentic aspects of German, Alsatian and Swiss art. Even the painters who had retained the influence of the Netherlands masters had emphasised their characteristically Nordic style. But at Augsburg he encountered a style of German painting that had gone to Italy for the training which had most inspired it.

It was not only in matters of business and general education that the Swabian capital maintained close relations with Venice. The artists active under the patronage of the Fuggers tended to believe that good painting hardly existed outside the frontiers of Italy and to feel that they could only learn their trade through direct tuition by the Murano masters. Consequently Dürer, by breaking his journey at Augsburg, was shortening rather than prolonging his approach to Venice. He unquestionably derived advantage from thus undergoing Italian influence at second hand, after it had been sifted and absorbed by the Swabian painters, who adjusted it to suit the German temper, ideals and limitations.

In the work of Hans Holbein, later to be called the Elder, to distinguish him from his illustrious son, Dürer noted a strong Italian flavour, more conspicuous, perhaps, in the domain of sentiment than in technique or aesthetic principle. Holbein, while he continued to adhere to the best precepts of Flemish painting, was already treating form in the manner of the Renaissance. But his eclecticism was one of time as well as space. He combined, with equal success, medieval practice and Renaissance innovation, German spirit and Italian taste. His personality, probably because of this very eclecticism, was less commanding than those of the masters Dürer had hitherto met. But his productions afforded to any young artist an excellent opportunity of acquaintance with and assimilation of the characteristics of foreign art. It was not Holbein's innate genius that was outstanding, but his ability to accept and utilise everything that he could turn to his advantage in the work of other men. He had all the merits, as well as the weaknesses, of the typical eclectic painter. The purely creative worth of his pictures, especially the great altarpiece he had just completed for the cathedral at Augsburg, deeply impressed the young Franconian by its triumphant versatility, grace and ease. But it is probable that Dürer profited even more by Holbein's effective transmission of the virtues of Flemish and Italian art. The son who was shortly to be born to the elder painter inherited the fluent brilliance of his style and would have suffered from it if he had not avoided the danger by lending his work foundations of a noble simplicity, masterful and sincere, the basis of the superb power and clarity with which he rendered truth.

Dürer also escaped the perils of the elder Holbein's consummate skill. It had simply taught him one more lesson, to be added to all he had learnt during his previous tour of Germany. He understood the precise nature of the older man's very remarkable achievement in digesting so many foreign elements, without either injury to his own creative gift, or interference with the tonic vigour of these alien importations. In any case Hans Burgkmair was at Dürer's elbow to warn him against succumbing too readily to the extremely potent influence exercised by Holbein.

Burgkmair was then only twenty-two. But he already had to his credit not only lessons from his father Thomas, a competent artist, and Schongauer, to whom he had been apprenticed at fifteen, but also the experience of travel in Italy, without which no Augsburg painter would consider himself capable of using a brush. But Burgkmair's robust and headstrong temperament had rejected a good deal of what he had seen and heard. He meant to go his own way without troubling himself much about instructions from other people, apart from a few studio tips which are always worth knowing. Dürer's interest in him was increased by the discovery that their aims were identical. They both intended to put new life into German painting by incorporating in it the best elements from abroad. Neither was satisfied by Holbein's eclecticism. Each considered that no elaboration of technique, no amount of theoretical research, would be worth anything unless inspired and coordinated by an authentic, powerful talent, aware of its own peculiarities, acting in accordance with its own temperament and determined to preserve its own nature from contamination.

Burgkmair's ideal resembled that already noticed by Dürer as represented by Hans Baldung Grien at Colmar. Both Burgkmair and Baldung had studied under Schongauer. Both had freed themselves from the meekness which can be as tyrannical a trait as the fiercest brutality. Burgkmair had declined to follow in the footsteps of any of the artists whose work he had examined. He had retained his originality both in Alsace and in Italy. Neither he nor Baldung would allow their essential characters to be weakened by the most authoritative, the most fascinating genius. Burgkmair, for all his Italian experience, declared that, though it might be necessary to have seen Venice in order to understand the latest developments in European painting, German artists must be careful not to paint like Venetians. For then they would lose their own special characteristics without being able to acquire, in any real sense, those of Venice.

Dürer did not need any such advice. Contact with the masters he had encountered on his first travels had made him proudly conscious of the force and originality of his own genius. The impression had been reinforced by the men he had met at Augsburg. His ambition was the same as Burgkmair's, but the two painters followed very different roads in their attempts to realise it. Dürer may have feared at one time that the prestige and overwhelming beauty of Venetian art might lead him astray. But now he knew that he could venture without serious risk into that enchanted city, so full of artistic genius.

After leaving Augsburg he found, in the towns where he stayed on his journey south, a new style of painting, very different from that of Swabia. The Tyrolean artists had also been influenced by those of Italy, but curiously enough it was not the grace and softness of Venetian art that had impressed them. The Italian master they most appreciated was not an insinuating Venetian, expert in glistening colour. He was an austere painter, stern and rugged, a sour and severe genius who used a cold palette and had won the devotion of the mountaineers by the qualities most calculated to appeal to them, energy, weight and the hardness of rock. His figures seemed to have been carved in marble. They had the serene and chilly grandeur of statues. Mantegna painted as though he were hollowing out stone or burning his forms into enamel.

Throughout the Tyrol, at Botzen, Innsbruck, Stertzing, Bruneck and Brixen, he was deeply venerated. The brothers Pacher, perhaps, would never have produced such strange and wonderful works if

THE MUSE THALIA. About 1495–1496.
BRITISH MUSEUM, LONDON.

they had not been acquainted with the lucid and glacial genius of Mantegna. Michael Pacher had completed, three years before, the great altarpiece commissioned by the Bishop of Brixen. The artist had just finished another, dealing with the legend of St Wolfgang. Its newly minted gilding, its warm, glowing colours, freshly laid, were dazzling. Dürer detected in Pacher's pictures the typical fervent Tyrolean realism and dreaminess. But they were lit by the gentle iridescence of the skies of Venice. The dramatic narrative animation, the sharp, restless line of the figures presented, lent Pacher's art a certain fantastic elegance. It gave Dürer a foretaste of Italy, but of an Italy in which sensuous charm had been whittled down by highland puritanism. Interest in the object for its own sake had, moreover, been combined with a tendency to introduce weird visions into the prosaic, workaday world.

But he had to tear himself away from these fascinating works. As soon as he had made a thorough study of Pacher's altarpieces and listened to what the great master had to tell him, the traveller set off once more. In a few days he would be descending, full of wonder, the Trento valley, a flourishing earthly paradise even more beautiful than he had imagined.

Italy at last! The trees in her favoured gardens seemed to grow and bear fruit simply by God's grace, without human intervention. The sunlight lay warm upon her gaily painted houses. The alternating purples and yellows of the Dolomites were here replaced by the rose and pale gold of vineyards where the vines were hung with garlands of grapes. At Trento, with its ancient cathedral and marble palaces, the luxury and elegance of the princes of northern Italy rivalled the splendour to be seen in Rome and Sicily. A broad, leisurely river, the Adige, traversed the fields of maize and the classical landscape of vines. The hills were crowned by the square towers of castles. Within the gnarled vinestocks on the slopes below, the flame that will burst out in the new wine smoulders through the winter sleep.

At Verona the wide streets were lined with Gothic palaces, and equestrian statues adorned the squares and tombs. The city had a grave beauty, refined and polished by centuries of enlightenment, the best in the thought and art of successive generations of its inhabitants. Political power constantly changed hands among the great families. But the tyrants who arose invariably sought popularity by a lavish patronage of art. Dürer wandered through the town in a state of rapture and amazement. He was captivated by the unrestrained gratification of the senses in all he saw. He realised that this art was also an art of living, free of the restrictions which the German burghers, emancipated as they might be by their prosperity, had not ventured to abandon.

The fantastic stone monsters, in rampant attitudes, on the fronts of the Romanesque churches bore some resemblance to those created by the Nordic imagination. But here they seemed quite mild and gentle.

Everything delighted him, from the gaiety of the swarming, half-starved occupants of improvised hovels on the steps of the ancient Roman theatre, with its antique columns, to the frescoes of Pisanello, where nimble saints equipped for the joust set out to do battle with dragons under the adoring gaze of fair damsels arrayed in the styles fashionable at the Courts of France or Berry. He admired the stately tombs of the arrogant robber-barons, with ladders in their armorial bearings, who were called by such nicknames as 'Mastiff' and 'Great Dog'. He strolled, at evening, along the banks of the Adige, where big waves slapped angrily against the spreading quays. He lingered in pleasure-gardens, among unfamiliar southern trees, bronze-leaved laurels, the tall, dark spears of the cypress, glittering pomegranates and velvety mulberries. He had longed to meet the illustrious Mantegna, of whose genius he had become aware through the works of the Tyrolean painters who imitated him. But Mantegna himself was in Mantua, whose princes would not let him go. Dürer saw, however, a number of his pictures in ecclesiastical and secular buildings.

The traveller had every inducement to remain in Verona. But now that he was so near to Venice his impatience was rising to a climax. He would not even wait to see Padua and study Mantegna's frescoes in San Agostino degli Eremitani and the stirring and sublime narrative with which Giotto had long before covered the walls from floor to ceiling, of a little chapel built by an extortionate money-lender to

HALF-LENGTH PORTRAIT OF AGNES DÜRER. About 1497.
KUNSTHALLE, BREMEN.

placate a jealous God. It is doubtful whether Giotto's work would have meant much to Dürer. But it is possible that he would have been astonished at the old painter's prophetic vision and might have realised that Scrovegni's chapel, erected to atone for usury, contained the seeds of all contemporary and even future painting.

In any case, his road led now to the sea. For he could no longer resist, as he steadily approached, the attraction of Venice.

Soon he could see the bell-towers perched on its islands like great birds, then the lagoon, alive with ponderous barges and light, swift galleys. The marble fronts of palaces were duplicated by their quivering reflections in the greenish water. The Byzantine domes, the dazzling mosaics that seemed to oscillate as if submerged at the bottom of the sea and the strange splendour of the dwellings of the citizens introduced the young painter to a different world.

He saw swarthy Croatians with long moustaches elbowing Turks wearing silk turbans. The flat, square caps of the Venetian merchants were scarlet and their robes were of brocade. The courtesans were more gorgeously attired than princesses and showed their handsome breasts. Pages followed them, carrying diminutive dogs, monkeys and parrots.

For some weeks Dürer experienced one shock of amazement after another. Then his curiosity began to abate and assume a certain pattern. At first he had given himself up to enjoyment of the spectacle of a life which itself enjoyed nothing more than the display of its own peculiarities. He had been absorbed in the incidents of the streets, the play of light in the sky and on the water, the pageantry of the processions of cloud above the gilded domes. But now he took up his sketchbooks, his box of water-colours and his silver point. He had never been much of an idler and was glad to resume the assiduous and painstaking industry to which he had been accustomed in Franconia. He eventually abandoned the seductions of the open air, entered the studios of painters, visited the famous galleries and spent much time in the churches, studying the beauty, both heavenly and earthly, of the Virgins there depicted, with the new-born Child in their arms.

It was at this time that he discovered the carved work of Carlo

Crivelli, then recently dead. This artist's Madonnas in burnished gold and angelic figures incised in rare marbles and gems exemplified a craft, that of the jeweller, which was already familiar to Dürer. He recognised its severe and meticulous style of execution and its extravagance of ornamentation, for instance in placing picturesque and over-decorative garlands of stone fruit above the lintels of the most nobly conceived doorways. But he was rather bewildered by these ostentatious and paradoxical, if agreeably ironic, devices. He felt more sympathy with the striking objectivity of Antonello da Messina, the Sicilian who had died some fifteen years previously, after travels in Europe extending from the Mediterranean to the fogs of Friesland. Antonello had digested in every country he visited all the styles of painting he had mastered elsewhere. His eclecticism was therefore very different from the elder Holbein's timid and even clumsy adaptations of foreign methods. The Sicilian had been at home everywhere. The ways of the Flemish masters were as familiar to him as those of the Tuscans. His widely ranging blend of regional manners constituted the first step towards a type of art that could be called European.

Dürer met some of his compatriots in Venice. They had come to the city, like himself, to study modern painting. A number of them had settled down there permanently. They seemed to have forgotten their native land and the petty, hidebound outlook of the ordinary German burgher. They had become Italianate in behaviour and even Italianised their names. Some were painting as well as the Venetians themselves. Dürer made friends, for instance, with Giovanni d'Alemagna, who had left Augsburg for Murano, and married a member of the Vivarini family, participating in its production of altarpieces, which were highly popular with the Church and the Brotherhoods.

The little island of Murano resembled an Eastern carpet floating on the lagoon. The Venetian patricians owned gardens there, where they sought relief amid flowering meadows and beds of flowers from the cares of business. The isle appeared posed so lightly on the water that an unusually big wave might have carried it off. Only the most delicate and fragile materials were created there.

DOSSO DI TRENTO. About 1495.
LANDESMUSEUM, HANOVER.

The Murano glass seemed weightless, transparent as water and iridescent as the sky. The dainty, frostlike patterns of Murano lace achieved effects of wonderful beauty, as of gardens under snow. Opalescent bulbs reddened in the glass furnaces. Bobbins clicked with a steady, reassuring rhythm, like that of the high heels of women on the pavement of a quiet street. And Giovanni d'Alemagna, the contented exile from Swabia, listened with only half an ear to the young traveller talking of Augsburg and the Fuggers.

It was through Giovanni that Dürer came to know Antonio and

Bartolommeo Vivarini, the first Venetians to break with the Gothic tradition of the previous century, remote from common life in its hieratic and ingenuous piety. The Vivarini brothers were gradually finding their own style, emancipating it from the influence of Pisanello and Gentile da Fabriano, painters from the mainland who had not surrendered to the spell of the 'Spirit of the Isles'.

The process was prolonged, like that of a war in which territorial gains have to be continuously renewed and defended. The Vivarini were acquiring artistic independence as they worked in their island solitude, far from the disputes of their colleagues. Their maturing art, unprecedented in its force and gravity, was soon to entitle them to be considered the true inaugurators of the new Venetian painting. But, for all their patience, they were not yet quite free of external influence. They were still encumbered by a certain degree of archaic mannerism, an excessive timidity in their approach to nature. The outlines of their figures retained the medieval aridity, with its stiff grace and shy reserve, and their colour sometimes remained within the conventions of traditional theory. But their impulse to innovation, their longing to shake off the fetters of the hackneyed styles inherited from Padua, Verona and Florence, continued strong enough to cause Dürer to pay serious attention to their work. He saw that the Renaissance spirit was breaking through the medieval trappings of their work. Alvise, the youngest of the family, in particular, who was nearest to himself in years and cast of mind, appealed to him as impersonating a type of energy capable of rejuvenating the ideas and technique of a whole artistic epoch.

Yet it was not from the Vivarini, valuable as their example had been to Dürer, that he eventually learned what he was looking for in Venice. He felt that his own style was already more advanced than theirs and that the Gothic backwater in which they still so fondly and so indolently lingered lay far behind the main streams to which he himself was tirelessly and eagerly attracted.

When the young Franconian enquired to which Venetian painters he should apply for lessons he had not been able to obtain anywhere in Germany, he was told to visit the School of St Ursula. In that building Vittore Carpaccio had recently finished a series of pictures dealing with episodes in the life of the saint. Dürer found there one of the most novel and exquisite productions of that highly imaginative and delightful, as well as profoundly reflective, man of genius.

Gothic elements had completely disappeared from his work. It was so fully and yet so unobtrusively winged by the great soaring spirit of the Renaissance that all nature seemed to be comprehended in his paintings. Yet their religious feeling was entirely serious and tenderly affectionate. His love of picturesque anecdote and entertaining detail did not prevent him from transcending the realism with which they were recorded. He knew how to tell a story and did so most admirably, mingling sympathy, humour and nonchalance in the narrative to a degree which concealed, as though by an excess of modesty, the powerful flights of imagination that sustained it. His genius was as much poetic as artistic, sensitive to the emotional element in human action, subtly intelligent and endlessly inquisitive. Though he illustrated with great charm the stately festivals of Venice, with their interminable processions through St Mark's Square, he loved even more a scene of warm domestic intimacy, such as the bright and peaceful aspect of a maiden's chamber, with angels entering upon a sunbeam, or a section of the harbour with ceremonial vessels rocking at anchor and the end of a Turkish carpet trailing in the water.

Carpaccio's intense efforts to apprehend reality, and to use this understanding in the fables he enjoyed, enabled him to attain 'states of grace' in which beauty is generously displayed and deeply felt. The eye dwells upon the vision indefinitely, at once drawn to it by a glimpse of revelation and checked by the modest and gentle reticence of the artist. Nothing could be more different from the style of the Murano painters. Carpaccio may have been trained in the school of the Vivarini, but he far exceeded it in his characteristic blend of objectivity and spiritual ardour. Nevertheless, the very highest rank must be denied him on account of his excessive love of anecdote and the very discretion of manner which is naturally deplored in some quarters as undue restraint or timidity. Dürer

The House by the Pond. About 1497.
British Museum, London.

appreciated to the full Carpaccio's mastery of landscape and space composition, the subtlety of his mobile and vibrant treatment of atmosphere and of the beauty of flesh given life and radiance by the spirit within. These merits, as well as the artist's dreamy, tender melancholy, elicited the admiration and even the astonishment of the Franconian visitor. He studied them intently, resolving to borrow from the master, if the occasion should ever arise, one of the picturesque details of common life that appeared so often in his work. But it was not from Carpaccio that Dürer obtained those dazzling, momentous revelations which ten years later, on his second visit to Venice, sent him back to Bellini, a genius of unrivalled eminence, he considered, in that city. 'He is still the greatest painter in Venice,' Dürer was to write at that time, faithful as ever to the admiration and affection he felt for the artist to whom he owed so much.

Bellini's personality, in fact, stood out with commanding and unquestioned authority among the multitude of Venetian painters engaged in working out the new style which was so swiftly to surpass, in the perfection and daring of its execution, every other Italian school of that age. He shared the aims, the researches and the ideals that inspired these men, but it was impossible to refuse him his place at their head. The returning traveller was right to regard him as 'still the greatest painter in Venice'.

Dürer never made a mistake when he gave high praise to an artist. He was instinctively drawn, like a thirsty man hurrying towards a spring, to Giovanni Bellini. The 'German tour' and the first stages of his Italian journey had taught him a great many important lessons. But he immediately saw that Bellini's career differed entirely from the tentative or bold experiments conducted by the Murano school or by Carpaccio. A genius was here manifest, one who was inaugurating a new era, opening up fresh paths through a world of beauty and truth, depicted at last in all their stimulating novelty.

No one could reasonably deny that Giovanni owed much to his father Jacopo, his elder brother Gentile and his brother-in-law Andrea Mantegna. Dürer was too discerning a critic not to recognise, for all his intense admiration of Giovanni, the contributions made by these men to the latter's art. But the young German had undertaken his long journey to Venice in order to examine in that city the latest and most important advances made in contemporary painting. In his opinion Giovanni Bellini surpassed all the other Venetian artists of the day. He was like someone standing on the top

AN APOSTLE. STUDY FOR THE HELLER ALTARPIECE. 1508.
KUPFERSTICHKABINETT, BERLIN.

HANDS OF AN APOSTLE. STUDY FOR THE HELLER ALTARPIECE. 1508.
KUPFERSTICHKABINETT, BERLIN.

of the bell-tower in St Mark's Square, high above the rose-coloured roofs and the greenish hues of the domes, the winding canals that resembled water-snakes and the swarming, shadowy streets. Giovanni's achievement had been unprecedented. No doubt many others had tried to do as well. If he alone had succeeded in realising the ambitions of a whole generation of painters, it was unquestionably as much to their efforts as to his own genius that he owed his triumph. Its origin may have been collective, but its execution had been so brilliant as to dazzle all who encountered his work for the first time. Such, to an exceptional degree, was the experience of Dürer, coming as he did from a Germany in which medieval ideals and customs remained as oppressive as ever and acquainted as he was only with such foreign masters as had too little in common with his own outstanding gifts to make any deep impression on him.

To an artist trained in the strict traditions of Franconia, modified though these had been to some extent in Dürer's case by what he had learned from the Swabian, Swiss, Alsatian and Tyrolean schools, the influence of Mantegna, the first traces of which he had found at Bruneck and then in full force on the other side of the frontier, where its despotic yoke was felt in all sorts of different ways at Verona, Padua and even Venice, could not provide the needful stimulus to independent creation. On the contrary, Dürer perceived in Mantegna's work the very elements which he knew were impeding his own. He wished to rid himself of some of them or at least to soften their effect by some process not derived from the crafts of the jeweller, engraver and die-sinker which still overshadowed his personal style. Since leaving his father's workshop he had been longing to produce 'pure' painting, in other words to attach less importance to the plastic problems for which Mantegna had provided such useful solutions and to contentrate mainly on pictorial values. He considered that Giovanni Bellini had been far more successful than anyone else in cultivating the realism, the complete expression of the whole of nature, which he himself so desperately desired to contrive. Bellini alone, he believed, could instruct him in these essential mysteries and show him the way to the goal his own German masters had once pointed out from afar.

PORTRAIT OF AN UNKNOWN MAN. 1500.
ALTE PINAKOTHEK, MUNICH.

Fate sometimes permits individuals, on their way through life, to meet those who can help them to a full understanding and effective development of the best that is in them. Such encounters may, moreover, take place at the time and place where they are most likely to bear fruit. This was the case at Venice with Giovanni Bellini, then at the height of his technical and creative powers, and Dürer, at the age of twenty-four. So fortunate an acquaintanceship with the ageing master in whom fifteenth-century Venetian painting had at last come to full flower naturally proved an immeasurable inspiration to the youthful genius, already afire with hope and expectation.

STILL THE GREATEST PAINTER IN VENICE

Ever since 1492 Giovanni Bellini had been working at the Doges' Palace. This astonishing structure, with its loggia at ground level and its vast, towering façade of rose-coloured bricks, edged with gleaming marble tracery, was constantly being remodelled by the government. As the scene of its deliberations and the dwelling of its Doge, the building was considered continuously in need of additions to its pomp and beauty. Until the beginning of the fifteenth century the Venetian love of splendour had been dominated by the Byzantine influence all-powerful in the city. But this subjection to a hieratic and stylised magnificence, most brilliantly expressed in the art of mosaic, was now on the wane. 'Painting with glass', which combined the solidity of precious stone with the fluidity of water, receiving and reflecting light in so many ways, suited the maritime atmosphere of the city to perfection. The popularity of mosaic work had therefore for long impeded the development of painting proper. Fresco, moreover, at the very period when it was most extensively practised in the rest of Italy, could not be undertaken in Venice with any hope of a lasting effect owing to the dampness of the air. The salt sea breezes attacked every surface except the glossy, invulnerable and unchanging materials of mosaic inlay. But the introduction of oil painting and the persistent pressure of the mainland schools of art gradually undermined the predominance of mosaic as a medium. For reasons connected with the Venetian climate this kind of work continued for some time to be produced as a 'national' mode of artistic expression; but painting first in an aqueous medium and then in oils eventually superseded it. The infinitely richer resources of the new technique fascinated the Venetian susceptibility to effects of colour. Mosaic work steadily declined to the point at which those who 'painted with glass' forgot the rules of their craft and the requirements of its materials and were content to copy and imitate pictures executed by other means, so that the true style and essential spirit of mosaic was lost.

The first Venetian painters came from the mainland. They were Gothic artists like Jacobello del Fiore, eclectics like Guariento, deriving from the schools of Tuscany and Padua, or mannerists of the dying medieval type like Gentile da Fabriano, whose Florentine tendencies remained permeated by the influence of the French miniaturists. Works by such mainland painters crowded the walls of the Doges' Palace or were superimposed, in that building, upon older productions, if no room could be found for them elsewhere. The Palace accordingly came to exemplify the whole process of the development of fashion and taste at Venice. It illustrated the replacement of medieval formality and piety by mannerism, the contrast between the Florentine style and that of Padua and Verona and finally the rise of indigenous Venetian painting, the work of native artists.

This evolution began with the exquisite productions of Giacobello del Fiore, whose angelic touch created a refined paradise, half Asiatic, half Christian. The Murano school, independent of outside influence in its neighbouring island, developed the first distinct characteristics of the style of the Lagoon. While the Murano artists Bartolommeo and Antonio Vivarini worked side by side with glass-blowers and lacemakers, the Venetian-born Jacopo Bellini attended the studio of Gentile da Fabriano in a most submissive way.

Or so it seemed. But in reality Jacopo Bellini had a strong personality. He collaborated with Gentile da Fabriano in the decoration of the Doges' Palace, and was fond enough of his master to name a

THE LARGE PIECE OF TURF. 1503.
ALBERTINA, VIENNA.

son after him. But Jacopo knew how to maintain his own originality and protect Venetian painting of which he was the 'father', from the domination of a prestige all too seductive and hence over-tyrannical. Even at Ferrara, where Jacopo met and competed with the best artists at the Court of the Este family, he was careful not to follow too closely the lead of a style which could never become acclimatised in his native city. His temperament was so thoroughly Venetian that he was able to undergo, without loss of his own individuality, the experience of artistic centres very different from that in which he had grown up. On the contrary, he took from them everything he felt he could use without prejudice to the new Venetian school, still poorly equipped to withstand foreign impressions. He introduced rigour and clarity of line into the art of Venice, a city where the aspect of forms tends to dissolve in the misty air. In this connection the legacy of the mosaic artists proved valuable. The sharply pointed crayon, the elegant, nervous calligraphy, of such draughtsmen as Pisanello showed Jacopo how the temptation to be vague could be resisted. At his death, about 1470, he bequeathed to his two sons, Gentile, who was legitimate, born in 1429, and Giovanni, born out of wedlock a year later, an excellent technique. Though built up from various sources he had made it entirely and uncompromisingly his own.

Gentile, however, who had developed a passionate interest in method, was not content to copy his father's manner. The artistic glory of Padua, at that time, was dazzling the whole Province of Veneto. Gentile set out for that city, where he discovered the grandiose and monumental austerity of Mantegna's work and introduced it into his own style. Being attracted by common life and being an adroit illustrator of the religious and secular ceremonies of his native Republic, he soon came to be considered a kind of national institution as a painter. The frescoes by Guariento and Gentile da Fabriano on the walls of the Doges' Palace were fading owing to the corrosive action of the sea air. Gentile Bellini was commissioned to restore them. When he reported that it was impossible to do so, the progressively minded government invited him to replace them by works of his own. In the midst of this undertaking he was sent on a diplomatic mission to the East, where he made a great number of drawings of exotic scenes. The sultan Mohammed II, in defiance of the precepts of the Koran, ordered a portrait from him and became so attached to the artist that he wished to retain him at the Seraglio. Gentile stayed at Constantinople till he grew tired of its attractions and was homesick for Venice. On his return he was more highly esteemed than ever.

When Dürer visited Gentile's studio the latter was engaged on a large picture representing a procession escorting relics through St Mark's Square. It might have turned out a commonplace, formal and tedious composition in the hands of a different painter. But Gentile's enthusiasm for every aspect of Venetian life lent his work on this official commission a lively charm which made a great impression on the young Franconian. The harmony of the general effect, the verisimilitude of the details, the masterly ease with which the movements of crowds of figures through a clear atmosphere were rendered, the simplicity with which the true nature of the action was conveyed and the dignity of the narrative style, all proclaimed the excellence of Gentile as a painter. Dürer's admiration would have been quite unqualified if the grace and facility themselves of the artist's manner had not suggested a certain complacency, the sort of pleasure sometimes felt by a story-teller in hearing himself talk. The beauty of the portraits of individuals which appeared in Gentile's large compositions, the exquisitely sensitive treatment of their lightly clouded skies, flower-decorated balconies and canals traversed by skimming gondolas, even the peculiar quality of Venetian air, at once substantial and delicate, as depicted by Gentile, could not in fact compare, in Dürer's opinion, with the fascination exercised by the work of his younger brother Giovanni. The latter's genius, Dürer found, threw into the shade the painstaking and delightful talent of Jacopo's elder son.

Gentile Bellini was a great painter, one of the masters of the new school which was then daily discovering previously unknown territory. But there were certain limits to his explorations. They were no doubt impeded by some lack of depth in his intuitive feelings. He was too easily satisfied by the outward aspect of people

94

and things. His portraits are not psychologically penetrating. He was restricted, by his love of the picturesque, to the illustration of familiar events. He did not suspect the existence of a secret life behind appearances. Absorbed in his task of historian, recorder and chronicler of the past or present glories of the Republic, he never went below the surface of human nature. The character of his fame confined him to the repetition of a few interconnected formal statements, expressed with refinement but not far-reaching.

In Giovanni's work, on the other hand, Dürer perceived an immense, luxuriant, profoundly suggestive and puzzling world he could not resist. Gentile's brilliant superficiality as a fashionable retailer of national anecdotes was here contrasted with his brother's silent, reflective personality, deeply engaged with introspection. Giovanni's versatile and unusual character could only be guessed, never wholly revealed, in his painting. For his natural reticence was so extreme that he seemed perpetually to be hiding behind or slipping noiselessly away from his picture. He did not resemble any of the artists Dürer had hitherto met. Throughout his travels he had never known a painter who seemed at the same time so easy and so difficult to understand. Giovanni either whispered what he had to say pictorially or hinted obscurely at it in one corner of the composition. In a city so given to demonstrative, sensuous and superficial pleasures as Venice, the younger Bellini was conspicuous for his meditative tendency, his love of solitude, the chastity of his affections and his equable, serious temperament.

His illegitimacy may have deprived him of the favours lavished upon his elder brother. It was soon in fact forgotten by society at large in the general admiration accorded to his genius. But there can be no doubt that he himself always remembered it. Without being in the least ashamed of the irregularity of his birth, he probably preferred the peace of isolation to the whirl of public commissions in which Gentile was involved. When invited to deputise for his absent brother in the decoration of the Doges' Palace, he readily accepted the opportunity offered him to cover such extensive areas with the figments of his imagination. Yet he was in reality little suited to the task: his deepest inclinations and feelings aspired to work of a more intimate, inward kind. He left his brother to depict public functions and go on diplomatic missions. Giovanni, too, would have been interested in the strange and seductive life of the Orient described with so much enthusiasm by Gentile on his return. But the younger brother considered, all the same, that communion with nature could have been secured nearer home.

His willing collaboration with Gentile in official painting was due less to any particular taste for picturesque narrative than to his love of the secret life and soul of Venice, its skies and waters, the boughs of its gardens overhanging the high walls low enough to touch the actual surface of the canals, the green moss that gave the ancient bricks a look of velvet and the strange reflections of sunlight from slabs of oriental marble on the palace fronts.

Loyal and modest by nature, Giovanni would never have dreamed of denying how much he owed to his teachers, his father Jacopo, his brother-in-law Mantegna and his brother Gentile, in the development of his gifts. But, like a rich man who takes little account of his minor obligations, he was perfectly well aware that his essential genius had not been conferred upon him by anyone save his Maker. His admiration for other talented painters was sincere and unassuming. He respected their art, knowing it to be the outcome of struggles which could be distressing as well as enjoyable. Dürer was strongly attracted by the peaceable and shy character of the artist, in which, as in his pictures, there were no violent contrasts, while his cordiality to foreigners and the freedom with which he disclosed his most cherished discoveries to his pupils, together with, finally, the complexity of Giovanni's personality, exceeding in resources and variety those of all his contemporaries, added to the impression he made upon the German visitor.

The meeting between Wolgemut's former apprentice and Giovanni Bellini was one of those decisive encounters, rare in Dürer's career, which affected him like a miraculous revelation. Bellini's work almost at once convinced him, to his delight, that he had at last reached the goal towards which he had been unconsciously travelling. His Italian experiences, he felt, had come to a head in Venice and everything that the city could teach him was to be

THE VILLAGE OF KALCHREUTH. About 1500.
KUNSTHALLE, BREMEN.

found in Giovanni's painting. He cultivated the artist's society, therefore, with a devotion both impassioned and deferential, retaining throughout his life, with his whole heart and soul, unbounded feelings of gratitude to the man whose pictures had unveiled so wonderful a world to him. Dürer's choice of Giovanni as a master whom he never ceased to reverence proved that neither Carpaccio's charm nor the agreeable naturalism of Gentile Bellini had distracted him from his true ideal.

Yet Giovanni Bellini's mind and productions were entirely different from Dürer's. The softly radiant light of the Renaissance that suffused the Italian's paintings had nothing in common with the medieval timidity, awkwardness and static quality by which Dürer's youthful work was still impeded. None of the artists he had so far studied had prepared him for the impact of Bellini. The influence of Mantegna, whose plastic sense had appealed so greatly to Dürer's longing to express form, actually ran counter to that of the great Venetian. The latter had freed himself at an early stage from the dictation of the Paduan style and thenceforth obeyed only the promptings of his own creative instinct. But Mantegna was undoubtedly at this time the most directly accessible of all living Italian artists to the German schools. His mastery of engraving, in the first place, recommended him to a country which had made almost a national institution of that art or at any rate regarded it as a rewarding aesthetic discipline. His austerity, too, confirmed the German painters in their reactionary tendencies, which would have been shocked by innovations of too startling a character. The somewhat self-conscious solemnity of the Nuremberg, Ulm or Augsburg schools could not accept without qualification the form given by Giovanni Bellini to Renaissance style. With their fidelity to medieval tradition, in spirit and feeling as much as in the manner of presentation, they felt more at home with Mantegna's works. Dürer himself believed that he was not destined so much to abolish these conventions as to bring them to a fuller maturity. He would therefore have been ready enough to join Mantegna's school at the Court of the Gonzaga family. If that artist had been resident, not at Mantua, but in one of the towns Dürer visited in Italy that year, it is possible that the German painter's career would have been very different.

However that may be, Dürer's quest for Mantegna led him to Giovanni Bellini. No meeting could have been more providential at that stage of his life, when he was on the point, after having learnt so much from masters so diverse as Wolgemut, Holbein the Elder, Schongauer, Witz, Herlin, Multscher and Pacher, of digesting all their various techniques and contrasting influences as a preliminary to the development of a purely personal method. For the very reason, perhaps, that such individuality, in Dürer's case, at its deepest, most significant level, bore little relation to that of Bellini, the younger man was able to profit all the more from contact with the Venetian. Dürer's originality, far from being paralysed, as often happens in such cases, was on the contrary enhanced by Bellini's influence, which assisted its rise and favoured its development. Albrecht did not become a German Bellini. He became a more complete and lively edition of himself. The most effective stimuli are not those which transform the recipient but those which bring into operation his own special characteristics along the lines most appropriate to their profitable exercise. Such results were obtained, for example, when Michael Pacher encountered Mantegna, when the elder Holbein gave lessons to his son, and during Schongauer's apprenticeship to Isenmann.

Dürer showed prudence in applying to so many masters while on the formative travels which took him from Nuremberg to Venice. But he showed even more of this quality in not permitting himself to be unduly dazzled by any of them, till the day on which he met the 'master of masters', Giovanni Bellini.

The visitor who came ashore on the Piazzetta in that year, 1495, could consider himself lucky. Carpaccio was finishing his paintings in the School of St Ursula. Gentile Bellini was working on his Procession of the Relics. Cima da Conegliano, famous for the delicate luminosity and melancholy of his scenes in fading light, was thirty-six. Palma, later to be known as Palma Vecchio, was then only fifteen. One of Giovanni Bellini's pupils was a boy of seventeen named Giorgione and another, eighteen years old, was called Titian.

Such was the Venice Dürer found on his first journey to Italy. By far the most eminent of the city's artists at that time was the sixty-five-year-old Giovanni Bellini. No genius was ever so continuously youthful, lively and resilient, in work after work, as the illegitimate son of Jacopo. His physical aspect alone, the refined features, long, thin nose and fine, brilliant eyes, the tight lips and curling hair, turning white, that fell to his shoulders, radiated a serene, well ordered disposition, equable and benevolent, though it could be imperious on occasion. A lucid intelligence combined with a generous heart could be divined in that noble countenance, together with a mind at peace and senses under due control. His person produced the same effect as his pictures, much placid and

OSWOLT·KREL·
1499·

Oswolt Krell. 1499.
Alte Pinakothek, Munich.

gentle strength, a kind of all-embracing contentment expressing the reconciliation of mankind and Nature.

Dürer had already heard of him from the Fuggers at Augsburg, for he was much admired by the great Swabian patricians. Some of the family had settled in Venice, where they enjoyed considerable prestige and had opened branches of their business. They were fond of ordering portraits from Bellini. He had painted, some years before Dürer's arrival, a picture of the young and brilliant Georg Fugger, lightly crowned with ivy-leaves, like a Greek god or one of the humanists of the day who liked to be compared with such a being.

The Fuggers had recommended the young Franconian artist to Giovanni Bellini. Dürer showed the latter his first works, some drawings and the water-colours he had painted during his travels. In these productions the objective rendering of nature was associated with a poetic feeling congenial to Bellini, who was himself enamoured of the effect, for example, of a rosy sky at sunset. They included Dürer's miniature, on parchment, of the Child Jesus holding a golden globe representing the world, the aureoled figure being framed in a window edged with ivy. This delicate little painting (p. 58), executed during the artist's 'German tour', is a proof of the skill with which Dürer was already ridding himself of the conventions and mannerisms that still encumbered the German schools. The figure lacks the naturalistic charm of Giovanni's *bambini*. But the handling of flesh and light forecasts the bold organisation of colour at which Dürer was then chiefly aiming.

He must have envied Giovanni his discoveries in this field, the rich variety of subtle hues all blending almost imperceptibly into one another, just as the tones of water and sky fuse together at the hour when daylight begins to wane over the lagoon. Bellini had found his favourite tints in nature, where they had always existed in the interplay of light and form, the rainbow, transparent depths of water and transitory cloud-patterns. Yet no one had noticed them before, or rather, if the Venetian painters had noticed them, such effects could not have been reproduced in the aqueous medium used, which only permits bright, cold colour schemes. But after

HERCULES. About 1500.

THE SMALL HORSE. 1505.   THE LARGE HORSE. 1505.

Antonello da Messina, some twenty years before Dürer's arrival, had taught the Venetians oil-painting, an art which had long been practised in Flanders, they were delighted to find that they could at last adequately record the scenes, in all their glistening beauty, which lay so near at hand.

Giovanni Bellini immediately made himself a master of the new technique and drew from it unprecedented results which revolutionised the current Venetian style. His methods in depicting the most elusive aspects of landscape, of sea and of sky expressed simultaneously all the rich variety of nature and the more fleeting imagery of the mind. He thus inspired Venetian painters to compete with the hours of the day and the seasons of the year in creating scenes, perhaps the most wonderful in the world, which their city

103

daily offered to them. His own supremacy was due both to a genius and a love of nature, a faculty for communion with its manifestations, which exceded theirs. He took to the medium as spontaneously and inevitably, one might say, as a bird sings. And Bellini's colour in fact, once he had freed it from the dry and artificial abstractions of the school of Padua, gave lyrical utterance to the true beauties of the earth. It was the first time that a European painter had performed the feat with such triumphant facility and grace.

To Dürer everything that he admired in Bellini's work seemed surprising and new. Its fluency, vivacity and variety of tone were not to be found in German or Flemish paintings, which also lacked Bellini's intimate feeling for nature, making each of his landscapes like a great hymn in which the artist's voice joined the chorus of the world itself. Both lagoon and mainland were so dear to him that he always found room, even in his portraits and religious compositions, for space leading the eye to imagine a blue gulf stretching to the horizon, a green slope warmed by the setting sun, a road winding among low hills or occasionally some solitary tree, its rustling boughs engaged in mysterious colloquy with the wind.

His landscapes were not merely picturesque accessories to the main subject, whatever it might be, but an integral part of it, an essential feature, painted with the deepest understanding and affection, of the whole picture. Dürer had noted a similar fervent love of nature, often expressed with touching awkwardness, in some of the German artists. He himself felt it and longed above all things to be able to put all reality into his work. But in Bellini's output he discovered a new facet of realism, its poetry, the linking of objective truth with lyrical intuition, the way in which the painter's vision of the actual world of forms kept pace with the poet's passionate pursuit of a hidden beauty beyond that world, his imposition, in short, of his own dreams and ideals upon the scenes presented to him by the universe.

It was not only in Bellini's landscapes but also in his portraits, religious works and imaginative compositions that he delineated both outward appearances and their inner significance. No previous

Two Musicians. Wing panel of the Jabach Altarpiece. About 1500.
Wallraf-Richartz Museum, Cologne.

painter had succeeded in giving such an impression of simultaneous fidelity to the real and ideal worlds. Some had confined themselves to exact reproduction of the object. Others had taken refuge in personal fancies abounding in chimerical images. Those who clung to reality only too often remained rooted to the spot, unable to rise on the wings of their inspiration. Those, on the other hand, who abandoned themselves too readily to the promptings of inspiration ended by losing sight altogether of the world as it is and producing only an illusory notion of it, quite unconnected with reality.

In Giovanni's work, however, the clear perception of objects and logically planned representation of them never clashed with his visionary powers. In his case no conflict arose between the world of appearances and that of the creative imagination. On the contrary, each complemented the other and only made its full impact in alliance with its contrasting partner.

Dürer had noted a poetic treatment of reality in the pictures of Conrad Witz. But there could be no comparison, he felt, between the latter's touching diffidence and the complete assurance, calm and apparently effortless, of the great Venetian. Bellini seemed to paint in a perpetual 'state of grace', with no trace of hesitation, uneasiness, doubt or anxiety, basing his work not only on a thorough understanding of the object to be depicted but also on his own self-control. It was only such personal discipline that enabled him to dominate external reality by himself entering into its essence.

His portraits combined attention to psychology with monumental feeling. The sitter's interrelated physical and mental characteristics were hit off so precisely as to lay his whole heart and soul bare. The first problem before the artist is one of form. But once this question has been decided, the next step is the most difficult. The material form, in its defined relations to space and light, has to be given spiritual life. The eyes, the muscular tension or relaxation, the movement of the lips or furrowing of the brow, must deliver the required message from within.

The imposing monumentality of these portraits succeeds, perhaps, better than any others, in conveying the imperious ambition of a Doge, the cupidity of a merchant, the frivolity of gilded youth, the speculative temperament of an artist and the angelic charm of adolescence. The deep interest they arouse is due to their invariable suggestion of Bellini's intimate knowledge of the sitter. His most striking capacity, one which Dürer, of all people, was best qualified to understand and attempt to exercise, enabled him to commune with every type of existence and animation. He saw a human face as simply another kind of landscape, its colours affected by the time of day and the season of the year or modified by the passage of a cloud across the sun. A landscape, again, was for him not merely a collection of trees and rocks, but a living, breathing creature, which might well be imagined to share the dreams and passions of humanity.

Bellini communed with nature and with mankind in the same way because he was spiritually and emotionally incapable of separating them. In his view each could only exist in mutual association and agreement. Consequently, the most impressive of his pictures display human action as deriving its highest level of significance from its environment. The joy of a mother embracing her child, the grief of apostles and angels mourning the death of Christ would be less intense, for Bellini, if the outside world itself, with its trees, clouds and waters, did not accompany the melody of these feelings with a sort of figured bass, the voice of all creation, issuing in an immeasurable and unique consonance.

He could not bear, in his affection for the animate and inanimate components of nature, to think of them apart. His 'Sacrae Conversazioni', to use the time-honoured term, suggest this special type of intimacy between individuals more successfully than pictures by any previous painter on this subject. It is hard to guess what his saints and martyrs, gathered about the Virgin, are discussing. Some seem to take no part in the 'conversation'. They are reading or plunged in meditation, visionary or troubled. They do not speak aloud. But their inner voices give unheard expression to a chorus of mutual regard, so fervent that no human utterance could ever make known the harmony and rapture of their feelings.

In order to enhance the intimate character of his 'Sacrae Conversazioni', Bellini broke with the traditional composition of an

YOUNG VENETIAN WOMAN. 1505.
KUNSTHISTORISCHES MUSEUM, VIENNA.

altarpiece, in which each figure had a panel to itself, separated from the rest by slender columns. He did away with these architectural divisions, which prevented any kind of plastic or moral link between the personages thus brought into proximity. After eliminating all such partitions and compartments, he assembled his figures in a group at the feet of the Virgin and introduced lutanists and flautists in the form of angels. The music they provided for an audience possibly surprised to find itself brought together in such circumstances set the key for the mood of the meeting, symbolising its harmony and general significance.

This new conception of the altarpiece was due to its correspondence with the artist's characteristic view of life as a state of concord and harmony. The impulses of heart and hand obeyed, in his case, an identical rhythm, which also coloured both mind and palette with the same range of hues. In his religious works he humanised divine elements in the sense of lending his supernatural beings the most perfect beauty conceivable in the human race, while the representatives of the latter, in their turn, were portrayed as spiritually ardent. The gravity of their looks, in every case, is instinct with a noble generosity and sympathy for mankind. Bellini dealt mainly with religious subjects. Pictures were favourite items of decoration in churches and convents; and of the commissions which Giovanni received he executed with most interest those for Madonnas, which allowed his marked feminine sensibility to express sentiments appropriate to the gentlest of mothers, and those for Lamentations over Christ, for the sincerity and meditative cast of his piety enabled him to excel in representations of the Passion.

Giovanni Bellini shows no sign either of the basic, ill-concealed paganism revived by the Florentines of the fifteenth century or of the austere and stilted religiosity imposed on Venetian art by the Byzantine tradition while Venice was still subject aesthetically, if not politically, to Constantinople. So religiously minded a painter as Dürer, whose art and life were deeply permeated by Christian thought, could not fail to sympathise in this field, as in others, with an artist who manifested his reverence for the divine beings he portrayed by endowing them with the most radiant types of human beauty. The young Franconian was much impressed by the tender respect which Bellini showed for all the concepts of Christianity and by his cheerful submission to its doctrines and regulations. Dürer never forgot the Virgins painted by Bellini; they profoundly affected his artistic responses and principles. He thought less now of Schongauer's Madonnas, which had so much attracted him during his first travels by the flowerlike freshness of their typically Alsatian charm. His cautious, diffident and shy temper must have caused him to wonder at the moral freedom of Venetian life, which had occasionally shocked the puritanical German burghers of the Middle Ages. But he never felt anything but affectionate veneration for the fleshly graces of Giovanni's Virgins.

When, at a later date, he began to compose religious pictures, he tried to follow Bellini's example in evading the two temptations which almost invariably entrap the painter, either an unnatural or an over-sensuous style. The German school in particular, seemed to have little talent for combining the attractions of the flesh with devout feeling. German artists tended to go to extremes in repudiating materialism on the one hand or a fanciful hieratic manner on the other. In so far as Dürer steered a middle course, he unquestionably owed it to the guidance of Bellini.

The days passed quickly in the company of that fascinating master. Moreover, the funds supplied to Dürer by the wealthy Pirckheimer were unfortunately running out, in spite of all the young traveller's efforts to economise. He realised that it was time to leave Venice. 'Oh, it'll be cold there!' he wrote, thinking of his return to Germany. But he knew that he had now learnt enough to embark without further hesitation on the production of an art of his own. He was impatient to start creative work in his turn. The admiration and study of others was all very well; but he felt that if he stayed too long in this foreign environment, the dangers of which were as serious as they were enticing, he ran the risk of becoming its slave. He could return later, he thought, as soon as his talents had taken firm root and had something to show. He would then no longer be the deferential student, but a master able to confront on an equal footing the most famous of the Venetians. A

THE HOLY TRINITY. 1511.

giddy abyss of ruin lurked behind the marvels to be viewed in the city. Its fragrance was never without a trace of poisonous air.

Dürer may well have felt that he was about to lose his individuality in a place itself suggesting the unreal. The time had come to return to prosaic, middle-class, down-to-earth Nuremberg. There he could recapture, even more effectively than the traditions of his race and soil, his own soul. There he could give free rein to a youthful genius already insistent upon taking wing.

RETURN TO STABILITY

A substantial world, energetic and robust, firmly based upon reality, received him. Coming from Venice, where everything tended to become transparent, Dürer was soothed to some extent by the very opacity of Nuremberg and its inhabitants. He was struck by the contrast between the old town, with its girdle of walls and towers, imprisoning it at the same time as they defended it against external perils, and the island city that seemed to float between sky and sea, precariously moored to a few piles and marshy shores. At Venice there were no walls or gates. The water flowed unhindered right into the houses, breaking against their façades and meandering in all directions.

At Nuremberg, on the other hand, there was nothing but solid ground. Instead of the reddish-brown, rippling waters of winding canals, there were streets, paved by a prudent municipality and swept every morning by order of the mayor. Instead of gilded palaces encrusted with oriental marble, where handsome courtesans leaned from the balconies of lanceolate windows, there were houses built of wood and clay, squat as country cottages, or ponderous medieval mansions filled with the pretentious treasures of the merchant princes. Their stone blatantly advertised its crude rusticity. Though the frontages were adorned with frescoes, statues, pinnacles, arcades and turrets, and the low-ceilinged, narrow apartments were crammed with heavy chests and earthenware stoves as big as dungeons, all their luxury amounted to no more than a bourgeois ostentation.

There was little opportunity for the exercise of an impassioned ingenuity among these typically methodical and sedate burghers. But the elder Dürer had long been acquainted with a strange artist who belonged to one of the best Nuremberg families. Like so many of his fellow-citizens he had a foot in both worlds, that of the ruling mercantile class and the less clearly defined circles in which artists moved. His rank entitled him to the former and his work took him to the latter. Hans Frey was hard to place, for he was both musician, jeweller and humanist. He played most agreeably on instruments made by himself; he read Latin authors in the original; he wrote light verse with ease and sang his own songs to his own accompaniment on the viol. But his local celebrity was chiefly due to the fountains he designed, in styles both charming and imposing. They were to be found in the gardens of the city and the interior courtyards of its houses. But also, since his craft as a jeweller was equal to that of the elder Dürer, he sometimes produced smaller specimens, in precious metals, which could be used as table decorations. They were adorned by him with dolphins, unicorns, seahorses, music-making angels and military standard-bearers. In addition, having found in old books descriptions of the mysterious fountains of Hiero, he invented a clever system of hidden pipes through which water could be conveyed until it splashed into the basins.

Frey and his wife had a daughter named Agnes, a few years younger than Albrecht Dürer. The parents on both sides had long been planning to cement the friendship between the two families by marrying the pair. Albrecht was unwilling to disappoint the promoters of this innocent conspiracy. His affections were not otherwise engaged; Agnes was pretty, unspoiled and seemed to have a gentle disposition. Ardent traveller as he had been, he now felt quite settled and allowed himself to be persuaded to take a wife and set up a home of his own. His love for the girl, whom he calls 'my Agnes' – he drew several charming portraits of her – took the place of any regrets he may have felt for his recent happy wanderings. It was, moreover, high time for him to establish a studio and begin work on his own account.

He was essentially a professional painter, that is to say, preoccu-

ST JEROME IN HIS STUDY. 1514.

pied by problems of the treatment of his materials. Colour organisation and lighting were what counted most with him and it was these effects which he had chiefly studied in the pictures he had seen and at the studios he had visited. Yet the art of engraving interested him nearly as much as that of painting. His own preliminary works, at the age of thirteen or fourteen, had been tentative woodcuts in which he naively attempted to imitate the mastery of such men as Schongauer. German art was in fact much influenced by engravings at this period. In the first place they were cheap: they could be easily and rapidly multiplied and sold at a price within almost anyone's reach. In addition to this purely practical advantage it was considered, in a country which has never lost sight of the educative function of art, that engravings were an easy means of improving general knowledge and taste even among the illiterate. Finally, the wide-spread diffusion of works in this medium enabled a painter to become known to a far greater public than could see his actual pictures. For panels were difficult to transport and their owners were reluctant to part with them, whereas bundles of engravings could be carried anywhere in the packs of pedlars.

Dürer would have been glad to paint some large pictures. But he could not do so until some private patron or church commissioned him. There were at the time many distinguished masters in Germany who were normally entrusted with such work. Orders were unlikely to be given to a young artist, still unknown, scarcely out of his apprenticeship, who had only just set up shop. Engravings were the best means of acquiring a reputation. As soon as prints bearing his initials began to be sought out by those interested in the art, he would also be asked to supply portraits and altarpieces.

For nearly half a century Nuremberg engravings had been as much in demand as those of Basle and Colmar. The first book-printing presses had been installed in the city by Johann Sensenschmid in 1470. Since then many more had been established. Those of Anthony Koburger now employed over a hundred workmen. The volumes produced were famous for beauty of type-face, perfect legibility and splendid illustrations. The art of engraving had been greatly stimulated by that of illustrated book production. For the purchasers of these early printed volumes enjoyed narratives of travel in remote countries and tales of ancient history, with plenty of pictures calculated rather to excite than to satisfy their curiosity. Their imagination never failed to respond to the stimulus of the astounding and the prodigious.

But Dürer was fond of engraving for its own sake, apart from the pecuniary profit it brought him. His interest in virtuosity revelled in the necessary simplicity of line, the richly sober effect of black and white, the enhanced plasticity acquired by a design in which colour played no part. He was also attracted by the actual methods of production, though he had never used a knife on wood himself. Artists generally left such work to specially trained craftsmen. But he took a sensuous pleasure in handling the paper, contemplating the gleaming black areas and inhaling the odour of fresh ink retained by the newly printed images. The abundance of subtle contrasts, moreover, provided by work in monochrome exactly suited a certain austerity in his character. He discovered, finally, that his colour sense was even more refined when he only had tones of black and white at his disposal.

At Koburger's printing works he eventually came to understand in detail the technique of engraving. He watched all the stages of production, both of designs and books, from the choice of ink and paper to the finished print, in which the machine obeyed the slightest variation of pressure applied by hand.

He was also able to examine at leisure, in his godfather's collection, the productions of Koburger's rivals. For the old master-printer still took a great interest in any new processes originated by those of his trade in other cities. Dürer could accordingly study a great number of Swabian, Rhineland and Franconian engravings, freely comparing the most varied styles and learning all that was to be known about methods of cutting, inking and printing.

German artists had experimented with copper engraving. But they did not succeed in it so well as the Italians. Either the familiarity of the former with wood made them unskilful in the treatment of copper or they preferred the popular appeal of the woodcut, with its heavier, more sensual effect. The first copper engravings were

116

humanist in feeling. They were produced for the most part by men of learning who had undergone the influence of classical literature. It is significant that the outstanding contemporary copper engravings were executed by Mantegna, who summed up in his own person Renaissance style, Italian national sentiment and the revival of the usages, thoughts, emotions and legends of antiquity.

Dürer's passion for the works of Bellini had not blinded him to Mantegna's merits. It seems, in fact, that the mutually opposed tendencies of these two painters, the plastic severity of Mantegna and Giovanni's refinement of colour, struggled for supremacy in the mind of the German artist. As a born painter he felt more drawn to Bellini; but as an engraver he could not fail to experience the deepest admiration for Mantegna's mastery of the burin. Dürer had brought back some of the latter's engravings from Italy and had copied such as he could not afford to buy. To judge from his drawings and copies of this period, he appears to have been even more impressed by Mantegna than by Bellini. For the style and emphasis of his first copper engravings have a great deal in common with those of Mantegna.

He was at this time still deep in the study of pagan mythology. It was therefore natural that he should deal in his engravings with subjects taken from antique fables as well as with Christian topics. It was less easy to sell the former than the latter, for the customers of all kinds who bought prints from pedlars or at fairs preferred illustrations of familiar tales. They had never heard of Orpheus, Heracles or Deianira. They were less interested in extraordinary scenes, depicting fabulous monsters, than in illustrations of the Biblical narratives treated in the popular, naturalistic way congenial to German taste.

Dürer's own style, confused by his extensive travels and the various ideas he had absorbed, was not yet mature. He was torn between two conflicting tendencies, that of the German medieval Christian tradition and that of Renaissance innovation, which involved the cult of antiquity and submission in all respects to Italian practice. Dürer was no pagan, either in thought or feeling. His birth and training, his character itself, forbade anything but an entirely superficial acceptance of Renaissance neo-classicism. Consequently, the few engravings he executed in Mantegna's manner are to be regarded as exceptional eccentricities on his part. They corresponded neither with his own most instinctive feelings nor with the preferences of his patrons. He drew like Mantegna out of sheer perversity or perhaps to astonish his fellow-citizens by confronting them with audacities to which they were not accustomed.

Eventually, however, he returned to engravings of the usual subjects in favour with both the lay public and the artists of Germany. These were either scenes of country life, to supply the demand of peasants to see themselves depicted in entertaining fashion, or else religious works, to stimulate devotion and protect the home against illness or damage by fire, as well as to safeguard the horses and cattle in the stable from the 'staggers' or foot-and-mouth disease. Dürer accordingly met the requirements of these worthy people by producing engravings in which the style of Schongauer is clearly recognisable. It was not that he thought Schongauer superior to any other master. He simply saw that this artist's delicate and elegant charm, combining piety with worldliness and sensuality with chastity, was best suited to the contemporary German type of religious feeling.

On the other hand Dürer's first engravings on copper, his *Holy Family with a Grasshopper* and *Virgin with the Monkey* (p. 142), contained novel and daring features, unconnected with Schongauer's manner, which connoisseurs were quick to appreciate. The conventional theme left them cold; but they admired the freedom of line, the mellow blacks and the bold treatment of textiles and faces. They also praised the originality of the landscape composition, the suggestion of clear, sparkling air, the facial beauty of the figures and the discreet realism which attempted no precise reproduction of natural features but an evocation of them, full of majesty and tenderness.

The most striking and up-to-date characteristic of these engravings was less their brilliant, effortless technique, though that was still a novelty in Germany, than their new vision of and feeling for nature. Hitherto landscape had been entirely subordinate to subject, playing a merely decorative part in the picture, and intended to relieve the

HEAD OF AN APOSTLE. STUDY FOR THE HELLER ALTARPIECE. 1508.
ALBERTINA, VIENNA.

solemnity of the Biblical episode with a lighter touch. No one looked for realism in such backgrounds. In view of their purely ornamental function it mattered little if they appeared as artificial and commonplace as stage scenery.

Venetian art had helped Dürer to rid himself of these stylised effects, still practised by the majority of his compatriots. Swiss and Tyrolese painters had also shown him admirable specimens of naturalistic landscape. Moser, Witz and Pacher, who loved nature both for its own sake and for the emotions it could communicate to mankind, had tried to represent what they had seen and felt in its manifestations. Bellini himself had brought nature into such close association with all the events of human life that a sunset, for instance, might play an integral part in one of his Nativity or Crucifixion scenes. He related, in fact, every aspect of land, sky and water to the gestures and moods of humanity.

The variety of the regions through which Dürer had passed in the course of his travels and the care he had taken with the drawings and water-colours he had made of the most attractive or unfamiliar of them had provided him with a great range of pictorial motives emanating from the most diverse sources. The experts to whom he showed these productions were loud in their admiration. For the works in question were the first, perhaps, in Germany to express a direct recognition of landscape as no longer a decorative accessory but as existing in its own right and at the same time capable of intimately affecting the mind of the spectator.

These water-colours were no doubt intended by Dürer, at the time of their execution, to serve merely as records. But even when they appeared to have no other than documentary merits, they were painted with a freedom which could only be due to profound penetration by the artist of the spirit of the place. They might merely represent a momentary and local aspect of nature. But they revealed in addition the fervent concord then subsisting between the landscape and the eye that observed it. The sky with its lighter passages and its clouds, the contours of the ground noted with a subtle understanding of geological variation, the picturesque detail of a castle perched on a hill or the houses of a village dotted along the shore of a faintly blue lake, are again significant of that love of truth so deeply ingrained in Dürer's art and character. But other sketches are fugitive impressions, only slightly tinted with colour, which resemble heartfelt, poetic confessions, insubstantial transcriptions of indescribable emotion in the painter as he watched the rose and green hues of a sunset, the sombre blue of twilight or sometimes only the simple reflection of a tree in water.

The remarkable modernity of these water-colours does not appear to have been much influenced by Italian practice. Italy played no more than a generative part in this section of Dürer's work. He drew his landscapes from the most fundamental depths of his own being. Direct and prolonged experience of the endless variety of nature developed simultaneously both his style and his sensibility. Yet it may well have been that Venetian art sharpened his faculties of observation. For paintings often call attention to appearances in nature that would otherwise have passed unnoticed. At the same time, the water-colours which at this date represented his boldest essays in innovation owed nothing to any of the masters he had studied. Their effect was due neither to aesthetic principle, technical skill nor the deliberate working out of theory. Their high value resides, on the contrary, in their immediate, involuntary, perhaps even subconscious quality.

A great painter had been born at Nuremberg. But the fact was not instantly recognised by the citizens. Dürer might have remained obscure for several years longer if he had not been discovered by a prince, in the modest studio he occupied, which was part of the premises of his godfather Koburger. Of the German rulers who took an interest in painting at that time the young Elector of Saxony was reputed to be both a generous and an enlightened patron. He had spent little time on cultural pursuits. Weapons and horses attracted him more than books. But he possessed a certain amount of innate good taste and showed a flair for picking out the most original of the artists in his territory, those most likely to render his reign illustrious. The elderly Wolgemut was one of his favourites. But he was more drawn to younger men of talent, whom he took pleasure in seeking out and encouraging. He had, for instance, at-

122   AN APOSTLE. STUDY FOR THE HELLER ALTARPIECE. 1508.
ALBERTINA, VIENNA.

tracted to his Court both Hans Burgkmair, whom Dürer had met at the Fuggers' house in Augsburg, and a still unknown Franconian, who had begun his career by producing woodcuts, like his father, and was called Lucas Cranach. This artist created works of an exuberant fancy and charm, with a fairylike grace marked by delicate sensuality, tender lyricism and humour.

Dürer was ordered to send some of his engravings to Weimar, where the Elector admired their originality and freedom both from German tradition and Italian influence. Frederick, called the Wise, knew genius when he saw it. He called for reports on Dürer's painting. The result was that one day, about a year after the latter's return to Nuremberg from Italy, he received a flattering commission. He was to paint the Prince's portrait.

The order was both a great honour and a severe test. Dürer had executed few portraits at the time, for the prominent citizens of Nuremberg still hesitated to apply to him. His models were his wife, his father and himself. His future career was now at stake. For if he contrived to satisfy Frederick his fortune would be made. The Elector set the fashion in German society, as the Medici and Sforza families did in Italy. Consequently, if he liked the portrait he had ordered from Dürer, the German nobility would follow his example and the Nuremberg burghers, unwilling to be outdone by the aristocracy, would in their turn patronise the successful artist.

Frederick the Wise lived up to his name by setting no restrictions on the imagination and spontaneity of the artists he employed. As they were usually young he considered that they ought to show proof of originality and independence. He was aware, through his connections with the Italian humanists, of what was going on south of the Alps. He was therefore by no means averse to the introduction at his Court of the new techniques invented in that quarter. But he did not want the German artists to imitate the 'foreigners' too slavishly. He shared the tendency of his time and place to look to the establishment of a German art firmly based on the national traditions, while at the same time warmly welcoming novelties from abroad. Frederick prided himself on being, like the merchant princes of Milan, Florence and Venice, a 'man of the Renaissance'. The phrase was not yet current: people in those days were more concerned to be than to define and explain their mode of being. But the ideas of the Renaissance were widespread, even in Germany. An unprecedented air was blowing from the south, keener, brighter and bolder than formerly, and redolent of new ardours.

Frederick, though he did not declare his aims in so many words, longed for a German Renaissance, in thought as much as in art. The most enterprising and, as some people considered, the most reprehensible of notions found an asylum at his Court. The Church sometimes complained that he was to blame for showing so much indulgence to certain opinions, not untinged by heresy, which had begun to affect German religious circles in the last years of the fifteenth century. The first works of the youthful Dürer showed no trace of conformist leanings. They were also as free from the influence of Franconian tradition as they were from that of Italian prestige. The shrewd Elector perceived at once that Dürer, of all the artists then working in Germany, was the most likely to give the national school an entirely fresh start. Cranach seemed still too subject to Gothic mannerism. Burgkmair's personal idiom was taking time to develop. He remained at present a disciple of the elder Holbein. Dürer, on the other hand, already conscious of his own powers, knew very well what both his genius and the age required of him.

His first portrait of Frederick (p. 140) – several others were to follow – made a thoroughly modern impression, though it had not broken with German tradition. The artist's realism is conspicuous in the precision with which details of costume and certain facial features are rendered. But the total effect of a vigorous and stately monumentality appeared strikingly novel. The Gothic concern with trifles in the interests of exact reproduction is quite absent. Dürer, by a stroke of genius, had passed beyond any such finicking attention to fact and incident. He had achieved, at a bound, the 'grand style', comparable with the best contemporary Italian work. He had sought to convey psychological truth, which he considered the essential element of a portrait; but he had successfully associated this preoccupation with a concentration upon his powerfully plastic sense of form. The sitter appears intensely alive in his own unique way, both

124

JACOB FUGGER THE RICH. 1520.
ALTE PINAKOTHEK, MUNICH.

125

physically and morally, yet this naturalism does not impair the plastic energy of the work.

The Elector expressed his satisfaction with the portrait. It lent, in fact, something of the dignity of a humanist to his gross, puffy and hairy countenance. He is not shown with any of the attributes of sovereignty. But the roll of parchment in his hand pleased him, for he was fond of being regarded as a man of learning, though horse-flesh and the sword were much more in his line. Dürer had won his stake. He had no intention, however, of exploiting the favour of the Prince by leaving Nuremberg to go to Weimar. For he suspected with good reason that a Court painter would run the risk of losing his aesthetic and personal freedom in the service of great lords. Dürer was not well off. But the proceeds from his engravings, which his mother and wife offered for sale at fairs, sufficed for his modest needs. Moreover, the Nuremberg burghers, roused by the partiality of the Saxon ruler for his works, were now hastening to commission altarpieces and portraits from him.

Frederick's portrait had been executed on the occasion of his visit to Nuremberg in April 1496. He subsequently tried to persuade Dürer to go to Weimar with him, but in vain. The young artist, after expending so much energy during his long years of travel, was in fact feeling the need of self-communion at the deepest level. He was afforded the opportunity for such introspection by the somewhat monotonous peace of his domestic hearth and his prolonged labours on still unfinished paintings ordered for churches or votive chapels. A further departure would merely have interrupted his meditations again.

The problems he was trying to solve were not solely aesthetic. His personal life was involved as much as, or even more than, his artistic genius.

When, therefore, he examined himself in the mirror, his troubled gaze reflected his troubled mind. The features he studied, those of the depressed, worried-looking youth shown in the Erlangen Library drawing (p. 29), of the desperately solemn young man in that of the Lemberg Museum or the dandified personage holding a thistle in the picture at the Louvre (p. 10), are in every case different aspects of the same complex individuality, one he was himself discovering. These three portraits all date from his years of travel. The two drawings have the spirited, frank, unhesitating quality of an analysis which has not yet ventured very far into the intricacies of character. The *Self-portrait* in which he holds a sprig of snakeroot is still too much concerned with outward appearances for psychological research to have played any great part in it. It was probably painted during his visit to Strasbourg: the influence of the older Alsatian masters is clearly perceptible. The thistle, a medieval symbol of masculine conjugal fidelity, as well as a certain deliberate severity of handling and the melancholy gaze, both reserved and challenging, complicate rather than elucidate the terms of the artist's problem. The pleasure he evidently took in composing a masterpiece at this early stage, presenting a romantic view of himself, not without a hint of eccentric affectation, merely adds a fresh intricacy to the traces of a private confession pursued by the investigator. The attractive warmth of the tones and the triumphant resolution of some particularly difficult plastic problems even suggest a certain degree of shallow complacency. This style is not that of the real Dürer, during his years of apprenticeship, or at any rate it only indicates one side of his nature. In condescending to reveal it he does not disclose any of the deeper levels of his mind. The haughty expression in fact appears to repudiate in advance any importunate curiosity.

Dürer saw nothing terrible in the mysteries of religion. It is even possible to detect a certain quietist serenity in his familiar treatment of heavenly beings. When Frederick the Wise ordered a triptych from him for the chapel of the castle of Wittenberg, the artist combined in it his memories of Italy with the suavity of the Schongauer tradition. The picture (p. 133) is full of a touching sweetness of sentiment. The Virgin who leans above the sleeping Child has the benevolence and grace of a Madonna by Bellini. She might have been seen in one of Dürer's childish dreams. The wings of the altarpiece, representing St Anthony (p. 136) and St Sebastian (p. 137), also prove that Dürer did not stand in much awe of the terrors of Holy Writ. The chubby infants representing angels have no diffi-

A German Woman from Venice. About 1507.

DAHLEM MUSEUM, BERLIN.

culty in driving away the demons tormenting the anchorite. The martyr's body is intact except for the wound in his side, which makes him resemble Adonis. He is simply a handsome lad of almost Hellenic charm. A flower in a vessel of transparent glass adds an idea of fragility to the calm, radiant figure of the saint.

There is some reason to believe that Dürer remained sensitive to the pagan seductions of Renaissance Italy. His taste for the nude defied the austere conventions of Franconia, which would have nothing to do with sensual treatment of the human form. As a young man he broke the rules by boldly engraving the unclothed figures of beautiful women in provocative attitudes. These audacities made his straitlaced mother blush. In order to advance a learned reason for exhibiting such products of a profane imagination and thus disguise their true import, he gave the four sturdy, appetising nudes, brimming with a hale, exuberant sensuality, whom he called *The Four Sorceresses* (p. 143), a fantastic setting. Anyone who cared to do so might guess the esoteric meaning of the cryptic letters on the sphere. Scholars might wrangle over the print of a worthy fellow asleep over his stove, unmoved by the allurements of a Venus of splendid proportions, attended by a Cupid on stilts. The Nuremberg humanists who met at Pirckheimer's house expatiated at length on the significance of this allegory. But it is possible that it may have been no allegory at all, merely the whim of a young artist annoyed by the puritanical conventionality of his fellow-citizens and diverting attention, by a pretence of mystery, from the simple pleasure he had experienced in delineating a massive abdomen, curving arms and robustly elegant legs. However that may be, Dürer seems to whisper to us, behind his hand, how sorry we ought to be for that poor fool deep in ridiculous slumbers with so glorious a creature within reach!

At Venice one could be as uninhibited as one pleased. Sexual freedom and gaiety were subject to no restraint or hypocrisy. Plenty of excellent nude models were to be had for the asking. But the timid, shrinking women of Franconia hardly dared to undress. Agnes herself, fond of her husband as she was, utterly refused to allow him to paint her without clothing. It was only possible to study human anatomy, to note how the limbs were attached to the body and

THE WOMEN'S BATH. 1496.
KUNSTHALLE, BREMEN.

moved in space, to observe the effect of sunlight or lamplight on flesh, by resorting to the greatest secrecy, concealed from prying or malicious eyes.

130

THE MEN'S BATH. 1497.

131

Dürer's mind, like his art, was still medieval, though he would have wished it far otherwise. He may even have intended to shock his fellow-citizens by the freedom which he claimed as an artist, for example in the coarsely sensual, almost pornographic, drawings he made in the public baths. It amused him to exaggerate his pagan sympathies in the desire he felt, like many other young people, to disconcert his neighbours. But his feeling for antiquity did not go very deep. His character, in spite of the many daring experiments he made, remained essentially pious, modest, serious and reserved. All the same, life would be very dull if one could not occasionally make a long nose at the philistines and thus obtain a little relief from all the disagreeable, graceless and scowling physiognomies one had to paint in order to acquire fame and fortune.

But the century was coming to an end. The moral and social foundations of society were reeling. Nuremberg too was feeling the repercussion of the great upheavals of the age. Dürer himself, for all the paganism to which he pretended, could hear the rumblings of an approaching storm within him, the groundswell of an anguished mysticism. He set down, like a seal upon the record of his happy youth, another *Self-portrait* (p. 145). It was one way of bidding his existing personality farewell. The young man in the picture is exquisitely, perhaps rather extravagantly, dressed. He has posed a rakish cap on his girlish curls and confronts the spectator with a cool, ironic gaze. The background, a memory of his travels, is mountainous. That gaze is directed simultaneously at the past and the future.

The past, his impetuous adolescence, had been full of reckless bursts of enthusiasm, intoxicating discoveries and uninhibited pleasures. Its irresponsibility took no thought for the morrow and left to maturity the task of unravelling the tangled skein of those riotous years. The Venetian dandy shown in the portrait seems only too confident in the seductive power of his effeminate grace and beauty. But just as, in the glimpse of landscape behind him, beyond the pleasing undulations of the plain, stand precipitous and frowning glaciers, so in the man's equivocal gaze a foreboding of tragedy can be discerned. The costume and the face itself are no more than the outer skin of a chrysalis, to be discarded by the future personality fore-

DRESDEN ALTARPIECE. CENTRE PANEL. VIRGIN AND CHILD.
DRESDEN, MUSEUM.

shadowed in that gaze when the coming tempest of conflicting emotions bursts upon him. The new Dürer was to live in fear, under the menace of the Apocalypse.

THE APOCALYPSE

In those days prodigious events occurred in Germany. The heavens were convulsed; giant meteors tore across the sky.

Celestial tumult was paralleled by social catastrophe. The prevalence of famine was regarded as God's warning to humanity, calling upon men to repent and atone for their sins. As though famine were not enough, it was almost immediately followed by outbreaks of the plague. Strange maladies ravaged the towns and the countryside. Drought scorched the harvests. Starving peasants infested the roads, as dangerous, in their misery, as so many packs of wolves.

In these conditions of acute suffering society was rent by class struggles. In the cities labourers rose against their employers and in the rural districts mobs maddened by hunger and distress rushed to storm the castles. The scourges of medieval times were reinforced by others, hitherto unknown, coming from unspecified, distant lands. Syphilis made its first appearance in Europe and instantly began to rage to such an extent that those whom the plague had spared now fell victims to its new accomplice.

The ensuing frenzy of migration in search of more favoured regions was not always due to the desire to escape famine or epidemics. It spread like the contagion of intoxication in a crowd, when even those who have not been drinking are affected. People left their homes without knowing why. They took to the road for no particular reason, driven only by a sort of purposeless yet irresistible impulse to wander. Such hordes of pious or ferocious vagabonds spread terror wherever they went. They took the form of long processions uttering plaintive cries, singing hymns or bawling ballads of a threatening character. The terrified inhabitants of the settlements they approached locked their doors and themselves issued forth to face the hazards of a nomadic existence.

Such a multiplication of calamities would have seemed less appalling if it had not been assumed that the anger of heaven lay behind their onset. All natural disasters were believed to be due to the wrath of God. It was to notify mankind of His imminent vengeance that He sent so many portents upon the earth. The signs were manifest to all who could read them. Nothing in nature, it was averred, happened by chance. If women gave birth to monsters and corn withered even before it was ripe, such evil omens could only mean that angels armed with swords were about to exterminate sinful humanity.

Such was the atmosphere in which the fifteenth century came to an end. It had been proud of its achievements, of its discoveries, scientific progress and advances in the understanding of the universe.

Accordingly, while the ravenous peasants were plundering districts not yet devastated by drought, long lines of penitents set out to weep and pray at Wilsnack, where three consecrated wafers were dripping blood. Elsewhere groups of the destitute, crazed by misfortune and fanaticism, gathered round the shepherd prophets who swarmed throughout the demented land. Anyone who could brandish a copy of the Book of Revelations might set up as a prophet, and the more fantastic his interpretations, the more numerous his disciples. In the disorder of the times such gangs of mystics, often rendered half insane by the crimes and debaucheries they had committed, constituted a danger to the State and were outlawed by ruling princes and municipal authorities. The visionary shepherd Hans Böheim harangued the vagrant peasants with the Book of Revelations in his hand and commanded them to perform a collective act of penance and then seize and share out the goods of others. This chieftain's hut soon became a focus of pilgrimage for his frantic followers and a hotbed of anarchy which terrorised the whole country with its revolutionary raids. Meanwhile, the night sky was streaked by dreadful signs of the wrath to come. Stars fell from the firmament, devils and apparitions stalked unimpeded through the streets of the towns, frightening the citizens out of their wits. Soon, it was foretold, a rain of fire would descend, the sun would turn dark as a woolsack and the heavens would be rolled up like a scroll of manuscript. Then the period of great abomination would begin, followed by the end of the world.

Dürer was familiar with the sublime and terrifying book written by St John in the island to which he had been banished. The young artist's religious feelings had been greatly stimulated by the apostle's visions. For Dürer, too, was conscious of having sinned. He may not have shared the absurd superstitions which caused so much panic among the ignorant in the wave of alarm that swept over Germany in those days. But he still stood too close to the childishly simple faith of the Middle Ages not to be affected by the deep and widespread uneasiness of the time.

The national crisis was both a social and a spiritual one. Dürer could not escape its influence. He suffered from almost continuous fits of unrest, which he made periodic attempts to overcome by applying himself to the pleasures of sensuous enjoyment or intellectual demonstration. But at bottom this 'man of the Renaissance' and friend of humanists possessed, perhaps, a good deal of the primitive mentality of a peasant or shepherd. Sometimes he felt the

DRESDEN ALTARPIECE.
LEFT-HAND WING PANEL.
ST ANTHONY. About 1496.
DRESDEN, MUSEUM.

authority of reason to be unques-
tionable. But his confidence in it
was repeatedly shaken by the disturbing impact of conscientious
scruples in his own mind or by
that of the outbursts of collective
mania he saw around him.

His high degree of sensuality
carried with it the bitter fore-
bodings of death and annihilation
that follow upon the exercise of
all carnal pleasures. He expressed
such feelings with tragic intensity
in one of his first engravings on
copper, entitled the *Incubus*. It
shows a terrified woman in the
grasp of a fierce-eyed, bony being
which is trying forcibly to lift the
hem of her dress. A little later he
subjected this theme, borrowed
from the *danse macabre* motif
which had so perturbed the Middle
Ages, to even more dramatic
treatment. In the *Incubus* he
had simply illustrated a woman
struggling in the grip of a monster
who is trying to ravish her. In
the *Walk* (p. 151), on the other
hand, which dates from 1497,
the figure of Death is left almost
imperceptible. At a first glance
there is nothing to be seen but an

DRESDEN ALTARPIECE.
RIGHT-HAND WING PANEL.
ST SEBASTIAN. About 1496.
DRESDEN, MUSEUM.

amorous young couple strolling through a rich, delightful landscape, plucking flowers and murmuring mutual endearments. But closer examination reveals a grinning death's head, crowning itself with an hour-glass, in the act of peeping from behind a tree. The lovers are not aware of this presence. Their ignorance is both sublime and distressing; they obviously do not realise that in the hour-glass brandished with menacing irony by Death the sands of their brief happiness are running out. Perhaps, if they did, they would not care. Perhaps they would remain as blissfully indifferent as ever, till the mocking skeleton darted from behind its tree and seized them by the throat.

Representations of the triumph of death were very numerous in the art of this period. But the most striking of them all is the Frankfort drawing by Dürer, executed at the same time as the *Walk*. On this occasion Death no longer takes the form of a lustful incubus or spies upon happy lovers from behind a tree. The victim is here a soldier, a type which Dürer knew well and had often drawn in his boyhood. He was familiar with both the Swabian pikeman, arrayed in plumed helmet and slashed breeches, shouldering a great glistening sword, and the heavily armoured cavalryman, bristling with spikes like a gigantic insect. In the drawing the horse seems either to have taken fright at a fallen tree barring the road or to have actually caught sight of a wild-haired apparition, its emaciated limbs wrapped in the rags of an old shroud. The phantom has certainly been seen by the dog, which is dashing away, with yelps of terror. Meanwhile, the horseman falls backwards, unseated by the sudden swerve of his mount, and at the same moment perceives the dread and hideous creature dropping from the air upon him like an enormous spider. The vertical composition gives the impression of figures hurled into an abyss. Its grim horror exceeds anything imagined by Baldung Grien, whom Dürer had known at Strasbourg, and shows what death meant for the conscience-stricken and visionary mind of the Nuremberg artist. He represented it in the form of a living skeleton of devilish aspect, seizing human beings and dragging them off to destruction, or else as that image of senility, with white hairs bristling from a noseless, fleshless skull, descending in an attitude of detestable cupidity upon the horseman. For Dürer, in short, death comes upon the individual at unexpected moments, as brutally cutting short the trooper's ride as it mockingly interrupts, with its hour-glass, the rambling lovers.

Such drawings and engravings, preceding by some years the famous *Knight, Death and the Devil* (p. 265), prove, in their sinister gravity, that Dürer's renderings of the figure and idea of Death were not mere flights of imagination, dismal fancies or adroit variations on the common *memento mori* theme. The images of death he produced at this period illustrate the aspect under which this concept occupied his mind. It was not regarded by him either with the philosophic interest of the humanists or the serenity and resignation of the Christian. He saw it as an *activity,* only too real in its direct and sudden irresistibly merciless incidence.

The designs he now began to compose for the Book of Revelations had not been ordered by anyone. It was in response to the bidding of his own thoughts and feelings, aroused by current public anxiety, that he abandoned work on portraits and religious paintings in order to devote himself to this urgent task.

Notions and representations of death were not, in Dürer's view, matters in which one could deal lightly with impunity. He had often engraved the armorial bearings of princes and burghers on his portraits of them. The sitters had always been anxious that he should not omit any quartering of their escutcheons. Now he invented the armorial bearings of death. In returning to the *Incubus* theme he introduced the variation of an apparent complacence in the woman's attitude to the shaggy skeleton's importunities. But the death's head on the coat of arms is designed with a ferocious and convincing naturalism, including the fissure in the skull through which the pride and glory of life may be supposed to have departed. Dürer now finds the idea of death summed up in the huge, bony brow, wretchedly inadequate nose, hollow eye-sockets and single jawbone equipped with only two loose teeth. He had stripped Death of all its romantic pretences, reducing it to the mere emblem, contained in the briefest possible, yet most tragically eloquent, outline.

He was obsessed by the thought of death, by anticipation of the

FREDERICK THE WISE. 1496.
DAHLEM MUSEUM, BERLIN.

end of the world and by that dread of the Millennium which then afflicted the whole of Germany. His Apocalypse engravings were no more than the expression of these feelings, the materialisation in plastic terms of an anxiety which had taken full possession of him. His passionate interest in painting was exceeded by his overmastering impulse to illustrate a book which described the end of the world. He had in view, moreover, not only his personal satisfaction but also the instruction and edification of the community. Consequently, he abandoned copper engraving for the time being and returned to the woodcut, the traditional, popular medium for illustration. It was no longer princely amateurs and middle-class patrons whom he wished to please, but the masses of the people. Accordingly Koburger, his printer, issued two editions, one with a German text for consumption by the populace and one in Latin for educated laymen and the clergy. As for the wholly illiterate, it was hoped that the engravings would be so readily comprehensible that the whole awe-inspiring drama of the Apocalypse would become clear even to those who could not read.

Dürer's cast of mind was essentially religious. The Apocalypse engravings reveal the fact more conspicuously than any of his other works. Yet he was also a man 'for whom the visible world exists'. He never doubted the reality of any object, even when presented to him in the flush of visionary intuition. He invariably set down what he saw without hesitation or ambiguity, in all its actuality, plastic life and material substance.

However far and high a man may go in exploration of supernatural mysteries, he can only interpret them in the impersonal language of the forms found in nature. He can express the ineffable, if at all, only by implying what lies behind and is actually obstructed by his words. If he is a draughtsman, he is forced to follow the text he is illustrating and reproduce what the author, in his capacity of seer, describes and shows to be symbols of certain forces, essences and ideas.

Dürer gives the impression of being able to enter this surrealist world by means of his very fidelity to natural appearances. There is hardly anything in his Apocalypse illustrations (pp. 154-5) which

141

THE VIRGIN WITH THE MONKEY. About 1498–1500.

THE FOUR SORCERESSES.

143

cannot be referred to human experience. Even the monsters he represents have no air of unreality or impossibility. The Apocalypse, in these works, is brought within the range of the perceptions and emotions of mankind. The vision can be understood by men but only by those for whom the sacred has become a living reality and the measure of all things.

The truly inspired artist is he who transcends the real by raising it to its highest pitch of intensity. There is no detail in the Apocalypse woodcuts that does not accord with objective and verifiable truth. The martyrdom of St John, for instance, is attended by persons who might be Nuremberg burghers. The setting recalls Nuremberg streets. The scene does not differ from that of any medieval execution, such as Dürer had no doubt witnessed. But the devilishly contorted features of the executioners exceed what would be normal on these occasions. Their grimaces express a kind of supernatural horror. Again, when John sees the seven candlesticks, they are depicted by Dürer with a realism which must be due to memories of the years spent in the workshop of his father, the goldsmith. The candlesticks are real from a human point of view, in so far as they resemble those used by men. But their heavenly reality, their supernatural existence and their prophetic significance are also evident, arising from some indefinable element in their presentation. It is not, strictly speaking, one of fantasy. And yet it precludes any suggestion that the objects in question are restricted to the commonplace functions of their nature.

These engravings were born of Dürer's imagination. But they were at the same time firmly based upon his observations and reproductions of the real world. The landscapes which appear in such cuts as those of *St Michael fighting the Dragon* (p. 155) or of the angel with the keys of the Pit obviously derive from the notes and sketches made by the artist on his travels. *The Great Whore* (p. 155) is founded upon some portrait of a Venetian courtesan. It might even be possible to identify this or that town, hill or wooded valley represented. But the detailed truth of the rendering is lost in the treatment by which the naturalistic features blend into the visionary atmosphere of the scene as a whole. It is more important to notice the submersion of all the separate items in the fervent wake, so to

SELF-PORTRAIT. 1498.
PRADO, MADRID.

145

speak, of the artist's inspiration. St John described what he saw in everyday language, for he had no other vocabulary. His illustrator would have misrepresented him, as a poet, in any but his own straightforward terms.

Dürer was well aware of all the difficulties involved. He began with a masterly exploitation of the plastic resources available for the evocation of mood. Each of his views is swept by violent winds symbolising the breath of prophecy. The angels' robes, the feathers of their wings and their long, curling tresses are wildly agitated. The dread heralds of the Apocalypse are borne at a gallop on wide horizontal swathes cut by the tempest through the landscape. Masses of cloud, rent from the air, are sent swirling into the fearful abysses of the world's end. The details in every case are those of natural phenomena. Yet at the same time they transcend nature without recourse to any of the distortions or stylisations generally employed to indicate the supernatural character of an object. The earth is never left behind. Its presence is always intimated by some reminiscence of its familiar aspect. But it is the earth of the Last Day, helpless in the hands of avenging angels, and scorched by the breath of demons and dragons. It is a world of the supernatural, which men tremble to behold, as the apostle trembled at the sight of the wonders revealed to him by God.

Dürer drew the immense energy which rendered such an achievement possible from two sources at once, spiritual and material. But it was perhaps by the latter, with which he never lost contact, that, like Antaeus, he was mainly supported. His visions invariably include aspects of nature. Land and sea shudder beneath the wings of his destroying angels. Surging waves, erupting volcanoes and showers of fire are accompanied by landscapes of smiling serenity, glades with boughs lightly stirred as the angels pass and smooth lakes unruffled by the aerial combat above them of seraphs and devils. Nature only takes part in the action when directly involved in its violence. Dürer may well have felt the need of some such provision of relief from the scenes of apocalyptic storm, some quiet spot of earth unscorched by infernal exhalations. The power with which he evokes the divinely imposed tragedy is still further increased by this contrast.

Dürer's Apocalypse series may therefore be regarded as inspired simultaneously by faith and love, the sacred and the profane dominions of his psychology. His love, moreover, is not only directed to the human victims lashed by fiery rain and cut down by the swords of destroying angels. It is given also to some individual tree, the foliage of which is modelled with such tender consideration, or to a single blade of grass drawn with such clear-sighted affection and intimate understanding of the vegetable world. Consequently, while actually describing the annihilation of the universe, he rescues the perishable from the void of its destruction, immortalises it by his art and preserves it for ever from change and decay.

For Dürer, besides being a seer and a devout Christian, was also a naturalist, in every sense of the word. He loved nature for its own sake and studied all its material manifestations. He believed in the reality of matter and of its visible characteristics.

The love of nature which appears in the Apocalypse engravings of 1498, as in all the artist's previous and succeeding works, complements, in short, his visionary faculty. These two traits, working in unison, enabled Dürer to associate, in creating so strange a work as the Apocalypse series, the most lofty spirituality with an objectivity as exact as it was sympathetic.

WOOD AND COPPER

Every kind of technique has, so to speak, a mind of its own, and every impulse of an artist's mind or sensibility chooses a different medium for the expression of its thought or feeling. Since Dürer returned from Italy he had been engraving with equal mastery on wood and copper. He took naturally to both procedures, for each accorded with a separate aspect of his character. He could not abandon one without prejudice to the other; for techniques are languages, and the meaning conveyed by certain words cannot be precisely and fully rendered except by those same words. An artist

LADY FROM NUREMBERG DRESSED FOR A BALL. 1500.
ALBERTINA, VIENNA.

does not himself arbitrarily select a medium: it is implied by the very nature of the idea he wishes to express. Particular materials are more suited than others to the representation of particular rhythms, inspirations of brain or heart and moral attitudes. An artist well enough endowed by training and temperament to be equally at home in any medium is hardly conscious of making a choice. For when the need arises he has already become merely the instrument of his creative instinct. Its blind intuitions and irresistible vitality dictate the proceedings of his intellect and hand.

If Dürer resorted to the woodcut for his 1498 Apocalypse series, it was not only because he would be assured of wider distribution owing to the artistic and economic conditions affecting the use of that medium; nor was it only because the public for which the book was intended was more familiar with the woodcut and more susceptible than others to its emotional appeal. It was above all because the pathos and mystery inherent in the subject could be better treated in the free style permissible to the wood engraver. The line, flowing as a pencil's, could convey depth, richness and flexibility, with a liveliness immediately obvious. Dürer would not have been able to incise on copper such shapes as he could cut in wood.

It was wood, accordingly, which he used for the first items of a series dealing with the life of the Virgin, which he composed at about the same time as those of the Apocalypse, though they were not published until some years afterwards. The Apocalypse drawings had been dashed off, so to speak, in a single effort, as though at the direct command of heaven. This rapidity of execution, suggesting that the artist worked in a kind of trance, ensured the spiritual and stylistic unity of the series. Dürer's creative drive seems never to have relaxed or hesitated till he had finished the work, as if he feared that the vision might fade and grow obscure or intractable. Thus the fifteen cuts which illustrate the book appear to have been done at a sitting, in one sustained burst of energy. Their power is that of elemental violence, the unresistable impetuosity of avalanche or flood.

The Life of the Virgin (pp. 166–7), on the other hand, and the 'Great Passion' woodcuts (pp. 178–9) begun at approximately the same period, show less unity and swiftness of execution. The subject did not, of course, demand such treatment. It had not the fiercely dramatic and hallucinatory qualities of the Apocalypse. Dürer, when he began these works, was in no such visionary mood. His brain was at rest and his conscience clear, whereas the illustrations to the Book of Revelations had required a prior condition of prophetic ecstasy, miraculously blind to all but spiritual phenomena. The scenes in the new series do not follow one another with the uncompromisingly enforced rapidity of the Apocalypse episodes. While the latter were designed almost continuously, the former are of the type which may take a lifetime to complete, against the setbacks of delays, interruptions and resumptions.

The Passion was Dürer's favourite subject. He dealt with it several times during his career, on varying scales and in different moods, using both wood and copper. For one series, known as the 'Green Passion', he resorted, for the sake of tragic emphasis, to a peculiar technique, combining pen and brush on a green surface. By this method the white highlights achieve a dramatic, explosive brilliance which lends them supernatural effect. To the end of his life he returned again and again to certain episodes, especially the Last Supper, of which he was particularly fond. Each rendering reflected his state of mind at the time. But the Apocalypse was never repeated. There was nothing he could add to or subtract from that series. The 1498 edition was reissued in 1511, unaltered in form and content. Though his other religious works show the influence of developments in his thought, social position and sentiments, the celestially inspired character of the Apocalypse did not admit of modification.

During the difficult years which saw its first publication, the troubled period of the turn of the century, Dürer gave free rein to the two sides of his nature in the production of woodcuts and copper engravings respectively. In the former he spoke as a man of the people, directly addressing ordinary men and women and dealing with the themes they preferred in such a way that they could not fail to be interested, moved and edified by his work.

When he treated profane subjects in this medium, which were

THE WALK. About 1496–1497.

also intended for popular consumption, he continued to restrict himself to ideas and feelings which could easily be communicated to the masses. The cuts he produced were calculated not only to attract or entertain them but also to appeal – though the response in this case may have been subconscious – to their resentment of class distinctions. It is significant that, while the first peasant risings in Germany were taking place and the country was restless, bewildered, impoverished and half starved, it was Dürer's intellect rather than his feelings that caused him to sympathise with the sufferings of the people. Reference to such woodcuts as *Samson and the Lion* and still more *Hercules and the Knights* proves the point.

The revolutionary cast of his mind appears more subtly in the copper engravings he executed at this period. These were not addressed to his humbler compatriots but to a more discriminating and refined public, the men of learning and the wealthy, cultivated merchants who were beginning to form a new aristocracy in fifteenth century Germany. Consequently, the rebellious spirit indicated in these works was not that of a proletarian but of an artist. Dürer's copper engravings, in fact, are even more influenced by the style of Mantegna than by that of Schongauer. They represent that side of his character which remained subject to Italian example. This was primarily because Italians excelled in engraving on copper, whereas the woodcut was a German speciality. The former medium, moreover, involved a whole train of associated ideas among which Dürer moved in dependence upon Italy.

There are obvious traces of Mantegna's manner in the *Hercules* woodcut. But they are confined to certain details. The spirit of the work as a whole is Germanic and medieval. On the other hand, the *Hercules* engraved on copper (p. 102), which followed two years later, is both ardently and awkwardly Italianate. The awkwardness is due to the barely intelligible handling of the allegory by an artist for whom classical mythology was not, as for the Italians, so familiar a subject as to be second nature. The very title of 'Hercules' seems ill suited to the scene, which shows a probably jealous woman attacking two lovers, a satyr and a nude nymph, with a stick, while a man wearing a grotesque helmet, shaped like a cock, tries to restrain the woman's frenzy. Here the same blind violence is depicted as in the drawing of *Orpheus Murdered by the Bacchants,* which is so thoroughly in the style of Mantegna as to suggest a mere copy of some work by the Paduan master. It would be interesting, in this connection, to investigate the significance of the 'Wild Man' theme in German art of the day. It has been held by some critics to have arisen from the shock administered to the thought of the dying Middle Ages by the discovery of hitherto unknown lands. Others have supposed that a 'Return to Nature' movement was responsible, impelled by some vague, unspecified and subconscious yearning for the barbaric freedom of primitive ages. This view would suggest that medieval man was already wearying of his characteristic civilisation and culture, so that the 'return to ancient ways', so constant and powerful an element in German mentality, then took to this strange mode of expression. The doings of 'wild men' were often illustrated, especially in tapestry, as though to compensate for the absence of brute nature from life indoors. Such figures were also used in heraldry, to support coats of arms. These facts prove that the conception had deep and widespread roots in the contemporary mind. In addition to actual images of the 'Wild Man' in person, the idea appears very frequently in the art of the time under more or less penetrable disguises. Nor can the possibility be ruled out, since art and life are so closely interconnected, that the Peasants' War provided on the material plane one of the manifold tokens of this preoccupation.

The theme of abduction is also prominent in Dürer's art and thought. Its most curious variant, since it is here coupled in a peculiarly intricate way with the notion of the 'Wild Man', appears in the copper engraving entitled *The Sea Monster* (p. 273), executed in 1500. The carrying off of a woman by a river- or sea-god is one of the most ancient conceptions in Greek mythology. The subject survived, grotesquely transformed, in the instinctive memory, the collective unconscious, of medieval man. It turns up again, for example, in the legend of the founding of the royal dynasty of Meroveus. The Renaissance revived it in such ingenious fables as the *Ambra* of Poliziano and Espinosa's *Fabula del Genil.* Dürer's treatment of the topic is singularly complex, highly characteristic of his

THE FOUR HORSEMEN

FOUR ANGELS STAYING THE WINDS

THE BATTLE OF THE ANGELS

THE WOMAN CLOTHED WITH THE SUN

THE REVELATION OF

ST MICHAEL FIGHTING THE DRAGON

THE WHORE OF BABYLON

THE SEVEN-HEADED MONSTER

THE ANGEL WITH THE KEY HURLS
THE DRAGON INTO THE ABYSS

ST JOHN (APOCALYPSE) 155

peculiar gift for fantasy, already noted in connection with the Apocalypse.

In the first place a most striking contrast is provided between the objective naturalism of a landscape so convincing as to appear to have been drawn on the spot, in a traveller's sketchbook, and the supernatural aspect of the sea monster. The creature swims in strangely stylised waves, bearing on its back a woman wearing only an elaborate and costly headdress. An agitated figure with beard, turban and scimitar, resembling a Turk, the arms raised in despair, races down the shore. In this case the theme of abduction is combined with that of the Wild Man, in so far as the triton is such a creature, rendered formidable to the highest degree by its hybrid character. At the same time it is evident from the extravagant artificiality of the woman's headdress that she was the mistress of the great fortified castle visible, which she had left to go bathing with her attendants. The triumph of barbarism over civilisation is illustrated in this engraving, as it is in the *Hercules* woodcut and even in the *Hercules* on copper, where the woman's murderous jealousy clearly indicates the most primitive mentality.

Dürer's Christian zeal found expression in his woodcuts. But he had also been influenced by the charm of antique legend and the revival of classical ideals of freedom in the sexual, intellectual and moral fields. His mythological compositions, however, lack unity. For he could not regard a myth as a biological reality. He saw it only as an extraneous, superimposed element. He was incapable of inventing an abstract landscape in which the spirit of fable could flourish. He had to show creatures as fantastic as the Sea Monster or the figure of Nemesis in settings so conventionally regional and naturalistic that in some cases it has been possible to identify the locality. He achieved perfect unity in his religious engravings, for the environment was then integrated with the event depicted. But in his evocations of legend he could not do so, since no connection then existed between the unreality of the figures and the profound truth to nature of their surroundings. Nevertheless, the impact of such works is all the more striking for that reason. The monster appears still more monstrous owing to its contrast with the familiar world around it. The sea-beast carrying off a woman through the waters of a Bavarian lake recalls the close association of the familiar and the fabulous characteristic of German fairy-tales. Magical events there take place in the midst of ordinary scenes. But in Dürer's mythological works the magic is bookish, intellectually contrived. It is both too clumsy and too ill-digested to be wholly convincing.

He was a great reader, interested in the literatures of pagan times. In his conversations with the Franconian humanists he became familiar with all sorts of strange and attractive stories. Willibald Pirckheimer, his friend from childhood, had the reputation of a renowned scholar and loved to show his erudition by quoting singular, obscure and allegorical passages from old books. It was to this learned and studious circle that Dürer owed the bulk of his knowledge of the written word, especially as concerned with antiquity. But the ancient world always remained alien to his spirit and temperament. He read the Bible more often than the Georgics or the Odyssey. He appears just as much at ease in the supernatural atmosphere of the Apocalypse, so far exceeding anything invented by the pagan imagination, as he seems awkward, stiff, baffled and inarticulate when dealing with mythology.

His allegories then become so hard to interpret that the ingenuity of commentators has ranged over a wide field and offered the most diverse explanations of them. It is, however, more important to discover what they meant for Dürer than to plumb the depths of secret significance attributed to them by resourceful philosophers or to investigate the mists of speculation thus created, even thicker than those already in existence. The anecdotal content of such a drawing as that known as the *Pupila Augusta* or the *Nemesis* engraving is unlikely to have been of much interest to the artist. No doubt there is a good deal of literature in his copper engravings on profane themes. But it is only in a secondary sense that the question of literature arises. The primary consideration is plastic. In the *Nemesis*, for instance, the main problem was to combine Bavarian or Tyrolean mountain scenery with the airborne apparition of a colossal female nude, to integrate this surprising figure with the familiar setting of a village among woods and stretches of water, to balance 'Fortune'

The Prodigal Son. About 1498.

on the globe in her traditional perpetual motion and to equip that stout matron's shoulders with eagle's wings beating upon the winds of chance. In comparision, the significance of the bridle and goblet she bears is of little moment. Nor does the name 'Nemesis' seem really suitable for this worthy Nuremberg citizeness, displaying in shameless nudity her vast stomach and massive thighs. Such a mythical personage would have been endowed with ideal beauty by an Italian artist. But for Dürer the allegory and the ideal were mere accessories, like the bridle and goblet, the latter, incidentally, drawn with the virtuosity of a master goldsmith. The essential features for him were the sensual vigour of the ungraceful body, the intense life of the region across which the 'goddess' moves, the quivering wings so closely studied from nature that one can almost visualise the artist's sketches, and the tactile values of flesh, metal, feathers and leather.

The powerful and direct naturalism of *Nemesis* has been overlaid by allusive or didactic elements which remain practically ineffective, such is the overwhelming effect of the purely formal objectivity. Yet, since Dürer's mythological figures are never real or convincing enough – nor even, one might say, sufficiently convinced of their own existence – to impose a personal atmosphere, his 'Fortune' flies in a void, a space which has neither consistency, depth nor actuality. It contrasts, therefore, all the more strikingly with the breathing, life-like and vigourous aspect of the landscape below. There is no connection whatever between the allegorical figure and its setting. They belong to entirely disparate worlds. The one is superimposed upon the other. There is no break in the intervening barrier, which is a moral even more than material frontier. The figure lends no life to the scenery: its detachment is as complete as if the halves of two different engravings had been brought together.

The unity absent from these mythological works is however splendidly achieved in the compositions based on either real life or a religious theme. The two famous prints executed in 1505, for example, called the *Small Horse* and the *Large Horse* (both p. 103), are wonderfully true to nature. The ruins in the background and the introduction of soldiers in fantastic armour do not affect the intense realism of these works. There is no point in suggesting that the four bronze horses Dürer had seen at St Mark's in Venice may have inspired the *Small Horse*. Its importance resides far less in any possible resemblances to what Dürer may have remembered or sketched on the spot than in the vitality and individual quality of the animal as rendered by the artist's creative realism. The beast is not simply any horse. It is one particular horse.

The points of resemblance between Dürer and Rembrandt are too evident to need any special emphasis. But it may be noted in the present connection that both were brought up on the Bible and temperamentally incapable of appreciating pagan mythology. Both were deeply religious men, of the type prone to supernatural visions. Thus in their studies of nature they became so possessed by the living reality of their subjects as to lend such external phenomena an intense vitality bordering upon the superhuman. Dürer's *St George*, also executed in 1505, is simply a magnificent specimen of contemporary German trooper, in spite of his halo and the vanquished dragon. Similarly, both the *Small Horse* and the *Large Horse* are wonderfully successful representations of individual animals. Their perfection is due to the absence of any consideration extraneous to the design and the object depicted.

Dürer could not give his forms mythological content by making his concrete objects embody a myth. But he triumphed whenever he was only concerned to endow an object with the highest possible degree of truth and life. As no alien or 'foreign' element then intruded upon his conception, the vital principle proper to what was being portrayed became visible and displayed its essential beauty, appealing to the emotions and senses alike. A great love, not only for horses in general but for these horses in particular, is vividly perceptible in these works, in which the animals' individualities are so powerfully rendered. The artist's affectionate understanding here transcends the character of the object he depicts. A similar heartfelt devotion and sense of communion is also evident in the *Prodigal Son* (p. 158), engraved a few years before. The perfect unity, in which the farm, animals and shepherds, all full of life and splendidly rendered, are combined, was only attained by Dürer at times when he himself felt completely in accord with nature.

LADY FROM NUREMBERG IN INDOOR COSTUME. 1500.
ALBERTINA, VIENNA.

Such close investigation and understanding of reality, intuitively as much as through the senses, sometimes brings about a romantically induced fusion between the observer and the phenomenon, a mutual intimacy amounting almost to identification. It was an ideal pursued by romantic painters in the eighteenth and nineteenth centuries as in the fifteenth and sixteenth. After 1500 Dürer reached a romantic conception of landscape which is extremely rare before that date. His *Sunset* of 1495, now in the British Museum, is one of the series of watercolours painted during his travels in which the young man's excitement is communicated with lyrical brevity, full of poetic zest. But these works are exceptional items in the great body of landscape notes. About 1500, however, and until the artist's second visit to Venice, he produced more and more romantic landscapes in the form of water-colour studies such as the *Castle at the Water's Edge*, now in the Bremen Museum, or the pen drawing in the Print Room at Berlin, representing a conversation between two hermits in a forest. Other such romantic landscapes of this period are mere décors for the main composition, to which, nevertheless, they supply the key-note and the tonal harmony.

Dürer seems in these years to have approached nature in the spirit of one seeking consolation from some great compassionate protectress, able to alleviate his sorrows and make him forget his troubles. He was in fact confronted by serious difficulties at the time. In 1502 his father died. The pious goldsmith had never been interested in making money; he had lived from hand to mouth, taking more pains over his work than over the problem of obtaining a fair price for it. Consequently, the family was left very badly off. His other sons either did not live in Nuremberg or were financially insecure themselves. So it fell to Albrecht to look after his invalid mother, the aged Barbara, now nearly blind. It was a further responsibility, in addition to those assumed owing to his recent departure from Koburger's establishment to set up on his own account. He now had his own printing-press. In order to increase the profits from his engravings he undertook their sale himself or sent his wife and mother to offer them to buyers at fairs and markets. The economic and aesthetic independence he had acquired and the niggardly payments he received for commissioned portraits and religious paintings forced him to deal with pecuniary matters which were a source of much personal irritation. To crown all his misfortunes, he fell ill in his turn, infected by a mysterious disease which was never properly cured and weakened him for the rest of his life, militating against his instinctive industry and even at certain periods making a hypochondriac of him.

Dürer's health was destined to play an important part in his life. His bodily sufferings affected his moral outlook, creating a peculiar atmosphere in his mind of varying degrees of distress and anxiety, with a paralysing effect upon his creative ardour. Eventually, from time to time, coinciding perhaps with the periodic attacks of his malady, he was seized with the desire to travel. He could never resist these impulses, cost what they might, in spite of his poverty and the commissions that poured in. He borrowed the necessary funds and left the pictures to be completed on his return. Few artists of his day travelled so much. It is known that, during his relatively short life, he visited Switzerland twice, Italy twice, the Low Countries for nearly two years, and Livonia in a long ramble that took him as far as Riga, in addition to his first long journeys as a student. He may also have been to France, England, Spain and Hungary, though there is no proof that he did so and nothing definite is known of any such wanderings.

He would not have been a German if he had not been given to the wanderlust so characteristic of his compatriots which is perhaps a legacy from their prehistoric nomadism. Any excuse would be enough to set him off on his travels. It might be the need to escape the plague, to wait upon the Emperor or to compare his own work with that of other painters and learn what they had to teach him. He alleged business reasons for these excursions, but in reality they were undertaken for his own pleasure. He never returned till he had spent his last penny and had nowhere else to go but the domestic hearth. It is doubtful whether, as has been asserted, Agnes was to blame for his frequent absences. He had called her 'my Agnes' in the halcyon days of their betrothal. He had painted for her the self-portrait which shows him holding a thistle, the symbol in the language of flowers for masculine marital fidelity. At this time, at any rate, she

BUNCH OF VIOLETS. About 1502.
ALBERTINA, VIENNA.

had not yet become the vixen she was afterwards affirmed to be. On the eve of his second departure for Italy he painted her portrait. The face is handsome, serious, tranquil, perhaps already somewhat heavy and inclined to puffiness. But the lips are beautifully formed, the nose perfect, the eyes full of mystery and intelligence. If this water-colour, now in the Bibliothèque Nationale, is really, as many critics believe, a portrait of Agnes executed between 1500 and 1501, it affords no ground for supposing that she was the cause of his leaving home for Venice.

DISENCHANTMENT

Morally, too, Dürer in 1505 was no longer the man he had been in 1496. The period of development from adolescence to maturity is always the most influential in the life of any individual. In Dürer's case it provided him with aesthetic and social experiences which ripened him and gave definite shape to his thought and feelings. Few external events of any importance occured. His mind, so to speak, was in retreat, taking stock of itself and of the aims suggested by his genius. He knew that, as a result of what his ⌐haracter and gifts had enabled him to learn during his first visit to Italy, he had created a new style. It was still a matter of wonder to his compatriots. Both the younger generation of artists and up-to-date connoisseurs had recognised it as exemplifying the direction that modern German painting should take. His versatile temperament had been lavished on a variety of techniques. He had employed both wood and copper for his engravings. In the 'Green Passion' the highlights had been stressed with white. The admirable warmth, sparkle and fluency of the paint in his more variegated works had built up, by its harmonious orchestration, such a major composition as the Paumgärtner altarpiece (pp. 169, 172-3). In certain of his portraits, conveying an effect of intimacy by a boldly impressionistic, unhesitating treatment, the light application of gouache allows the canvas to play its part by making use of its texture and grain, so that an extraordinarily lifelike representation is given of the sitter. Dürer had further enriched his methods by the addition of the Italian and Netherlandish procedures made available to the traditional art of medieval Germany. Finally, he had studied the general technical problems involved, digesting treatises on geometry and perspective, analysing the geological components of landscape and familiarising himself with the organic structure of plants and animals.

THE MEETING OF JOACHIM AND ANNE
AT THE GOLDEN GATE

THE MARRIAGE OF THE VIRGIN

THE VISITATION

THE CIRCUMCISION

THE PRESENTATION OF CHRIST
IN THE TEMPLE

THE FLIGHT INTO EGYPT

REPOSE ON THE FLIGHT INTO EGYPT

CHRIST TAKING LEAVE OF HIS MOTHER

THE VIRGIN

167

The ten years thus spent had turned the youth into a man. The lad with the thistle had become a grave, even stern personality, signing his works, for the first time, in Latin. He called himself now *Albertus Durerus Noricus,* no doubt under the influence of Pirckheimer and his learned friends, who enjoyed talking in the most admired idiom of that language. The *Self-portrait* in the Munich Pinakothek (p. 213) is the most striking illustration of the classical manner adopted by Dürer on his emergence from the whirlwinds of the Apocalypse. It carries classicism to an almost academic point. There is something cold, rigid and artificial about this work, which has neither the physical interest nor the psychological penetration of the earlier *Self-portraits.* It might be supposed that the artist had intended to produce a 'type' and only used himself as a model, on this occasion, for that purpose. He may have originally meant to execute a somewhat stylised head of Christ, in the Italian manner, and then been induced by the mysterious image, familiar yet unknown, presented by his mirror, to abandon his first idea and concentrate upon a portrait.

However that may be, the painting has a disturbing, disconcerting effect. It is not intimately revealing like the Louvre and Prado *Self-portraits.* The artist seems to have been bewildered by the stranger substituted, in the mirror, for his own person. The stylisation with which he began appears to have taken charge of the entire work, guiding its development, arresting every impulse to investigate the sitter's psychology and treating it, instead, with the kind of academic stiffness already noted. Perhaps Dürer had noticed an abstract formation of masses within the architectural volumes presented by a human face and expressed it by the pyramid of hair, a shape he inverted in the opening of the furred mantle. The structure before him was thus summarised by the interpenetration of two triangles known as the 'Star of David'.

In the other *Self-portraits* the spectator has a feeling of close acquaintance with the artist, while the latter in his turn seems in perfect agreement with his inner personality, the daily secret companion of every individual. But here for the first time Dürer sees himself through different eyes and has unquestionably fallen under his own spell. He was to rid himself of it in another *Self-portrait* of this

PAUMGARTNER ALTARPIECE. CENTRE PANEL : THE NATIVITY. About 1500.
ALTE PINAKOTHEK, MUNICH.

169

period, one full of picturesque fancy and good humour, that of the Jabach altarpiece, where he is depicted as a drummer. Two musicians had to be represented on one of the wings. Dürer gave one of them his own features, making him an eccentric-looking personage with long curling hair, garbed in a style of mingled splendour and negligence appropriate to a wandering instrumentalist who is not above buffoonery, and looking a bit of a tramp. The gaiety with which he set to work in this case contrasts so conspicuously with the mood of the Munich *Self-portrait* as to illustrate once more the intricate tangle of complex and mutually contradictory strands that render his character such a puzzle. The drummer is a jovial figure of romance. But this style hardens, in the Munich portrait, into a classicism like that of Ingres. The face has the inflexibility and impersonal dignity of a mask, hiding the restless turmoil of anguish and passions within.

Such was the man who now left for Italy. He was thirty. He had already known death, in the persons of those he loved; he had borne crushing burdens of economic responsibility. He did not set out, on this occasion, in the carefree spirit of youth: the home from which he was parting lay under the continuous menace of poverty. The landscapes he was about to visit were already familiar; no dazzling series of discoveries awaited him this time. There is no reason to suppose that he had lost the faculty of wonder so early in life. On the contrary, his thirst for new experiences remained insatiable, but he would no longer be tempted by each of them to open his sketchbook and box of colours. Nor did he intend to delay his journey by calling on foreign painters. He seems to have been preoccupied at this stage far more with his own work than with that of others. It was more himself than anyone else whom he was seeking in this return to Italy. He was less extrovert in his maturity than he had been in adolescence, more inclined to absorption in his own concerns. Nor should it be forgotten that his reputation was now made and his fame assured. His resumption of travel may well have been due in part to a wish to know more of his own renown and find out how far it had spread to foreign lands. No doubt his own estimate of it was somewhat exaggerated, for at Venice he refused invitations to dinner in case someone should try to poison him. In fact he was already a prey to suspicion, part of the cost of fame. He feared the Venetian painters might consider him a dangerous rival likely to rob them of their customers and therefore due for removal by means of a good dose of 'poudre de succession'. Was it not common gossip at Nuremberg that Regiomontanus had died that way, shortly after reaching Rome, at the hands of jealous competitors in the scientific world?

He was less trustful and careless now. Venice was no longer the inexhaustible source of enchantment it had been for him ten years earlier. The city had not changed in that decade. But the traveller had altered much. His fear of poison kept him aloof from the local artists, whose studios he now ceased to frequent in the old nonchalant way. He was also concerned to maintain his present reputation as a painter and consequently not to go about much or show himself too easy of access. He intended to impress the Italians by the dignified behaviour suitable to a 'master'.

It was the wrong frame of mind in which to confront the city. Venice is always gracious to those who desire her and solicit her favour. But she readily returns mistrust with interest and can then be ironical even with those who please her. Dürer's vexation at finding his glory less on the shores of the Adriatic than by the banks of the Pegnitz no doubt caused him to lead a retired life, exacerbated by disdain and wounded vanity. He sought out new friends among the Swabian or Franconian merchants at the German Club, where they met to discuss their affairs. The circle was dominated by the Fuggers, who were surrounded by the most distinguished members of the German colony in Venice. Dürer was already charged with plenty of commissions from his fellow-citizens. Pirckheimer, a leader of fashion, had asked him to look out for hats of the latest style. As this friend had always treated him with such consideration Dürer felt bound to do what he could for him.

The visitor had been disillusioned not only by Venice but also by Venetian painting. Once he had dashed excitedly from one church to another in search of new pictures. But those days were long over, like those on which he had walked across the isle of

Murano to call on the Vivarini
brothers, stood for so long to admire the newly finished paintings
in the School of St Ursula and
passionately adored the still incomplete compositions of Gentile
or Giovanni Bellini.

'It's always the same, time after
time,' he wrote one day to Pirckheimer. The monotony of the
Venetians' work wearied him. He
may have blamed them for not
developing as fast as he had himself during these last ten years.
Or he may have been angry with
them for not overwhelming him
with cries of delight and surprise
as they had on his former visit. It
may well have been Dürer's fault,
not the Venetians', that he took
less pleasure in their productions.
In any case, whether truly disappointed in his expectations or
prejudiced by ill-temper, he now
found less attraction in what had
previously so inspired him.

He might have learnt much still
from the Venetian painters he had
thus grown to despise. He was
too good an artist not to have
understood their new tendencies,
which he professed to regard with

PAUMGARTNER ALTARPIECE.
LEFT-HAND WING PANEL.
ST GEORGE. About 1500.
ALTE PINAKOTHEK, MUNICH.

such indifference. Carpaccio was decorating the Slavonian Church (San Giorgio degli Schiavoni) in a new style, different from that of the School of St Ursula. Giovanni Bellini, near his end, was beginning to interpret mythology in images full of splendour and mysterious fascination. Moreover, two startling men of genius, Giorgione and Titian, had already appeared among Giovanni's pupils, whom Dürer had not deigned to notice. It seems strange to say, 'It's always the same', when Cima da Conegliano was at the height of his powers and reputation, when Mansueti and Basaiti were introducing new feeling into landscape and the young Palma – later to be known as Palma Vecchio – was endowing portraiture with an unprecedented glory of sumptuous colour. Was Dürer really so unconcerned with the abundant originality of those young men, Cariani, Lotto, Savaldo and Pordenone, who were so constantly giving new directions to Venetian painting at this time?

If he kept the rising generation at arms' length, it was only to his

PAUMGARTNER ALTARPIECE. RIGHT-HAND WING PANEL. ST EUSTACE. About 1500. ALTE PINAKOTHEK, MUNICH.

173

own detriment. But his injustice to Giovanni Bellini is hard to account for. At seventy-five that artist, to whom Dürer owed so much, was far from exhausted. He was still tirelessly engaged in fruitful research, still young in spirit, rejuvenated by the eternal freshness of Greek mythology, to which the former painter of Madonnas and Lamentations had turned in the evening of his life. In anyone but Dürer such incomprehensible disparagement of the aged Giovanni would be absurd. But some excuse for his attitude may perhaps be found. In the first place Dürer's personal development and that of the Venetian School proceeded at different rhythms, in different directions. The creator of the Paumgartner altarpiece had every right to consider himself a master. Such lessons as he might have still learned from the young successors of Giovanni Bellini would perhaps have been of little value to him at this date. To be favourable, an influence must be brought to bear at the proper time. Dürer was not ready in those days, either aesthetically or psychologically, for the message a Titian or a Giorgione might have conveyed to him. He may have even felt instinctively that any such example might do him harm and impede his progress.

Nor had he, on this occasion, come to Venice to sit at the feet of others. He meant to practise his own art there. He had felt isolated from the city while working in his German environment. He proceeded to live on the shores of the Adriatic almost as if he had never left Nuremberg. In Venice his compatriots appreciated his fame, welcomed him warmly, monopolised him and overwhelmed him with orders. They were very proud of having the greatest of German painters living among them. Exiles soon contrive to transplant their native institutions. Dürer could easily fancy himself at Augsburg. For he found in the Fuggers' mansion and at the headquarters of the German colony the same customs, ideas, outlook and habits of thought as prevailed in Germany itself.

Celebrity often proves a heavy burden. Ten years before, Dürer had been merely a young, unknown painter in Venice, an apprentice on his travels, like so many others. His present solitude may sometimes have been irksome, though Venetian hospitality and friendliness to strangers render the possibility unlikely. Yet his very isolation had at least the great advantage of allowing him to be his own master, free from social obligations, obedient only to his own impulses and at liberty to yield to them at any moment. He had not yet drunk the cup of glory to the dregs. At present he had simply savoured its happy intoxication, the sparkling warmth of its heady draught. He enjoyed to the full the praise lavished upon him by his fellow-countrymen. He snubbed the Venetians who appeared insufficiently convinced of his title to fame. The 'great man' sunned himself, unconsciously, among those who really believed him 'great', thereby risking the loss of independence in matters of the utmost importance to him.

He now occupied, in the greatest comfort, a fine house which the Fuggers had placed at his disposal. The leading members of the German colony begged him to paint their portraits. As they had their own churches, as well as their own banks, wharves, warehouses and schools, Dürer was given a number of commissions for pictures to adorn their chapels. Even if he had wished to take some interest in the work of other artists he had not the time to do so. He was too busy himself to find leisure for such studies. This situation may, after all, have been the best for him. For he was now ready to condense and consolidate, in direct self-expression, all the lessons previously learnt in the years of apprenticeship and practical experience.

Naturally enough, while working for Germans in German surroundings, he allowed full scope to the essential characteristics of his race. The *Feast of Rose Garlands* (pp. 196–7), painted for the church of St Bartholomew in the German quarter, followed the best Franconian tradition. The italianate features of this production have no effect whatever on its profoundly Teutonic quality. It is true that the older convention for the structure of altarpieces is abandoned. The saints or donors formerly represented in rows along the wings are now grouped around the Virgin in an unprecedented manner, the crowded composition itself suggesting the packed congregations attending important ecclesiastical festivals. But there is no trace of anything like Giovanni Bellini's spacious and orderly designs. Even the landscape is northern and the colour organisation, so far as can be judged in the damaged state of the work – often more seriously

175

damaged by repair than by the accidents of time – retains certain crude and over-insistent notes in its lively execution.

Compared with previous works by the German schools the picture makes a strikingly novel impression. It is above all remarkable for the intensely romantic and emotional treatment of the faces, for the dramatic vitality of the landscape, foreshadowing the styles of Ludwig Richter and C. D. Friedrich, and for the high piercing tones of the chromatic values. A gulf yawns between this painting and the Paumgartner altarpiece. Dürer himself appears in the panel, in a guise so different from those of the former self-portraits that he would be almost unrecognisable, were it not for the long, curling hair, practically the only feature this version has in common with the Munich image of the artist.

For the first time since the drawing produced at the age of thirteen the aquiline gaze, revealing the painter's personality at its deepest level, recurs. The fierce, burning stare fixed upon the spectator seems predatory, as though taking possession of the observing mind by indisputable right of actual ownership. This figure is no longer that of the preceding portraits of himself, all more or less superficial, telling a story or illustrating a phase. If ever an artist for once in his life manages to confess his passions and anxieties, to drop the mask and speak without extravagance or dissimulation, I believe that Dürer did so in this case. The achievement is of such importance that it tempts the critic to neglect the formal beauty and psychological acumen displayed in the other portraits shown in the painting, those of the Emperor Maximilian and Pope Julius II and those of the Fuggers, the merchants and the princes who lend the sacred scene aspects of an earthly humanity, vigorously objective, incomparably evocative of the living presence of the model.

These portraits are so numerous, judiciously observed and realistically rendered that they detract from the religious character of this work. The ideal – idealised – beauty of the Virgin has an almost conventional air among so many faces scored by worldly experience and secret passions. There is no suggestion of genuine piety in the picture. It is too full of mundane phenomena to call up thoughts of heaven. The fervent devotional feeling of the two *Depositions* of 1500, of the 1504 *Adoration,* of the Life of the Virgin or the 'Green Passion' is here almost wholly absent. The most striking feature of the large religious works executed by Dürer during his Venetian period is actually their lack of religious sentiment.

It may be conjectured that the particular kind of stereotyped charm, the mere pretence of spirituality, characteristic of the *Feast of Rose Garlands,* the *Madonna of the Goldfinch* and *Christ Among the Doctors* was paralleled by a change of heart. The production of a quantity of specifically orthodox paintings succeeded years of ardent faith, passionate devotion and visionary mysticism. The influence of Venice may have seduced the artist from his instinctive piety, one of his most important personal traits. His correspondence at this date reveals a superficial morality, a levity and an ironic cast of mind. He gives free rein to the love of pleasure which was another of the dominant features of his mentality. He boasts with ingenuous vanity

THE ANNUNCIATION

CHRIST TAKING LEAVE OF HIS MOTHER

THE LAST SUPPER

CHRIST ON THE MOUNT OF OLIVES

THE SMALL

CHRIST BEFORE CAIAPHAS

CHRIST ON THE CROSS

CHRIST APPEARS TO MARY MAGDALENE

CHRIST AND THE DISCIPLES AT EMMAUS

of the praise accorded to his work, of the throngs of Italians as well as Germans who visited his studio and of the compliments paid him by Giovanni Bellini.

Fewer and fewer traces of spirituality, more and more of sensuality, are to be found in his output of this period. The *Madonna of the Goldfinch* is no more than a girl in the bloom of youth. She is painted in those graded tones of pink and red which in Dürer's pictures invariably strike the observer as a gratuitous display of carnal attractions. The *Virgin with Animals* water-colour (p. 200) is another example of remarkable dissimilarity from his previous style, being simply the fanciful depiction of a grotesque menagerie. Dürer did not possess the typically Italian sense of balance, which enabled the sacred character of a production to be relieved by sensuous elements without degrading or cheapening its appeal.

He subsequently visited other parts of Italy, including Florence and Rome. He came to know artists of whose genius he had often heard. He saw the actual paintings he had formerly only known through engravings and copies. The indifference he showed to Italian pictures other than those of Venice would be astounding if it were not obvious that he had really nothing to learn from them. The lavish banquet offered by Italian aesthetic achievement to a foreign artist may endanger his talent. The most gifted painters risk the loss of their originality by contact with Italian creative work. Dürer may have mistrusted his own powers of resistance. In Rome he only wished to meet the Emperor Maximilian, whose portrait he had just introduced among those of the *Feast of Rose Garlands*. He wanted to be appointed Court Painter to the monarch. There was one other man in Italy, however, whom Dürer was particularly anxious to cultivate, as a necessary adviser at this point in his career. This personage was not one of the great painters, sculptors or architects of the century. Yet Dürer felt sure that he had much to teach.

The two men had already met several times. On the first occasion, at Venice in 1495, Dürer had been completely absorbed by the Venetian school. He was at that time captivated by Bellini. Again, five years later, when Jacopo de Barbari passed through Nuremberg in the Emperor's train, Dürer paid hardly any attention to the artist.

THE LAMENTATION FOR CHRIST. About 1500.
ALTE PINAKOTHEK, MUNICH.

But now all his thoughts were engaged by the single image of the man, whom he regarded as unique. Scorning Giorgione and Titian, Dürer pursued this minor figure from town to town, reduced to despair when he missed him, yet all the more impatient to catch him up. When at last he encountered him at Bologna, he was crushed by disappointment to find that either Jacopo did not possess the secret he was supposed to have or would not reveal it. Dürer, in his discouragement, felt that Italy had nothing more to offer him. He left the country, determined never to return.

THE GREAT SECRET

At the time of Dürer's first visit to Venice, when he became so fascinated by the art of Giovanni Bellini, an illustrious guest of the Republic was studying methods of defending the city against a Turkish attack then believed to be imminent. This expert was not a professional leader of troops, military engineer or strategist. He was a man of universal genius, active in every department of science and art. He would turn from the practice of painting and architecture to the invention of ingenious flying-machines and from the wet clay of a projected statue to the design of war-chariots equipped with scythes. Or he would elaborate strange theories, demonstrating the secrets which lurked beneath the cunning disguises of nature.

The Duke of Milan had given Leonardo da Vinci permission to come to the aid of the Venetians. That eminent man was never disconcerted or surprised by any commission. He would sketch the plan of a brothel as willingly as the complicated machinery of a self-propelled airship. He embarked upon his new task with the energy he applied to everything he undertook, from the most trivial to the most grandiose conceptions. At this date he was forty-three. He had already executed a number of suavely intriguing pictures, in which enigmatically smiling Madonnas confronted the mysterious gestures of angels. He considered painting, incidentally, one of the subordinate manifestations of his genius. He enjoyed employing his multifarious gifts in all kinds of directions, any one of which would have been enough for an ordinary man. But his all-embracing ambition was such that he felt himself an ignoramus if he neglected any field of human knowledge.

Dürer was at his period an unknown German apprentice-painter, badly in need of polish, intimidated by the succession of wonders presented to him, continuously captivated by the beauty or strangeness of what he saw and above all devoted to painting. He knew Leonardo's work by reputation. But the artist of the *Virgin of the Rocks* and Wolgemut's pupil differed so much intellectually that even if they had met, which is by no means certain, there is no reason to suppose that they would have had much in common. The young Franconian, entirely taken up as he was by the new methods of the Venetian school and so assiduous in his visits to the studios of Carpaccio, the Bellinis and the Vivarinis, took no account of the chance that put three men in his way with whom he later tried in vain to renew acquaintance.

He was chiefly exercised at that time, in fact, by a problem of technique, to which the Venetians eventually gave him the key. He was convinced that Mantegna could show him how to deal with the conception of form he had in view. He shared, in short, the enquiring and aspiring attitude of all the German schools at the end of the fifteenth century. They regarded the leadership of Padua as self-evident. In the German centres frequented by Dürer between the Rialto and Merceria districts he must have met a Venetian painter who had acquired some renown in Franconia, Jacopo de Barbari, known at Nuremberg as Jakob Walch. He owed his reputation mainly to his engravings, signed with the *caduceus* or messenger's wand; his paintings were few and less familiar. They had not yet attracted the attention of connoisseurs.

The young Dürer instinctively cultivated artists likely to assist him in getting rid of the complex accumulations of ignorance and contradictions in which he was floundering. His principal anxiety at the time was to free himself from the style of the old Franconian masters who had taught him. No doubt he still could not quite see which way his own genius was going and it was for this reason that he

THE LAMENTATION FOR CHRIST. Detail.

tried to clarify it by requesting certain artists to show him how they reached their best effects. Da Vinci, in that case, could only mislead a young German who considered the 'trade' he had learned from Wolgemut to be the rudiments of a pictorial science which the admirable Venetian discipline could not fail to perfect. While Dürer relied on Mantegna for instruction in plastic values, he learned from the Bellini and Vivarini brothers to appreciate the exquisite colouring of the universe and reproduce it in his work. He did not concern himself with the mysterious problems of invisible form. He was not indifferent to them, for he took an interest in all artistic questions. The reason was simply that different subjects call for attention at different stages of one's career. Dürer already had enough on his mind at that period. He may not, therefore, have paid much attention when Jacopo de Barbari told him that a close friend of Leonardo da Vinci had accompanied the latter to Venice and that this friend, an eminent scholar, had taken advantage of a stay in Nuremberg to arrange for the publication of some of his books by the famous printers there.

Dürer asked what the books were about. One was a Latin treatise on commercial accountancy, said de Barbari, entitled *Tractatus de Computis et Scripturis;* and another, a very bulky volume, dealt with mathematics: it was called the *Summa de Aritmetica.* The author, de Barbari added, had astonishing powers. He could solve all the riddles of the universe with his figures. All its forms were in fact governed by a certain law of proportions. If they obeyed its principles they were beautiful and if not they were ugly. Jakob Walch was full of admiration for so exceptional an intellect, capable of manipulating at will the components of matter itself. By way of proving the importance of Luca Pacioli's discoveries he cited the treatise by Piero della Francesca on proportion, the Diagram of the mathematician Hippocrates, Fibonacci's mathematical series and the commentaries by Campanus on the books of Euclid.

Pacioli's devoted pupil quoted in support of his master's theories the *Metaphysics* of Aristotle and the *Theaetetus* and *Timaeus* of Plato. Dürer had not learned Greek at school in Nuremberg and cared little for Plato's *Dialogues.* He was bewildered by de Barbari's talk and not much enlightened by hearing that the 'soul of the world' had a number.

He left Venice that same year, without having met either Leonardo da Vinci or the celebrated mathematician of Borgo San Sepolcro. Ten years passed, during which he reflected deeply on aesthetic problems. He also listened to a number of learned discussions by the Nuremberg humanists, which familiarised him with the names of Plato and Aristotle. As his art and technical skill developed he was drawn to the study, among others, of human anatomy. In seeking an answer to the question why some forms are regarded as beautiful and others ugly he remembered the theories of Jakob Walch and the allusions the latter had made to treatises by Luca Pacioli. Dürer saw now what Jean Vignot had meant when he said that there was no such thing as art without science. That great French architect had been called in a century before to advise the builders of the cathedral at Cologne. Apparently his contemporaries had also misunderstood the phrase, which meant that art is only possible if founded upon scientific knowledge of the structure of the universe. In other words, the clever use of brush or pencil serves no purpose if the artist is ignorant of the principles governing the composition and motion of the earth. For no science can exist without taking account of the universe as a whole and no art can be complete without a substantial basis of scientific data. *Ars sine scientia non est.*

The theory of proportion, however, was not new. It had been known and applied in the ancient world. The medieval architects built their cathedrals by the rule of the Golden Number and the Nuremberg goldsmiths automatically worked in accordance with the same great principle of harmony whenever they manufactured a chalice or a censer. No one saw anything miraculous about the science of proportion. It was not even given a special name. It had become simply a collection of studio precepts, a technique habitually applied by hand and brain and never called in question. Long before Dürer began to reflect on the Golden Number and Divine Proportion he had instinctively obeyed their laws, as a youth, while working as a jeweller. But doubtless he never dreamed that such principles might be equally useful to a painter. He did not become consciously aware of them until he started to draw the nude human figure and found himself obliged to take steps to represent the ideal he had intuitively conceived.

Accordingly, after returning to Nuremberg, Dürer set himself to rediscover on his own account, with the help of books he had brought from Venice and others in Pirckheimer's library, the laws of 'divine proportion' which he might have learned from Pacioli. He was convinced that they contained the 'great secret', that their figures would explain the entire structure of the world, since a single principle controlled the universe. 'That which is below is as that which is above' was a phrase occurring in the Books of Hermes, which were much esteemed by the Nuremberg students of the occult. In spite of the danger still involved at that time in the pursuit of studies which might easily give a scholar the reputation of a wizard, the most outstanding minds of the day were attracted to obscure doctrines of this kind. Dürer was certainly aware of a work published by Johannes Reuchlin in 1494 on the Sacred Tetragram YHWH, the supernatural properties of which the author expounded in his *De Verbo Mirifico*.

Reuchlin was a remarkable man. The scientific theories he had imbibed in so many European universities, those of Heidelberg, Basle, Paris, Poitiers, Orleans and Tübingen, were certainly calculated to arouse both admiration and distrust of him among his fellow-citizens. He had graduated not only in jurisprudence but also in medicine and in addition wrote comedies in imitation of those by ancient dramatists. While on a visit to Florence he had made friends with Lorenzo the Magnificent and attended the gatherings of the Florentine Platonic Academy under the Tuscan pines in the gardens of Careggi and Poggio a Caiano. He had discussed scholarship with Ermolao Barbaro and Argiropulo and learnt Hebrew under the Rabbi Obadiah Sforni of Cesena. At present he was teaching Greek and Hebrew at Ingolstadt.

Like Pico della Mirandola, he had been led by the study of oriental languages to investigate the secrets of the Kabbalah, which instructed mankind in everything of which it would otherwise be ignorant in regard to God, the world and humanity itself. The

THE YOUNG JESUS WITH THE DOCTORS. 1506.
GALLERIA BARBARINI, ROME.

Kabbalah enabled its devotees to enter into relations with angels and devils. For these reasons Reuchlin, who was said to know more about it than anyone else in Germany, was suspected of heresy by the Holy Inquisition. The humanist, a man of high character, was not afraid of compromising himself by defending such causes as liberty of conscience and the supreme authority of the intellect, which he regarded as sacred. For the sake of the books he loved he had entered upon disputes with all sorts of civil and ecclesiastical bodies.

Not a great deal of evidence was required in those days to prosecute a man for practising the Black Arts and selling his soul to the Evil One. Reuchlin's scientific knowledge alone laid him open to suspicion. But the great Hellenist did not hesitate to face the anger of influential persons when it was proposed that all Jewish books should be burnt. The Emperor himself was too tolerant by nature and too devoted a friend of learning to have made any such suggestion on his own initiative. He had been persuaded by a renegade Jew named Pfefferkorn, who wanted to show zeal for his new faith and injure those who adhered to his old religion, that it would be a pious action to send to the stake such Hebrew works as affronted Christianity. In theory, these alone would be destroyed. But it was only too easy to understand how greatly those in charge would be tempted, in view of the difficulty of discriminating between subversive and innocent works, to fling every book written in a foreign script, whatever its subject, into the flames.

Reuchlin, deeply shocked by the announcement, called in person on the Emperor to request that such philosophic works as the Talmud and the Kabbalah be exempted from the holocaust. Pfefferkorn, fearing the exposure of his malicious motives, retorted by accusing Reuchlin of heresy. The Inquisition immediately intervened, instigating formal proceedings against the 'Cabbalist', who was supported in his turn by the humanist fraternity.

It is easy to guess where Dürer's sympathies lay. He had not only always struggled, himself, to defend freedom of thought. The nobility and generosity of his personal character also set him at the side of the man who was fighting for the honour and dignity of learning. Furthermore, Reuchlin was an expert mathematician. He had read all the Greek, Italian and Jewish books dealing with the problem of numbers and it was through him that Dürer hoped to reach clarification of the points on which Jacopo de Barbari had been unwilling or unable to enlighten him.

The determination with which Dürer pursued his mathematical studies for many years after returning from his second visit to Italy proves that he was devoting his intelligence to the search for some kind of rational explanation of the world. He may have felt the need to balance, by the exercise of reason in this way, the opposition of the two chief traits in his character, mysticism and sensuality. Logical certainty was required to reinforce tentative, empirical understanding. His instinctive, intuitive apprehension of beauty demanded confirmation by the authority of reason, the support of objective, scientific standards of judgment.

He had begun by trying to find ideal beauty in the living model, but he soon gave up the attempt. It was difficult to persuade the men and women by whom he hoped to be inspired to pose for him in the nude. The extreme rarity, moreover, of faultless figures rendered this expedient impracticable. He turned, as he had occasionally turned in the past, for his mythological compositions, to drawings by Pollaiuolo and Mantegna. He copied Italian engravings of Greek statues, for the originals did not exist in Germany. He also examined engravings by Jacopo de Barbari, believing that this artist must have used the 'great secret' of the Golden Number in designing his nudes.

He was not content with the mere reproduction of such works. He measured the figures, breaking down their proportions into geometrical shapes. Starting from the navel, he calculated the vertical proportions of the anatomical structure. For two-dimensional design he reduced the figure to a series of rectangles, for which he substituted polyhedra when representing the third dimension. He measured the sides of these geometrical forms and worked out the degrees of their angles. He tried to determine why a certain relation between the width of a chest and the length of a finger indicated harmony and resulted in beauty.

Such studies led him from the observation of concrete, living phenomena to recognition of the formal abstractions underlying them. In the process of analysing the human body or that of an animal into geometrical patterns he came to attribute more importance to the latter than to the actual frame they composed. The obsession with abstractions which affects students of geometry and mathematics developed in him a passion for crystalline formations. Though he had as yet no proof of their organic life, he instinctively divined it and regarded such bodies as fundamental constituents of the universe.

For all Dürer's mysticism and sensuality, he came near to idolising abstractions. Like Fra Luca Pacioli, he designated the dodecahedron 'the most noble of all solids', as if its discovery among the components of a living being conferred a special excellence upon both the figure and the phenomenon itself. He was dazzled, like the exponent of occult doctrines Fautrieus de Rembrandt, by the mere contemplation of the pentagram, named in the Kabbalah as the key to all things. He spent weeks, possibly months, working at the construction of a regular pentagon, corresponding with the famous Diagram of Hippocrates, in the hope that it would enable him to solve all formal problems. The intoxication invariably produced by exclusively intellectual operations took further hold of Dürer in his studies of the heptagon and the cubo-octahedron. He began to take an acute, almost morbid pleasure in evolving all kinds of polyhedra.

He was impassioned by everything that attracted him. Imitating Paolo Uccello and Piero della Francesca, he embarked on the double task of first dividing the living body into its geometrical elements and then building it up again on that basis. The second stage had been child's play for the Italians, no doubt, he supposed, because they knew the 'secret'. But it proved agonising to Dürer. He experienced all the torments of a mind concentrating upon knowledge of itself, its exhaustion under the strain, the exasperation of its original devouring thirst for information by further, equally intense longings. Sudden bursts of rapture when he believed success within his grasp were followed by abrupt disappointments at the detection, behind the mirage, of vast spaces of unexplored territory, jungles of enigmas, deserts of unanswered questions.

Attracted on the one hand by Reuchlin's mathematics, which in the end invoked divine authority, and on the other by those of Pacioli, with his worship of the numbers and geometrical figures he believed, in defiance of the teaching of his Franciscan Order, to contain the idea of Deity, Dürer became an omnivorous reader. He annotated Euclid and Vitruvius. Passages he could not understand were translated for him by Pirckheimer. But he continually felt the need to resume contact with Jacopo de Barbari and consult Pacioli.

The latter, however, eventually died without having revealed the essential secret. His last books, which remained unpublished, dealt with chess, the peculiar properties of certain numbers and mathematical posers. Such were the hobbies of the great scholar towards the end of his life. In order to free himself from the diabolical fascination of numbers, to exercise their power, the friend of Leonardo da Vinci had come to use them as playthings for his personal amusement. But Dürer could not believe that was his last word. He was sure that Pacioli had passed on to Jacopo de Barbari, orally, in the greatest secrecy, his mysterious legacy. Then Jacopo died in his turn. No one knew whether he had confided his discoveries to anyone else. It was said that he had left a manuscript, the only copy of which had been acquired by Margaret of Austria. Dürer would have given anything he possessed to get hold of it.

'The excessive use of reason causes melancholy,' he noted at a later date, remembering the years of enthusiasm and despair. Fortunately, he had never been wholly possessed by these fevers of the intellect. He had always remained in the first place a painter, even when lost in the labyrinth of mathematics. He had never abandoned his faith even when reason appeared to him capable of accounting for all things human and divine. He had not been in love with geometry for its own sake or for the acute and subtle delights it afforded him; he always regarded it as a mere tool for the acquisition of knowledge. He never woke his placid wife in the middle of the night, like Paolo Uccello, to tell her that perspective was a wonderful thing. Man remained for him the measure of all things, man in the flesh. Nor did the temptations of rational thought disturb his religious convictions when he engraved, in the very midst of his mathematical researches, his two Passions and the Life of the Virgin, when he issued a new edition of the Apocalypse and produced his Great Passion on copper, a work which at least equals his woodcuts in emotional power, nor when he painted two imposing religious pictures, the *Martyrdom of the Ten Thousand* and the *Triumph of the Trinity*.

192

HEAD OF THE CHILD JESUS. 1506.
ALBERTINA, VIENNA.

193

Many of Dürer's engravings provide no clue to the meaning which he attached to them. But he gave the above title to one which has been the subject of a great deal of commentary and exegesis. The name he applied to this work (p. 219) does not make it any easier to understand. In fact, it calls for more explanatory annotation than any other picture in the world, with the possible exception of the Mona Lisa. As in the case of Goya, whose engravings bear legends of a monitory rather than definitive character, the word MELEN-COLIA inscribed on the long scroll shaped like the wings of a bat raises more questions than it answer. Why did Dürer portray 'Melancholy'? What is the significance of the attributes of the female figure shown? What, in short, was the view taken of 'Melancholy' by a man who had reflected deeply on the problems of being and knowledge, consulted the most learned of the Florentine humanists and eventually worked out a philosophy of life? His philosophical opinions were closely associated with his professional activities and productions, which they illuminate in a remarkable manner. He applied himself, with characteristically medieval industry, to the development of a complex, perhaps even indeterminate, idea in his mind. He was fond of posing riddles in some of his compositions, puzzling to ourselves, though his contemporaries were probably able to interpret them without difficulty. For the men of his time were more familiar with the language of symbol, allegory and what might be called intellectual assonance. Accordingly, Dürer's *Melencolia I* carries in its very title, placed below a rainbow, in the dim effulgence of a comet, as though on the first page of a book, a whole set of conceptions and convictions with which the educated classes of the Middle Ages and the Renaissance were perfectly well acquainted. Once in possession of this key to the picture's intention they could easily comprehend the whole of it, though in modern times the vocabulary of allusion and image so often employed by Dürer is only acquired with considerable effort, through an erudition by no means easy to attain.

But whatever explanations may be given of a work enigmatic in so many respects and however minutely its various elements may be

analysed, its sensuous and even sensual appeal enraptures the spectator even before his emotional sympathies or intellectual curiosity are
aroused. The beauty of this engraving is enthralling. The variety of
tone obtained by the subtle treatment of the copper is prodigious.
The cutting and pricking of the surface are boldly and accurately
executed, the mellow and sumptuous effects of the inking most notable. The dense and heavy atmosphere conveyed, the sense of bitter
disenchantment, of nerveless and hopeless discouragement, can be
fully appreciated without attention to the allegorical content of the
objects by which the giantess, seated in an attitude of deep meditation, is surrounded. She might be the sister of Michelangelo's *Night*.
Nor is there any reason to suppose that the sculptor had not the
Four Temperaments in mind, whether consciously or subconsciously,
when he carved the statues reclining on the cenotaphs of the two
Medici dukes.

Attempts have sometimes been made to elucidate Dürer's *Melencolia* by referring to certain biographical details which may have
helped, in fact, to create the mood responsible for producing this
strange vision. In considering how far external events may account
for the inception and character of a work of art, it may be noted
that the year 1514, the date of this engraving, was an important
one in the artist's life. His mother had just died, after a long illness.
For some time the aged Barbara Hofer had been blind. She is said
to have recovered for a moment, on her deathbed, the beauty of her
first youth.

The *Melencolia* must have been influenced in some degree by
Dürer's grief for his mother's death. His sorrow may have been
accompanied by a certain amount of remorse. For, though Barbara
had occasionally shown evidence of a tyrannical temper, he on his
side must often have adopted, in his rebellious fits, an aggressive and
inconsiderate attitude. If this affliction did not directly inspire his
great engraving, it is at any rate strongly marked by his feelings at
the time. Death, more than anything else, induces reflection upon the
vanity and impermanence of human endeavour.

The first 'still life' compositions painted were called 'vanities'.
Originally subordinate items in a picture of wider import, they

THE FESTIVAL OF THE ROSE-GARLANDS. 1506.
PRAGUE MUSEUM.

eventually acquired independent existence and were prized for their
own sake. They continued, however, to carry a certain moral implication. The apparently casual juxtaposition of objects conveyed a
warning of mortality.

Dürer's *Melencolia* may also be regarded, from a certain stand-
point and to a certain degree, as a 'vanity'. The disorder in which
the various tools used by mankind lie scattered on the ground, the
sleep of desire symbolised by the infant Eros seated dozing on a

The Festival of the Rose-garlands. Detail.

197

millstone, and the silent bell which no one will ever trouble to ring again, all convey the same message as the 'vanities'. It is possible that, in the atmosphere of suffering and death that prevailed in Dürer's house at the time, he was affected more powerfully and deeply than usual by the tragedy of man's mortal condition, a cruel lesson for anyone to learn and perhaps even more so for an artist, naturally impelled by his creative impulse to ignore, or at least to forget, the fragility of all human achievement.

In any case, however reluctant he may have been to accept this melancholy conclusion as to the transitory nature of life on earth, public events gave him cause enough for depression and anxiety. The world he knew seemed to have been shaken to its foundations. Seamen were exploring unknown lands. From the heights of the isthmus of Darien, Vasco Nuñez de Balboa gazed for the first time upon the ocean later to be named the Pacific, though he himself was content to call it the South Sea. The Portuguese were carrying their trade and political power into Malaya, India and even China. Wars were raging in Italy, Scotland and Burgundy. The Turks were conquering the Christian kingdom of Armenia. Unrest and disaster were rife throughout the world. In the little town of Nuremberg merchants and men of learning waited impatiently for news. Each announcement, whether from Europe or the East, and however belated, excited the minds of the citizens to an extraordinary degree. The Franconian humanists were as 'European' in their outlook as Erasmus of Rotterdam and certainly more so than the philosophers of Florence and the sages of Rome. The very word 'humanists' indicates their keen and instant response to every idea and occurrence of interest to humanity. It was a time when the massive solidarity of the Middle Ages, rooted in a common liturgy and faith, was on the verge of breaking up, while the passion for education and the longing to render it truly comprehensive in both thought and feeling was about to replace the Christian sentiment of 'catholicity'. The primacy of intelligence, erudition and reason was being affirmed, a primacy which could only be justified by taking the whole field of human nature, without exception, for its province.

In Germany political and religious problems were particularly threatening. The old feudal and princely order of society was crumbling. The Reformation hat not yet, strictly speaking, taken place. But the new theology summarised in the works of Martin Luther was already undermining orthodox religion. Nine years before this date the young Luther, as a graduate in philosophy of the university of Erfurt, had been prostrated, like St Paul on the road to Damascus, by a flash of lightning. He had thereupon entered an Augustinian monastery, been ordained and become a monk. Transferred to Wittenberg, he taught philosophy at the university there. Even before taking his degree as doctor of theology he was appointed to deliver lectures in public on the Bible. The freshness and penetration of his comments on the text both impressed and disturbed the ecclesiastical authorities. But it was only after receiving his doctorate of theology in 1512 that he ventured to launch fiery denunciations of orthodox Roman doctrine. He had then been friendly for some time with Eobanus Hesse, a scholar full of rustic energy, and with the amazing Ulrich von Hutten, who was destined to take a leading part with Sickingen in the forcible establishment of the Reformation. Three years later the storm burst. The Lent sermon on the foundations of Christianity was pronounced. The ninety-five theses were posted up at Wittenberg and the controversy over Indulgences began.

The spirit of the Reformation had not been the growth of a mere few years in Germany. Such ideas had been in the air and adopted by German thinkers long before Luther's polemical exchanges with Tetzel, the Augsburg hearing and the Leipzig debate. In a certain sense the revolution, if only as general unrest, may be said to have started even before Luther took up the sword with which he both wounded himself and influenced the destiny of mankind. Conceptions, accordingly, which had troubled the national conscience long before their formulation in the ninety-five theses, must have affected the mind of Dürer, so sensitive to every change of direction in religious thought and feeling.

He did not dread the onset of melancholy. He often yielded to it in his bouts of ill-health. More than one self-portrait reveals his obsession with this mood. He had read, moreover, the statement by Ficino that 'all men who have excelled in art have been melancholy.'

A distinction was also commonly made at the time between morbid and healthy types of melancholy. The figure in Dürer's *Melencolia* does not therefore represent either melancholy as the Romantic and Baroque ages understood it or the characteristic temper of the end of the Middle Ages. His engraving illustrates, rather, a resistant and salutary sort of restlessness, resembling the recuperative weariness of an athlete or that of an artist after a productive period of toil.

One of the problems presented by this celebrated work will never be solved. The stroke following the word MELENCOLIA on the pennant displayed by the bat might be either the letter 'i' or the Roman figure 'I'. Critics who take it for the latter assume that this plate was intended to be the first of a series. The second plate, they maintain, which was never executed, might well have represented a second kind of melancholy. Those commentators who prefer to read 'i' have no probable explanation to offer except to regard it as a Latin ejaculation – 'Away, Melancholy!'

It may not, then, be out of the question to suppose that Dürer meant to convey a number of different feelings in this image. They may have included his discouragement after so many fruitless endeavours to detect the 'secret', his subsequent distrust of physics and mathematics which did not appear, after all, to provide keys to the mystery, and at the same time his unshakable confidence in the power of human reason to dissipate the nightmares symbolised by the bat. He knew that science could never supply an answer to every question. He understod its limitations. Nor could he, in view of his keen recognition of the claims made by spiritual and artistic activities, confine himself to the guidance of scientific enlightenment alone.

Neither the bankruptcy, therefore, nor the apotheosis of science is implied by this engraving. It illustrates the prolonged effort, or at least one of the aspects of it, made by the human spirit in pursuit of truth. The character and extent of such studies are indicated by apparatus and instruments surrounding the winged woman, with her coronet of foliage. It would be useless, in a work so complex, to seek for any unmistakably symbolic object. For similar compositions, such as the *Nemesis* and *Despair,* are full of puzzling detail.

THE VIRGIN AND CHILD WITH ANIMALS. About 1505.   201
ALBERTINA, VIENNA.

THE MOCKING OF CHRIST

CHRIST BEFORE PILATE

THE FLAGELLATION

ECCE HOMO

THE 'LITTLE'

PILATE WASHING HIS HANDS

CHRIST ON THE CROSS

THE DESCENT FROM THE CROSS

THE RESURRECTION

COPPERPLATE PASSION

The bell, the tablet inscribed with cabalistic signs, the scales, the enormous polyhedron, the carpenter's plane, the compass, the infant asleep on the millstone, the closed book and the crucible on the stove can all be given a wide variety of meanings. The sleeping hound recalls those placed on tombs, at the feet of reclining effigies of the dead. It is in this connection that a resemblance becomes apparent between Dürer's wide-eyed giantess and the *Night* of Michelangelo. The sculptor's famous sonnet may contain a clue to the mystery. Or it may be found in that Faustian dilemma, both tragic and passionate, in which the desire for knowledge mingles with doubts of the value of knowledge for its own sake. 'Philosophy, alas, jurisprudence, medicine and thou too, drear theology! All have I studied so deeply, with such ardour and patience! And yet now, poor fool that I am, no wiser than before!'

On one point, however, there can be no hesitation. At the end of Dürer's long pursuit of the 'secret,' which he never in fact abandoned, he discovered that either it did not exist or, if it did, it was a multiple secret and could be reached from different directions. He concluded that, while the excessive use of reason should be guarded against, it was equally dangerous to allow it to slumber; for then such monsters as Goya beheld approach the sleeper. Science was necessary for the acquisition of knowledge in its own field. But it was only one method of solving the problem and a precarious and inadequate one into the bargain. After having practised simultaneously, for several years, both scientific research and artistic creation Dürer had begun to lose faith in mathematics as the best standard for the judgment of art. He no longer believed that the Golden Number could be found by using such tools of measurement. He had come to regard it as only one of the elements of aesthetics, not the ubiquitous and omnipotent reality itself.

If it is assumed that the giantess with the coronet of foliage has despaired of attaining ultimate truth by means of the instruments she has been using, it may also be noted that these do not include any of the artist's implements, such as the brush, the burin or the chisel. Her tools are, on the contrary, those required by the scholar and the artisan. They have nothing to do with artistic creation. The impli-

STUDY FOR 'THE KNIGHT, DEATH AND THE DEVIL'. 1498.
ALBERTINA, VIENNA.

cation may be that if melancholy has its injurious and dangerous sides, they may kept at bay by the practice of art, with its constantly renewed pleasures and regularly increased bursts of energy.

Finally, as a man of religion, Dürer has unquestionably something more to say. It is probable that the three most important engravings he executed this year, the *Melencolia,* the *St Jerome* (p. 114) and the *Knight* (p. 271) – the latter is actually dated 1513 but belongs to the same spiritual series – all fall within one category of thought. Perhaps they should even be considered together, in the hope that they will afford evidence in this way which is not forthcoming when they are studied separately. They are not, strictly speaking, religious works at all, at any rate so far as their subjects are concerned, since for the truly religious man all phenomena bear the divine imprint and the underlying form of the spirit. Nevertheless, it is in these productions that the most important revelations of Dürer's religious development and of his relations with the Reformation are to be sought.

His whole heart and mind were with the Reformers. His writings prove that he looked forward to such a movement and embraced its cause with enthusiasm as soon as it took shape. He never actually met Luther. But he became so devoted to the doctrines of the man whom Hans Sachs called the 'Nightingale of Wittenberg' that when he heard a rumour which afterwards proved false that Luther had been arrested, he gave violent expression to his feelings in his diary. He called down the vengeance of heaven, in apocalyptic language, upon those who had been stupid and criminal enough to misrepresent the Reformer's apostolic mission.

For some years before Luther's teaching was explicitly formulated in his famous Theses it had been afflicting the German conscience. The boldly defiant stand beginning to be taken by a mere Augustinian friar against the Roman Church hardened the revolutionary temper which already prevailed throughout the country. Political as well as religious interests were involved in the crisis. Consequently, not only selfless but also base passions were aroused in the course of the agitation. Luther had simply intended, at first, to do away with certain abuses, but he eventually found himself the leader of an actual rebellion in which varying degrees of conviction and ambition inspired the minds of his followers.

The Reformation was not, in all probability, the work of the 'Wittenberg Nightingale' alone. A man of destiny is a much the victim as the creator of circumstance. On this view the germ of Luther's ideas already existed in Germany at the end of the fifteenth century. Many Germans were thinking along the same lines as he. Above all, the collective unconscious of the nation was tending towards the intellectual upheaval of which he became the apostle. The ferment was expressed, involuntarily or otherwise, in the works of artists, the writings of humanists and the deeds of men of action. Accordingly, Dürer's great trilogy of engravings, issued in 1513 and 1514, illustrates, for those able to detect the inner meaning of these works, his doubtless unconscious participation in the early stages of the movement that was to culminate in the proclamation of the ninety-five theses.

The subjects of the *Melencolia,* the *St Jerome* and the *Knight* appear to be very different. Nevertheless, taken together, they illuminate Dürer's religious thought at the time. The phase may be considered as temporary in the sense that, dispite the general continuity of his ideas in this direction, the *Apocalypse* of 1498 (pp. 154–5), the Vienna *Trinity* of 1511 (p. 111) and the *Four Apostles* of 1526, two years before his death, if regarded as evidence of his most fundamental beliefs, express their convictions in noticeably variant terms. The years 1513-14 were those in which Luther's opinions began to assume their final form. He was about to pass from the preaching of theory to practical action. In this connection the three engravings might be seen as a triple portrait of the man, or rather a three-faced image of him. The *Melencolia* would then represent the doubts and visions of his meditative period, in the guise of a massive, crouching figure that suggests, like that of Michelangelo's *Night,* the possibility of a sudden and terrible awakening. The *St Jerome,* on the other hand, implies the personality of the doctor of theology and translator of the Bible. As such, he would claim the special respect of those who were already secretly thinking of reform. Lastly, as the *Knight,* he assumes the moral armour – even before donning that of St George

ADORATION OF THE MAGI. 1504.
UFFIZI, FLORENCE.

– of an active combatant against ecclesiastical abuses and the sale of indulgences.

Thus in these three works Dürer may have represented, though perhaps unintentionally, three aspects of the man of destiny soon to arise in the person of Martin Luther. The artist's intuition and foresight, the turmoil of his creative inspiration, may have prefigured the image of a foreordained leader, certain to make his appearance, as indeed he did during the ensuing years, with the moral lineaments then traced by Dürer with no direct awareness of their prophetic nature. The *Knight* was engraved first. For Dürer's Faustian subconsciousness, a characteristic of his race, must have suggested to his mind the phrase of Goethe's hero: 'In the beginning was the deed.' But in Luther's own life events proceeded in a different order. He had first, as a young man, known the anxiety, the torment and the bewilderment arising both from his own troubled mind and the public events in which he saw the omens of disaster. Secondly, he had turned to theology, translating and commenting on the Bible. It was only thirdly that he had taken up arms.

These three idealised attitudes to life, so rarely combined in a single individual, had been conjured up by Dürer in his great trilogy, not with deliberate purpose, but simply because the burin had expressed his metaphysical position in that way. Yet it was also true that he had recognised three separate elements of his own personality, intellectual, spiritual and practical. He had, moreover, tried to promote their alliance in action without running the risk of injurious or destructive consequences to any one of them. This series of engravings, accordingly, constituted a moral portrait of himself as much as of Luther, presenting manifold facets of the artist's own psychology, a confession of the various impulses directing his energy to creative labour, to speculation or to a contemplative state of mind.

The three works, therefore, when viewed as a whole, summarise Dürer's philosophy. Melancholy may be overcome either by creative activity, that of the artist, by practical action, that of the knight, or by prayer and contemplation, typified by St Jerome. No one can escape fate. The Divine Will has determined in advance the course of each individual's life and his soul's salvation or damnation. Such was the form taken by fatalism in the doctrine of predestination, which was to be one of the main pillars of the Reformation. This theory, informally current in Dürer's native environment prior to its definitive statement by Luther, was interpreted by the artist both in the *Knight* and in *Melencolia*.

In the latter work he stressed the incapacity of human knowledge to reveal inner truth. The phosphorescent gleam in the baffled, anguished gaze of the woman, under her coronet, reflects the realisation of man's inevitable ignorance of the essence of things, however great his erudition in other respects. Dürer had reached this conclusion after several years of search for the 'secret', a search which he continued, however, as long as he lived. He saw that humanity is predestined to remain unenlightened, or perhaps even worse off, in the darkness of pseudo-science. Books and scientific apparatus, in whatever quantity, he felt were but feeble aids to the operations of intelligence and could guide it only a little way.

Of all the heroic medieval virtues to which Dürer, though a 'man of the Renaissance', remained devoted, the chivalrous temper seems to have been one of the most attractive. Memorable images of the Knight appear in his engraving of St George, a figure which might illustrate the noblest of legendary epics, and in the *St Eustace* (p. 173) and *St George* (p. 172), portraits of Lucas and Stefan Paumgartner respectively, of the wings of the altarpiece presented by that prominent Nuremberg family. Dürer's affection for the Knight was not limited to the active and heroic aspect of such an individual. All the details of knightly equipment, body-armour, helmet, sword and other weapons, fascinated the artist.

He had at times, while apprenticed to his father, decorated with the chisel armour used at tournaments or in war. He had hammered out the griffin on a casque and embossed armorial bearings on a shield. He was not a military man like his friend Willibald Pirckheimer, who commanded municipal troops in the Peasants' War; but he was interested in all that concerned a soldier's life. As a child he had been fond of visiting cannon-foundries. Towards the end of his life he applied a great deal of ingenuity to designing types of artillery and siege-proof forts. Medieval chivalry stimulated the flamboyant side of his imagination, his view of life as heroic adventure, equally stirring in his own case and that of any soldier. The Knight in the engraving of that name, sternly impassive, indifferent to the supernatural perils that accompany him, does not even notice the snake-crowned, ghastly figure showing him an hourglass nor the boar-headed monster, an emissary from hell perhaps, awaiting the moment at which the sands run out for the seizure of its prey. Yet the Knight is well aware of all these lurking dangers. He pays no attention to them because he knows that the hour at which fate strikes can never be postponed and that a man can do no more, if he deserves to be called a man, than fight the battle of life, whatever its outcome, to the best of his ability.

The hour-glass appears in all three engravings. It is perhaps their sole common motive. But its significance varies according to whether it is held by Death, or hung up in the study of St Jerome or on the wall overlooking the sea, near which Melancholy seeks to evade Time and where everything in her environment connotes measurement and can therefore only increase the dramatic tension of her anguish in the contemplation of space and the passing moment.

The Knight is not conscious of time. For he is engaged in action. The dynamic quality of his existence itself sublimates, if it does not transcend, any such idea. The hour-glass here has a direct meaning, since it is held and presented by the hand of Death. St Jerome, however, does transcend time by living in the domain of the spiritual, of eternity. The light by which his apartment is flooded is that of a soul at peace with itself. Time has ceased to exist for the saint. Persons and things, as such, have passed, for him, out of the temporal into the eternal mode of being. They share the immortality of the spirit, are themselves spiritual beings, even the good-natured lion tranquilly dozing beside his friend the dog. The Knight's dog, like his master, is an active, urgent creature, almost a beast of prey. Nor does the dog in the *Melencolia* engraving sleep so peacefully as St Jerome's. The hound quivers, as such animals do in the grip of nightmare. Bred to race and leap, it curls up uneasily between millstone, polyhedron and sphere, captive, like Dante's mysterious greyhound, of the lacerating dreams of an intelligence that cannot rest.

Here the hour-glass is hung between a pair of scales resembling those flourished by one of the horsemen of the Apocalypse and a bell fated to ring at some as yet unknown moment of achievement or annihilation. The glass in flanked, too, below the bell, by a squared board of magic numbers, all adding up to the same total, as if there were but one solution to the riddle of human life. The base of the hour-glass is touched by the tip of one of the wings of Melancholy and is perhaps the cause of her mood. For Dürer the thought of time was one of the most disturbing that can afflict mankind. He did not, like Rembrandt, succumb to the horror of its endlessness and incessant decay. Dürer's entire work, on the contrary, bears witness to his energetic endeavours to arrest and pin down the relentless flux that Heraclitus posited. The concept of time, among all those which gallop so fiercely through the mind of Melancholy, is one of her chief tormentors. Its power is enhanced by the instruments that surround her, with which she may measure the impermanence of life and realise its precariousness and inadequacy. The patience inherent in the sombre resignation of her gaze, in the kind of tense despair that possesses her, represents the effort made, in her struggle against the hour-glass, to escape from and triumph over Time.

MAXIMILIAN

The day on which Dürer met in real life a personification of Melancholy and the Knight combined in a single individual was one of those important occasions by which a man's subsequent career is profoundly influenced. The artist's fame had attracted to him the most flattering attentions on the part of the German princes. The Elector of Saxony, after patronising him in his youth, continued to show him friendship and favour in his successful maturity. Dürer's portraits of the Elector during these long years of intimacy illustrate even more vividly than those by the monarch's Court Painter, Lucas Cranach, the development of his subject's character. The young humanist of 1496, generous, impulsive, hot-tempered, discriminating and capable of deep feeling evolved into that hirsute, benevolent and incalculable personage, Frederick the Wise.

He was a strange mixture. With typical medieval piety he collected every relic he could lay his hands on, apparently supposing that God would favour him in proportion to the quantity of holy bones he packed away in his chests. At the same time he aspired to the freedom

SELF-PORTRAIT IN A WIG. 1500.
ALTE PINAKOTHEK, MUNICH.

213

of conscience and judgment claimed by the men of the Renaissance. Though his behaviour, character and temperament remained Gothic, he had been strongly influenced by Italian culture. He had a sincere love of art and literature, but his interest in patronage perhaps included a wish to emulate the refined princes of the peninsula, such as the Este, Sforza and Medici rulers, or those who had so greatly extended the range of French art, the dukes of Berry and Burgundy.

His chief rival in the pursuit of relics and works of art was Albert of Brandenburg, Archbishop of Mainz. But the latter's zeal doubtless lacked something of the Elector's naivety and sincerity. For the prelate, who enjoyed an enormous prestige in Germany at this time owing to his office and his rank, united haughty ambition with an indulgence in coarse sensuality vividly noted by Dürer in his portrait of the Cardinal in 1518. Albert's Court at Halle was renowned for its splendour and the pomp of the festivals and religious ceremonies over which he presided. Determined not to be outdone in magnificence by the Italian ecclesiastical dignitaries, he gathered about him the most fashionable and inventive artists he could find. Of the rising German painters he was particularly attracted by two men whose eccentric talents appealed to his taste for the beautiful and strange. He admired the voluptuous and sombre allegories painted for him by Baldung Grien in the dusky hues of night, shot by stormy gleams. He was delighted and flattered by a portrait of himself as St Erasmus, executed by Mathias Grünewald, following a freakish custom prevalent in Italy.

The cardinal-archbishop, in his vanity, was not content with a local reputation. The portraits of himself that filled his palace at Halle must be multiplied, he considered, until all Europe knew and admired his supercilious features. Since Dürer was at the time the most famous of all German engravers, Albert of Brandenburg was willing to associate his own glory with that of the artist. The portraits he ordered from Dürer were engraved on both wood and copper. Large numbers were printed and distributed wherever the ambitious prelate wished his name and face to be known. The artists he honoured with his commissions did not have a very easy time of it; for the Cardinal, a more domineering character than Frederick the Wise, ruled his painters, as he ruled his clergy, with a rod of iron. Though munificent as any Italian patron, he was not always quite so gracious.

Dürer had thus to submit to the caprices of two patrons who were not perhaps so appreciative as they might have been of the stature of the artists they employed. But he now encountered one whom he came to regard as the very incarnation of the imperial idea in all its true grandeur, which included the almost magically radiant atmosphere in which Maximilian I journeyed about his empire.

He had been crowned King of the Romans in 1486. Seven years later, on the death of Frederick III, he assumed the imperial dignity. But his reign proved far from tranquil. The rivalries which had, as usual, accompanied his election left the country in a state of unrest and instability which rendered his tenure of the double office of king and emperor extremely precarious. The title of Holy Roman Emperor still commanded great respect, but Maximilian had inherited the legacy of Charlemagne without possessing the means to defend it from aggression. A formidable task confronted the young elective sovereign and the slender resources at his disposal.

The fiercely independent German nobility of the day stubbornly maintained their authority and privileges. At times, therefore, the imperial power existed only in theory. Maximilian, so poor that he used to say he possessed nothing but his saddle and stirrups, was mortified by the contrast of so much splendour and destitution. As a Habsburg, he was proud of belonging to one of the most ancient and glorious of royal dynasties. As an Emperor, he regularly displayed a fanatical concern with every question that affected his domains. He considered his rank not merely political, but also religious and sacred. He had felt the ceremonies of his coronation to be as mysterious and impressive as an act of incantation. His anointing, the ritual by which the crown, globe, sceptre and sword were delivered to him, seemed to have invested him with a kind of supernatural majesty, as the representative of the Divine Will on earth. He saw himself as chosen by God, not by the few princes who had quarrelled over his throne with the selfishness and savagery of wild animals. He had been obliged to drive as hard a bargain for his Empire as he did in

ADAM AND EVE. 1507.

216   PRADO, MADRID.

negotiating with moneylenders. He had been forced to make promises to some and browbeat others. He had, in short, only obtained the crown of Charlemagne after a hard struggle, through intrigue and diplomacy, compromise and stipulation. On his eventual succession to the throne he had found himself, he said, more forsaken than anyone had been since Christ.

In order to reach the imperial eminence to which his boundless ambition aspired he had necessarily suppressed the speculative and extravagantly optimistic side of his nature, always in conflict with his sober political judgment. After subordinating his dreams to the harsh requirements of reality and thus acceding to the position he desired, he became the loneliest man on earth. Poised between heaven and the world, at a height from which the swarms of mankind resembled an antheap, and imprisoned in the imperial purple, burdensome as a porphyry sarcophagus, he nevertheless continued still to long for power with such eagerness that on the death of Julius II he entered upon negotiations with the Sacred College with a view to having himself appointed Pope.

Consequently, the idea of empire was now personified in a mind at once mundane and given to wild schemes, intoxicated by history and legend. The urgency of Maximilian's will to power was such that he sincerely believed it feasible for a single individual to wear both the crown of Charlemagne and the triple tiara of St Peter. The feverish and fantasy-ridden passions of the old Hohenstaufen rulers revived in this Renaissance monarch, like them infatuated with omnipotence, not only so as to assuage his ambition, pride and love of power, but above all to experience the prodigious sensation of dominating the world and holding the fate of humanity within his grasp.

Maximilian's political talents were not free from romantic colouring. His conception of the Empire was in fact more fanciful than realistic. Bursts of enthusiasm for far-reaching plans alternated with stupefying fits of depression which left him troubled and suspicious of all things and all men, himself in particular. Weighed down by his rank and yet impatient to raise it still higher by the conquest of more power and authority, he lived, in imagination, in a period which could perhaps be compared with that of Charlemagne and the great

ADAM AND EVE. 1504.

MELENCOLIA I 1514.

German Emperors of the early Middle Ages, but had nothing in common with the degenerate realities of the first years of the sixteenth century. Blind to contemporary conditions, Maximilian dwelt in a haunted, chimerical world of shadows. He refused to permit the crude light of day to invade the fairyland he had devised, the realm of his choice. He surrounded himself with all the illusions conjured up by man to veil the disappointing and too prosaic facts of life.

He expected literature and art, in which those discomfited and defrauded by a cruel experience of reality find such precious consolation, to provide him with the visions he needed. Five years after his accession he endowed a college for mathematicians and poets. His intention was to encourage science and art. But he probably desired even more that those whom he invited to join this establishment should record his acts and glorious deeds, reciting or depicting them for the edification of posterity. Above all, he hoped, in enlisting their services, that their books and pictures, like flattering mirrors, would furnish him with his own ideal view of himself. Maximilian was not vain. But, like Hamlet, he lacked self-confidence and therefore longed to acquire it from the testimony of others.

His continuous concern with this species of propaganda, designed to spread his fame in the present and perpetuate it for the future, suggests that he may have felt it necessary to have his virtues enshrined in some permanent form before he could believe in them.

There were flatterers and courtiers among the members of the kind of Academy he had set up. Their praises of him sometimes bordered on the sycophantic. But their excessive adulation did not vex the Emperor, who was already dazzled by his own aspirations. Like actors who pay a 'claque' to applaud them and then forget that the acclamations they hear are furnished by their own employees, Maximilian asked nothing more from his 'College' than support of his ideals. He wished it to surround him with a wall of books and pictures, a continuous exhibition of thrilling images of his power. It was not vanity that impelled him to this course, but on the contrary a possibly undue modesty and the fear that his real empire might never be so impressive as the one in his dreams.

He engaged the best German artists to carry out this task and to

THE EMPEROR MAXIMILIAN I. 1518.
ALBERTINA, VIENNA.

221

banish from his mind the precarious nature of a sovereignty exercised in such conditions of poverty, uneasiness and princely defiance of his authority. Innocently enough, he had himself indicated the sort of themes and treatment he wanted, based upon both his own life and romances of chivalry, with the strange result that he appeared in them under the guise of such medieval paladins as Freydal, Theuerdank and Weisskunig. The chief author of these fanciful chronicles, packed with complimentary allegory and learned conceits, was Max Treitzsauerwein. The Imperial Councillor of Nuremberg, Melchior Pfintzing, sometimes lent his aid in their production. The writers piled one romantic and alluring episode on another. They showed Maximilian, as a youth, at the Court of sixty-four princesses, who were one and all dumbfounded by his virtues, accomplishments and exploits. He appeared on all occasions as the flower of chivalry both ancient and modern, the rival of Perceval, Amadis and Lancelot. By a refinement of courtly pedantry the names the poets gave Maximilian only served to reveal his true personality the more clearly. Eventually the emperor, in his desire to bring under his own direction the unreal scenes through which he intended subsequently to move, and so that he could himself arrange the ritual of this extraordinary cult of hero-worship, entrusted his personal autobiography to Treitzsauerwein. It was to form the basis of an epic, *Weisskunig*, which was never completed.

Fate also ordained that another great work ordered by the emperor was to remain unfinished. It was his vast tomb, commissioned to compete with that of Pope Julius II, whose body, however, like that of Maximilian, was never laid to rest in the gigantic sepulchre he had commanded. The emperor's glory survives only on paper; he was denied the opportunity to record it in permanent form. A lifelong wanderer, he could erect no memorials in the shape of palaces, columns or statues. He loved books because he could take them everywhere with him, to relieve the loneliness of his endless journeys. And the care he took to confide to paper alone the task of preserving his renown proves how implicitly this eccentric harbourer of vain visions relied upon the written word and the engraved figure. Fortunately, his trust was rewarded in the end.

Maximilian I and Dürer had so much in common, both intellectually and psychologically, that they were bound to be greatly attracted by each other when they met. Unfortunately, it was long before their respective paths crossed. When, in 1506, Dürer painted the emperor as one of the figures in his *Festival of the Rose Garlands* (p. 196), the artist had never seen him in the flesh. The portrait was executed after a drawing by Ambrogio de Predis, in which the lineaments of the Habsburg sovereign were softened and rendered insipid by the Mannerist style of the Lombard School, influenced by Leonardo. Maximilian and Dürer met for the first time in 1518, in the artist's little room at Augsburg, when the emperor posed for him. As a result of this sitting, which may have been the only one given, Dürer produced the charcoal drawing (p. 221) he used for the two posthumous portraits he painted of Maximilian in the following year.

The penetrating intuition of the artist's imagination showed him in the emperor's features not only their own essence but his own. He saw the consciousness of vocation, a devotion both eccentric and practical to the chivalrous ideals of the Middle Ages and the ambition to give the highest possible expression to the idea of Empire. But he saw, too, that sunlike personage given to nocturnal unrest, shadowy visions, the agitation of a mind at grips with oppressive problems, material and spiritual. All these elements appear in the portrait of Maximilian with a pomegranate (p. 224). The fruit alludes to the Kingdom of the Shades of which the emperor was by then a subject. But it may also represent the fruit of the Tree of Knowledge, to eat of which meant death.

The intellectual sympathy between the two men would have made Dürer the ideal illustrator of a glorious reign. It is easy to imagine the quantity of monumental works he would have produced in different political and economic conditions. Unfortunately, the emperor possessed only 'card houses'. The Triumphal Arch consecrated by Dürer to the glory of the monarch remained a sketch. A huge woodcut, over 100 square feet in area, it represented such a monument as is erected for royal processions, but one of enormous size, lavishly heaped with statues, reliefs, portraits, allegorical

POTENTISSIMVS · MAXIMVS · ET · INVICTISSIMVS · CÆSAR · MAXIMILIANVS
QVI · CVNCTOS · SVI · TEMPORIS · REGES · ET · PRINCIPES · IVSTICIA · PRVDENCIA
MAGNANIMITATE · LIBERALITATE · PRÆCIPVE · VERO · BELLICA · LAVDE · ET
ANIMI · FORTIDVDINE · SVPERAVIT · NATVS · EST · ANNO · SALVTIS · HVMANÆ
M · CCCC · LIX · DIE · MARCII · IX · VIXIT · ANNOS · LIX · MENSES · IX · DIES · XXV
DECESSIT · VERO · ANNO · M · D · XIX · MENSIS · IANVARII · DIE · XII · QVEM · DEVS
OPT · MAX · IN · NVMERVM · VIVENCIVM · REFERRE · VELIT

THE EMPEROR MAXIMILIAN I. 1519.

224   KUNSTHISTORISCHES MUSEUM, VIENNA.

figures and inset coats of arms. So fantastic an edifice, impossible to build, suited well the ruler it was designed to celebrate. The structure, baroque in spirit if not in form, constituted a vast folio of history and anecdote for the proclamation of Maximilian's mighty deeds. The general plan and decorative scheme belonged to the Renaissance. But Gothic ideas and sentiment are evident in the swarming, inexhaustible proliferation of a succession of shapes without functional purpose, multiplied simply to indulge the super-abundant energies of a wild imagination.

There is almost nothing in this engraving to recall the Roman triumphal arches of which Mantegna and his pupils were so fond, though Dürer had seen reproductions or versions of such memorials in Italy. Plastically, psychologically and technically the work suggests a paper building, made of engravings or the pages of a book laid side by side instead of being bound in the normal way. The actual material of the cut is not stressed by the artist, wood being an unsuitable medium for the illustration of didactic narrative. The phrase 'card house' comes immediately to mind when the composition is viewed as a whole. But the wealth of invention shown in the details, their variety and their masterly fusion of Renaissance feeling with late medieval forms are most remarkable. The foliage borrowed from the plastic vocabulary of the Flamboyant style is used with a dynamic freedom, in its complex architectural setting, that anticipates the German Renaissance, itself essentially a transitional movement from the Gothic to the Baroque manner. Plants are conspicuous, naturally enough in the art of a country so largely given over to forests. Yet the mass of precise, minute, anecdotal detail combines to give the edifice in its entirety an effect of imposing solemnity, of truly imperial majesty. The artist's analytical method produces in the end a great symphonic harmony. For the 92 distinct engravings constituting the work only acquire their due plastic and educative significance as a coherent body.

Ever since the time when Dürer, as a child, had been fascinated by the annual ceremony of the display of consecrated objects at the church of the Holy Spirit in Nuremberg, he had been deeply conscious of what the words 'Holy Empire' meant for the men of his day. He had often walked in the procession of his awed fellow-citizens to gaze reverently upon the sceptre, crown, orb and sword laid out in their shrine. The emperor Sigismund, reluctant to expose these treasures to the risks of war and travel, had entrusted them to the Nuremberg municipality in 1424. On the second Friday after Easter the precious casket was taken down from the high shelf on which it was usually kept and the people of Nuremberg, proud of the priceless articles confided to their care, brought their wondering, shy children to view, with astonishment and veneration, the sword of Charlemagne and the crown of St Stephen. Dürer's goldsmith father took the opportunity to call his son's attention to the beauty of the ancient enamels, gems, cameos and chased work in gold. The boy's childish bewilderment may have been the germ of the profound devotion he felt as a man for the idea of empire. He expressed this sentiment when he painted, in compliance with the only order the town councillors ever gave him, portraits of the two emperors Charlemagne and Sigismund.

The night before the regalia were exhibited they were placed in one of the rooms of the Schopper family's house in the market-place. The apartment had come to be regarded as a sort of Imperial sacristy. The two portraits commissioned from Dürer by the municipality were to be hung there. Many sketches for these works survive, showing that Dürer had studied the coronation apparatus itself in order to depict the robes and jewellery worn by his two subjects. But, just as in the case of his Triumphal Arch, the precision and objectivity of the detail blend into the stately final effect. It is of little consequence that Dürer, after taking Sigismund's features from contemporary documents, used the councillor Stabius as a model for Charlemagne. The important point is that both images shed a convincing radiance of imperial dignity, due even more to the power and authority expressed in the faces than to the historical accuracy of the accessory adornments.

Similarly, it is not the accessories in Dürer's portrait of Maximilian that suggest his model's imperial office. Nor did the artist trouble to embellish a countenance unpleasing enough with its enormous nose, pendulous chin and heavy jaw. Yet the total physiognomy asserts the genius, magnanimity and keen intelligence which, coupled with

ST EUSTACE. About 1500–1503.

a frank and unassuming good nature, were basic traits in the emperor's character. It is a true likeness, worthy of a painter who never failed in any such work to bring out the psychology, together with the social and political aspects of his sitters, rendering them as types without detracting in the least from their unique individuality.

It even seems that imperial grandeur is still more evident in this simple portrait than in the picturesque luxury and glitter of the Triumphal Procession executed by Dürer in common with Burgkmair and Springnikler in conformity with Maximilian's own directions. The objects here, too, seem to be made of paper. The advancing chariots, in my view, are much more the outcome of creative imagination than of historical study. Literary sources for this pompous masquerade, devised on the lines of Italian *trionfi,* were provided by Stabius and Pirckheimer. They lavished upon the scene all their erudition, knowledge of ancient literature, ingenuity in the presentation of allegory and mythological scholarship. It does not matter, in this case either, whether these sumptuous vehicles ever paraded in the streets, any more than it was important to ascertain whether the Triumphal Arch ever existed as a real building. Everything connected with Maximilian was bound to carry the signs of unreality and fantasy. He was not even buried in the magnificent tomb he had caused to be erected. It is as though his fame were destined to survive on paper alone.

Dürer's *Procession* may have been inspired by similar Italian works. But it has not the classical simplicity of Mantegna's or even Marcantonio's productions of this kind. The style is Baroque and the themes Gothic. The Gothic elements are already almost Baroque, as in Burgundian art, which clearly served as a model. The Renaissance decoration is itself treated as if it were derived from Flamboyant. An interest in mechanics, shown for example in the self-propelled vehicles, is also characteristic of the spirit and art of the end of the Middle Ages. It may be added that in this series of woodcuts which when aligned as a whole constitute the *Procession,* the respective contributions of Dürer and Burgkmair are easy to distinguish. Burgkmair's are entirely in the German Gothic-Baroque manner, hardly influenced at all by the Renaissance. Dürer's on the other hand strive to achieve a delicately harmonious design by clear and simple means, with much reminiscence of Italian practice. As in his *Triumphal Arch,* classical conventions and those of Gothic decoration are associated without strain.

He thus inaugurated a new style peculiar to himself, neither Gothic nor Renaissance, and not as yet Baroque, though heralding and foreshadowing that movement of a later age. Medieval as he remained in thought and feeling – in his illustrations of the *Freydal* poem, for instance, which resemble miniatures in manuscripts of the Middle Ages, while Burgkmair's drawings for the *Weisskunig* are much more modern – Dürer attained vigorous originality both in the *Triumphal Arch* and those parts of the *Procession* which he engraved. He had acquired a personal idiom which could not be brought into line with the fashions of any period or regarded as specifically German or Italian. His evocation of the idea of empire transcended the limitations of time and space. To evoke the universality contained in the idea he created the novel plastic language, entirely his own, which has no equivalent in the German Renaissance, except in the numerous works directly inspired by his own production. Even the necessity of collaborating with artists so different from himself as Burgkmair, far from paralysing Dürer's initiative, lent it wings. The superficiality of Burgkmair, admirable enough in its way, cannot compare with Dürer's 'imperial' vision, much more deeply based in a complex of intellectual and emotional factors. These enabled him to create an artistic medium capable of expressing profound moral sentiment.

He retained, accordingly, only so much of the Renaissance vocabulary as could be used together with the medieval admiration of heroic qualities that was represented by, for example, the idea of empire. Maximilian's personality was essentially of the Baroque type. Yet, like Luther, Hamlet and Savonarola, he was cast in a thoroughly medieval mould, only superficially coloured by the light of the Renaissance. Dürer, on the other hand, in escaping from the Middle Ages, overshot the mark. He announced, without realising it, the first stage of the Baroque movement. It was as though the Renaissance in Germany was not, as it had been in France and Italy, a biologically

Antiphona· Post partū vir=
go inuiolata permansisti:dei
genitrix intercede pro nobis·
Versi·Diffusa est gratia in la
bijs tuis·Respon·Propterea
benedixit te deus ineternum·
Pater noster·Et ne nos indu
cas intēptationē·Benedictio
Recibus et meritis bea
tissime gloriosissimeq3
matris semp virginis Marie:
omnium sanctorum et sancta
rum perducat nos dominus
noster iesus christus ad regna

PAGE FROM THE PRAYER-BOOK OF THE EMPEROR MAXIMILIAN. 1515.
STAATSBIBLIOTHEK, MUNICH.

inevitable development, but simply a very brief and relatively unstable period of transition. The various sides to Dürer's character, furthermore, correspond with the different epochs that shaped his mentality. His style is by turns medieval, Renaissance and Baroque, dependent upon the kind of work he was doing. Its nature dictated his allegiance to one era or another, as well as his typically German resistance to uncompromising acceptance of Italian influence.

The medium also dictated his procedure. It has been suggested that paper gave the *Triumphal Arch* a look of that material. But in the case of the *Procession* woodcut the vehicles appear to compose an enormous centrepiece for a table, in which the artist's recollections of his goldsmith's work seem to outweigh his painting experience. He was also inspired by processions which he had actually watched, such as that of Maximilian's entry into Nuremberg in 1512. His father, moreover, had assisted in the construction of a fine arch which was set up right in front of his house in the year of Albrecht's birth, on the route of a triumphal procession escorting Frederick III. When, however, Dürer turned to illustrate Maximilian's *Book of Hours*, his freedom was restricted both by the general plan of the work and by the intervention of collaborators. Jorg Breu, Cranach, Baldung Grien, Burgkmair and Altdorfer all participated in the project. Mathias Grünewald was the only one of the leading painters in Germany who was not engaged on this occasion.

The book was being printed by Schönsperger of Augsburg for distribution to the Knights of St George, an Order founded in 1469 by Pope Paul II and the Emperor Frederick III for active service against the Turks. The work was to be a gift from Maximilian to the new crusaders and he ordered it, perhaps with a view to emphasising its significance in the history of chivalry, to take the form of a manuscript. Although by this date (1512) the art of printing was fully developed, Vincenz Rockner was commanded to cut type in imitation of the calligraphy of ancient manuscripts. At the outset, therefore, inconsistency arose between the nature of the printed book and the medieval appearance given to it by the lettering and the use of parchment instead of paper. The discordant effect of so ill-advised a union of ancient form and modern methods of production was increased by the excessive number of artists called upon to contribute illustrations. A grouping of such diverse styles as those of Dürer, Cranach, Altdorfer and Grien would have resulted, if the book had ever been issued, in a most extraordinary collection of samples, representing every tendency in the painting of the day.

Unfortunately, none of the artists concerned could be regarded, strictly speaking, as a miniaturist. On the contrary, the outstanding feature of Baldung's work, for example, was its monumentality, while Altdorfer's strength lay in his visionary renderings, through multifarious detail, of enchanted forests. Moreover, like all the undertakings of this unlucky emperor, the book could not be completed. It was begun in 1513, but the printing remained unfinished at Maximilian's death on 12th January 1519. The Knights of St George never received the gift he had meant for them. But Dürer's part in the work (p. 230) to which he applied himself with passionate interest as well as delight, survives as one of the most curious specimens of his glorification of the emperor.

The style of decoration was imposed by the medieval typography and supporting material. Nor did Dürer feel inclined, at this period, to design religious allegories in the margin of the text corresponding with its meaning. In this attitude he much resembled Jean Pucelle, who had not scrupled to exercise his jocose and captivating fancy, typically medieval in its easy-going irony, on the borders of pages containing written prayers. Like Pucelle, Dürer gave his imagination free play. Instead of inviting the reader to study illustrations bearing some relation to the text, Dürer attempts to distract him from prayer and meditation by letting loose upon him a whole menagerie of comical creatures, herds of monsters pursuing one another amid decorative foliage and sometimes blending with the leaves and boughs. The spirit at work in these cases is not that of the humanists. It is the boisterous gaiety of popular verse narratives. Fantasy and realism are combined. The procession of exotic beasts may be beautiful or absurd. Lonely hermits, bagpipe-playing peasants, fully armed foot-soldiers and horsemen struggling with skeletons and apparitions are represented, comprising an entire world of tireless fancy, drawn by turns from everyday reality and waking dream.

A wide range of sentiment is also expressed, including tender affection for animals, a feeling for landscape that makes every touch tell, faultless objectivity and unlimited invention. The illustrations are, moreover, notable for their arabesques, a reminder that Dürer rivals Leonardo as a designer of interlacing figures, for the vigour of their statements and for a monumentality that imparts surprising grandeur to these light sketches. The artist did not approach his task with any strictly illustrative end in view, involving some adjustment to the text. He simply took advantage of its white margins for the casual depiction of his whims of the moment, some jocular caprice, note of piety, realism or curious enquiry into the exotic or unfamiliar. With all this playful mockery a discreet, barely hinted, emotion lends these small pictures a dynamic life, both secret and miraculous.

Dürer's work for Maximilian brought him little financial gain. The artists employed by that needy monarch earned more glory than money. Dürer received a bare 85 florins for the two portraits of Charlemagne and Sigismund. For the municipality paid no more than the emperor, though it was far richer. No remuneration was forthcoming for the illustrations to the *Book of Hours*, as the volume was never issued. Maximilian was by nature generous, but he could only be so with other peoples' funds, since he had not enough of his own. As some compensation for what he owed Dürer, he requested the Nuremberg treasury to exempt the painter from taxation, a step which that body took with reluctance. But this concession did not enable the artist to meet his expenses. The emperor then promised Dürer 200 gulden for the *Triumphal Procession* engravings. But this sum was never disbursed. Maximilian told Dürer to ask the Nuremberg authorities to pay it in the Emperor's name. But unfortunately the councillors had already been annoyed by an annuity of 100 florins to Dürer imposed by Maximilian upon their budget.

Their resentment was increased by the new demand upon their resources. After 1515 they made difficulties about the payment of the pension. They found one plausible excuse after another for withholding the 200 gulden. The climax came when, upon Maximilian's death, the wealthy aldermen of Nuremberg took advantage of that event to pass a resolution against further payment of the pension.

They maintained that, since the emperor himself had granted it, the artist's right to receive the annuity ended with the life of the person who bestowed it.

Long and troublesome negotiations ensued between Dürer and the councillors. The latter's philistine attitude to artists had always been conspicuous. The authorities were for ever bullying those unhappy members of the community, restricting their freedom, prosecuting them for slight offences and censuring them for nonconformity. But the withdrawal of Dürer's pension did not render him destitute. He earned enough to live in comfort: he had even been able to buy a fine house, where he lived at his ease with his wife. It was the injustice of the municipality's cancellation of the pension, rather than its loss, which provoked him. Consequently, when the aldermen told him, with sly grins, that if he wished to continue to receive it he had better apply to the new emperor to confirm the grant, Dürer at once determined to do so. Maximilian's successor was then at Antwerp. That didn't matter, for Dürer had never been to the Low Countries and he was always glad of any excuse to travel. He had an even better reason for leaving Nuremberg, for the plague had just reappeared in the city. Accordingly, on 15th July 1520, he set out with his wife Agnes and their maid Susanna to appeal to the generosity of the Emperor Charles V.

JOURNEY TO THE NETHERLANDS

He was destined to travel in triumph. But first he paid a visit, as was customary at the time, to the Sanctuary of the Fourteen Saints. It had been for half a century the most renowned place of pilgrimage in Franconia. Dürer, as a good Christian, always invoked the protection of heaven before embarking upon any project. He would have thought it foolish to start on such an important expedition without securing in advance the blessing of the Saints to help him on his way.

Armed with their benediction and also with a number of engravings, which he intended to sell or give away to meet the

THE MINSTER AT AACHEN. 1520.
BRITISH MUSEUM, LONDON.

expenses of the journey, Dürer took his place in the coach with his maid and wife. The latter was now a respectable matron of about fifty. He had never taken her abroad before. Probably he had never hitherto been able to afford transport, board and lodging for two. Or perhaps on previous occasions he had meant to enjoy a freedom which the company of his wife would have considerably restricted. Her character is hard to ascertain precisely. Of her contemporaries only Pirckheimer, Dürer's friend since childhood, mentions her; he had certain reasons for disliking her and may therefore have been unjust in his estimate. The silver-point drawing of 1521 shows her as a stout, placid creature who retained nothing of the pensive and romantic charm of her youth. The sketch-book portrait, on the same sheet as that of a little girl in the local costume of Cologne, is even less attractive. The child's smooth features emphasise, by contrast, those of Agnes, whose face is heavy, with an almost wild glare in the eyes, while the pursed lips indicate greed and avarice. The drawing Dürer made of her that day at Cologne seems to prove Pirckheimer's charges. It is easy to imagine the woman as a jealous shrew, herself terrified of the plague and by no means inclined to stay at home while her husband sought safety and distraction abroad.

She insisted, moreover, on travelling under her own name and sharing Albrecht's triumphs. Her participation, however, was by no means always complete. Quite often she and the maid supped alone together, while her husband was being entertained by the local nobility and painters' guilds. But whenever she did happen to be invited to the banquets given for him she took great pride in accompanying her illustrious spouse and put on for the occasion the grand dresses she had brought with her to do him honour. Their life together may not have been without its stormy passages. But Dürer remained attached to her. He notes with much satisfaction, in his diary, the manifestations of sympathy and respect accorded to Agnes in the towns where they stayed.

At Bamberg the travellers turned west for Frankfurt. The Bishop of Bamberg, Georg Schenk von Limburg, in return for a painting, an edition of the Apocalypse series and some other engravings, entertained Dürer at his house, granted the artist exemption from taxation and gave him certain letters of introduction to save him trouble on the journey. Dürer distributed his works pretty freely among the prominent people he met. Such generosity cost little, made him useful friends and increased his fame. But he also gave away a considerable number of prints by his colleagues, especially Schäufelein, whom he much admired, and Baldung Grien. In thus advertising possible rivals he acted out of pure liberality of spirit and because he thought these artists should be better known.

At Frankfurt he was received by one of his old friends and first patrons, the draper Jakob Heller, who had ordered from him the famous Assumption altarpiece, the wings of which were decorated by Mathias Grünewald. Heller naturally made much of Dürer, who received from his host, before leaving for Mainz, a case of wine to enjoy on his journey down the Rhine. More hospitality awaited him at Mainz: Peter Goldschmidt and Veit Varnbuler entertained the couple regardless of expense, loading them with presents, provisions and a supply of the exquisite gold-coloured wine grown on the banks of the Rhine ever since the time of Charlemagne.

Dürer reached Antwerp on 2nd August, a fortnight after his departure from Nuremberg. Next day the mayor, who had been notified of his arrival, received him at the Town Hall. The ceremony was no longer one of friendly welcome, such as had previously marked his progress, but a solemn, official affair, attended by all the municipal authorities, who were delighted to show their appreciation of the celebrated painter in this way. After the banquet Dürer was taken by the mayor to his private residence. The spacious apartments, up-to-date decoration and large garden deeply impressed the guest, who noted in his diary: 'I never saw anything to equal it throughout Germany.' Indeed, the mayor's prodigality and love of display were so extreme that he had built at his own expense a new street, very long and wide, which ended at his own house. On the following day a less formal and probably more enjoyable reception was held, to which both Dame Agnes and her maid were invited. On this occasion it was the Antwerp artists who entertained the travellers, making the occasion, in their casual way, a family affair. The best known painters brought their wives to enliven the feast, at a table laden with jewelled ornaments of every kind and appetising dishes. When Dürer entered the room, everyone rose and bowed deeply; after this mark of respect the guests resumed their seats and attacked the food with great gusto. With the dessert the City Councillor, Adrian Herebouts, made his appearance, followed by two footmen bearing four pitchers of wine, a gift from the Lords Paramount of Antwerp. Then Master Peter, Carpenter to the Municipality, appeared with wine in his turn. As liquor equally potent had been flowing freely throughout the meal, the guests were in jovial mood when the party broke up at an advanced hour of the night. Dürer was escorted, to the sound of music and by the light

AGNES DÜRER AND A GIRL FROM COLOGNE. 1520.
ALBERTINA, VIENNA.

of torches, to his inn, that of Jobst Planckfelt, where he and Agnes
were destined to stay for nearly a year. They behaved just as if they
were at home, with Agnes doing cooking and Susanna the house-
keeping. Dürer himself spent very little time there, overwhelmed as
he was by visitors and invitations.

Antwerp had already become the main centre of trade with
Europe, the Orient and the New World, to the detriment of the celebrity and prosperity of Venice, which were beginning to decline.
The most important representatives of sea-borne commerce, the
Portuguese, had established offices and banks at Antwerp. They
were rich and cultivated men, as much interested in foreign painting
as in their own. More than one fine German or Flemish picture
found its way to Lisbon, where it hung beside the works of Grão

Vasco and Nuno Gonçalves. A Portuguese merchant, in order to obtain the good graces of Agnes Dürer, presented her with a green parrot, which talked like a man and filled the inn with its raucous mimicry.

Dürer lost no time in calling upon Quentin Matsys, the most fashionable Flemish painter of the day. The elegant, mannered charm, the kaleidoscopic brilliance of colour in Matsys' work and the somewhat extravagantly dramatic atmosphere of his big altar-pieces were highly appreciated by the German visitor. But he never regarded Matsys as the greatest of the Netherlands artists whom he studied at this time, or the most congenial to himself. He found he had more affinity with Joachim Patinir, whose wedding he attended. Patinir showed him some fine romantic landscapes, full of mysterious overtones and enchanted perspectives, beckoning the imagination into a maze of subtle, haunting suggestions of tranquillity. Dürer was also much attracted by the pictures of Barend van Orley and in particular of Lucas van Leyden, the youthful genius whose visionary fervour found dazzling expression in his religious paintings and whose engravings were already famous. 'He's only a little fellow,' Dürer noted in his diary. But Dürer's portrait of the 'little fellow' admirably reveals his sitter's quiet, thoughtful simplicity, dignified composure and eyes alight with sensitivity, gentleness and ardour.

Albrecht was never mistaken in the works he admired. His instinct and his taste led him straight to what was best and most significant in the painting of his day. As on his early tour of Germany and his two visits to Venice (though on the second of these he was less attentive, owing to an excessive preoccupation with matters not strictly relevant to art), Dürer made himself acquainted, during his stay in the Netherlands, with the rapidly developing tendencies of contemporary practice. The thirty years thus spent coincided both with the rise of Renaissance style in northern Europe and the imminent approach of the Baroque period, already forecast in so many different ways.

The diary he kept on his travels records an abundance of concrete detail but very few aesthetic judgments. His encounters with artists and their works are briefly noted. Of Patinir he only writes that the man was a good landscape painter. He does not mention any of Patinir's pictures, nor does he refer, except casually, to the van Eyck brothers and Memling. It is as though Dürer had passed through Flanders, then so fertile in masterpieces, with the indifference of a philistine.

Though he says so little of the great Netherlands painters he met and the outstanding productions of Flemish art he saw, it is certain that these experiences deeply impressed him both psychologically and professionally. Such an artist as Dürer could not have summarised in a few lines his opinion of, for example, the *Mystic Lamb* altarpiece. It may be conjectured that his visual memory of works of art was better than his recollection of everyday matters. It is likely that, though he never forgot a picture, he was obliged to jot down the sums spent at the inn or the apothecary's shop. He required memoranda only for such insignificant details of ordinary life, written down simply to be rid of them. He did not need to note profound emotional or intellectual exitement.

He always recorded his impressions, very important to himself, of any object new to him, such as the branch of coral given him by the landlord of his inn in exchange for a portrait, whereas six other persons whom he 'counterfeited', to use his own expression, neither paid him nor presented him with the slightest token of their gratitude. Whenever Hindu textiles, exotic fruits or shells of grotesque shape were brought him, he immediately described them, with a few accurate and vivid phrases, in his notebook. His wonder at the bones of the Antwerp 'giant' – clearly those of a prehistoric animal – is that of a simple-minded tourist. But his delight in the treasures imported from Mexico by the Spanish conquerors derives as much from his artistic interests as from mere curiosity. The magnificence of the skulls in rock crystal, the carved gems, the daggers with their mosaics of precious stones and the feathered robes, which constituted part of the booty of Cortes, inspired Dürer to fervent eulogy. His sentences still glow with the pleasure and admiration he felt in contemplating these masterpieces of Mexican art. By his equal enthusiasm for the most exquisite and striking productions of the Aztec goldsmiths and

240

PEONIES. About 1505.
KUNSTHALLE, BREMEN.

for what was merely outlandish and strange, he simply proves that any novelty could exercise upon him the same power of suggestion. His imagination and knowledge of form were as much absorbed by a Brazil nut as by a Toltec breastplate. He applied no aesthetic standards to such articles. But with greater wisdom than that of the philosophers of art he knew how to find in all things whatever they had to offer of enjoyment, instruction or stimulus.

For the same reason there are more drawings of animals and monuments than of landscapes in his sketchbook, which amounts to a series of illustrations to his diary. The landscapes appear to be mostly of a documentary nature, but Dürer's genius lent the slightest of his scenes the vivacity and expressive power of a major work. The sketches made during his earlier travels are full of a romantic love of nature. They clearly indicate his intention to form a collection of picturesque fragments for insertion in future paintings. But the sheets relating to this later journey prove an equal measure of what might be called scientific interest. The same feeling led him to produce a large number of portraits, especially of people conspicuous for their racial traits or unusual garb. His drawings of monuments have the precision of an architect's blueprint, though formerly, in the Tyrol, he had concentrated on the pictorial values of the castles he drew. In the same way, his studies of dogs or lions are more learned than artistic. They are records as coldly accurate as those executed by Pisanello or Gentile Bellini on their travels. They cannot be compared, for instance, with Rembrandt's sketches of animals, where the creature's inner nature and organic mobility are as evident as its outward aspect.

Every page of Dürer's notes and sketches at this period – the two collections should be studied together – proves that he was in search of both instruction and amusement on this journey. His prolonged stay in the Netherlands was of course undertaken ostensibly to obtain confirmation by Charles V of the pension granted by Maximilian. But he could have arranged this matter through friends, without leaving his native city. It is probable that the recreative and educative aspects of travel were in the forefront of his mind. The ingenuous interest he took in every public event is most evident. He rushes from an inspection of the triumphal arches erected for the Emperor's entry into the town to watch the procession for the Feast of the Assumption and gives as minute a description of it as he does of Charles's coronation, as king, at Aix-la-Chapelle. 'I have seen many strange things,' he often notes. For his curiosity never relaxed: he remained as alert in the Brussels or Ghent zoological gardens as before the paintings of Raphael or Michelangelo's *Madonna* at Bruges, a work which, incidentally, he believed made of alabaster. He was perpetually dashing off in different directions to see masterpieces or join friends in excursions near and far.

He made Antwerp his headquarters, but he was by no means tied to that city. At the end of August he left Agnes with her maid at Jobst Plankfelt's inn and went off with his friend 'Tomasino', short for Tomaso Bombelli, a rich Genoese merchant who had been appointed Treasurer to Margaret of Austria. The two men visited Malines, where the Archduchess, Maximilian's daughter, lived. Their object was partly to appeal for her support in the matter of the pension; but Dürer also wished to present to her the portrait he had executed of Maximilian, based on the drawing he had made in the 'little room' at Augsburg. In exchange, he hoped to obtain from her the famous 'book of secrets' by Jacopo de Barbari, which he longed to possess in order to perfect his professional erudition.

Unfortunately, the Archduchess did not seem to care much for her father's portrait. She politely declined to accept it. The artist, in his vexation, bestowed it upon 'Tomasino', who gave him a piece of English cloth for it. As for the 'book of secrets', it turned out that Margaret had just promised it to her favourite painter, Barend van Orley. After this failure to achieve what had perhaps been the primary purpose of Dürer's visit to the Netherlands he turned to seek an audience of Charles. But the new emperor was very busy in connection with his forthcoming coronation and also besieged by other suitors. It was not until 12th November that he ratified the pension.

Dürer might now have returned to Nuremberg, richer by a hundred florins a year but poorer through his inability to obtain Barbari's book. But he continued to stay in Flanders, still given up to the

YOUNG HARE. 1502.
ALBERTINA, VIENNA.

244

pleasures of travel with no specific object. Delighted to find his fame as great abroad as at home and to be entertained by the artists and other prominent persons he met, who admitted him to their intimacy, Dürer prolonged a visit which had ceased to have any practical end in view. But journeys are not necessarily undertaken for financial profit. With his pension assured, he could give free rein to all his inquisitiveness and zest.

On 27th August, at Brussels, he was introduced to Erasmus, whom he painted, inscribing the portrait 'Erasmum Roteradamum'. None of the artists of the day who attempted representation of the great humanist caught so well as Dürer the mixture of ironic detachment, sociability, scepticism and love of hard work that lay at the root of his subject's character. Soon afterwards, when Dürer became an impassioned supporter of Luther, he was to implore Erasmus to abandon his neutral, good-humouredly sarcastic view of the Reformer and lend him active aid.

The religious controversy had already grown embittered. Dürer, who could not remain indifferent to the crises of conscience that afflicted both individuals and society at large, had for long been sure of his own position in the matter. Whenever a new book by Luther came out, the painter at once bought it, noting in his diary his devotion to that 'admirable man'. Consequently, he could not understand the attitude of Erasmus, his determination to maintain the judicious outlook of a 'clerk' and the independence of a humanist, who had no business to interfere in ideological or political strife, except from far 'above the battle'. Dürer could not see the truly heroic side of such 'intellectual' disinterestedness, which deliberately refrained from all but logical thought, so as to preserve opinion and judgment from any distortion by the emotions.

The profoundly antagonistic temperaments of artist and sitter render Dürer's portraits of Erasmus somewhat theatrical and superficial, as if there could be no spiritual communication between the two men. The painter recognised the writer's genius, though it always remained alien, almost hostile, to his own. The sarcasm, like Swift's, of the *Praise of Folly* was very far from any mood of Dürer's. For the latter invariably 'committed himself', and deeply, to one side or

1520

erasmus ror roterdam

ERASMUS OF ROTTERDAM. 1520.
LOUVRE, PARIS.

THE SCHELDT GATE AT ANTWERP. 1520.
ALBERTINA, VIENNA.

the other of any question. He felt Erasmus's detachment to be a sign
of a certain emotional poverty or intellectual timidity. He could not
see that it requires true courage to refuse to participate unreservedly
and blindly in any movement and how much easier and more con-
venient it is to join a popular cause, whatever it may be. The isolation of Erasmus between the Reformers, who blamed him for not
ranging himself openly on their side, and the Church, which complained of his sympathy with modern ideas, implies a heroism
characteristic of the Renaissance humanists. Both Luther and Dürer
were still too medievally minded to be capable of the supreme virtue
of declining to enter a conflict the merits of which can only be
assessed by a lucid and impartial intelligence.

247

Dürer and Erasmus, then, came from different worlds and belonged to different periods. They were distinct not only as creator and critic respectively but even more in their religious views, which were diametrically opposed. It is therefore not surprising that there is much less about Erasmus in Dürer's diary than there is about the Antwerp carnival, the horse fair, the women of Bergen op Zoom or even the bones of the 'giant'. I doubt whether Dürer would have taken as much trouble to meet the illustrious philosopher as he did to see the whale stranded at Zierikee.

With his usual insatiable curiosity he rushed off as soon as he heard that a sea-monster had been cast up on a Zeeland beach. He forgot that the month was November, with its wintry storms. He had no sooner returned from Cologne and Aix-la-Chapelle, where he had attended the Emperor's coronation and stood up for the painter Stefan Lochner, than he took to the road again. He dismissed from his mind the friendliness of the princes he had met and the gifts of Raphael, to whom he had sent his own portrait in exchange for a picture. He paid no further attention even to a recent, short but subversive publication by Luther, that 'pious man', or to the sulks of Dame Agnes, who complained that she was being left alone too often and took her revenge by spending a lot of money on trifles. He could think of nothing but the whale. He had just finished a portrait for which he had received a hundred oysters. Many of his patrons paid in kind and were satisfied with a sketch on a restaurant table in return for their hospitality. But now he packed his bag.

The weather was bad, the sea rough. The boat was nearly wrecked off Armuyden. During the gale Dürer worked with the sailors and gave them his advice. The party had a narrow escape. Eventually, six days after leaving Antwerp, they arrived at Zierikee. Too late! Dürer learned, to his consternation, that the whale had been carried off as it had come, in one of those squalls to which both fish and seamen must submit. The voyage had not been a waste of time, for nothing is wasted on a man who knows how to use his eyes. But it had a disastrous effect on Dürer's weak constitution and he began to suffer from various aches and pains which he explained to his doctors by diagrams sketched on his own person. He had caught a fever.

1508

THE LITTLE OWL. 1508.
ALBERTINA, VIENNA.

From now on the diary refers in almost every entry to expenditure on doctors and drugs. The malady mystified the physicians. Throughout the ensuing winter he remained at Antwerp, suffering from the consequences of his unlucky excursion to Zeeland. In April he was shaken by an even severer attack of the illness. To crown all his misfortunes, money was getting scarce. He would have been in want if the innkeeper had not agreed to lodge him free of charge in return for a portrait. Worse was to come. The event occupies several pages of his diary, where as a rule notable occurrences are given only a few lines. He had never known so fierce an inward struggle.

Luther was the cause of it. After the Leipzig debate the Reformer had entered into relations with Erasmus, whose indifference had disappointed him, and with two other men, Hütten and Sickingen, who were to give the Movement a new direction. The alliance of the theologian with these men of the sword began a phase which had not been anticipated. Offensive action replaced learned dispute. The Church fought back, condemning 41 of Luther's theses in the bull *Exsurge*. It was followed on 3rd January by the bull of excommunication. On 16th April Luther was called before the Diet of Worms.

On 17th May Dürer, still at Antwerp, was told, probably by some Augustinian friars he knew who favoured Luther's ideas, that the Reformer had just been arrested and imprisoned. But the rumour was false. The truth was that the theologian, knowing himself to be in danger, had taken refuge in the castle of Wartburg under the name of Junker Georg. He was safe there from any assault except those of the devil, to which he was often exposed.

Amid all this uncertain information Dürer was only sure that the man he loved best in the world had been the victim of a criminal attack. For the Emperor, after having given him a safe-conduct and a herald to escort him, had treacherously caused him to be carried off by ten horsemen posted at the edge of a wood. The painter was in despair at this outrage upon a soul illuminated by the Holy Ghost. 'I know not whether he still lives or was murdered,' he wrote. Tortured by such doubts, he covered page after page with abuse of the 'anti-Christian papacy', disconsolate lamentations, curses, prayers, denunciations, digressions on history and finally the most

250

heated confession, or rather profession, of faith ever written.

'O all ye pious Christians, join me in heartfelt mourning for this man, the instrument of God. Pray that another may be sent in his place, as enlightened as he. What ails thee, Erasmus of Rotterdam, in this momentous hour? See what tyrannical political violence and the powers of darkness have wrought! Hear me, Knight of Christ, ride beside Him, defend the truth, grasp the martyr's crown! If you do not so, you are truly but a wretched little old fellow!'

This verbose address to Erasmus, through which sounds the appalled anguish, the genuine despair, of the writer, shows how utterly these two great men misunderstood each other. Dürer could not appreciate the 'scholar's' point of view; and the latter for his part would probably have smiled at the almost insane violence of the other's prolonged effusion. Yet Dürer's grief over the disappearance of the 'man of God' was a sign of that generosity of heart for which he was so conspicuous. His religious ardour was coupled with an unselfishness never limited or qualified. These tearful, exclamatory pages reveal the misery he felt at being so far from the scene of action. He would have ridden, if he could, beside Sickingen and Hütten, to win the 'martyr's crown' he wanted Erasmus to assume, though it was hardly in the latter's line. Dürer no longer wished to travel. He did return to Malines in another attempt to get hold of Jakob Walch's book. He also attended the King of Denmark, who had ordered a portrait, to Brussels. He received cordial hospitality both from the King and Charles. But now he was feeling homesick.

Famous as he had never been before, in high favour with ruling princes, on intimate terms with such great artists as Lucas van Leyden, Barend van Orley and Joachim Patinir, he had nevertheless already taken leave of the fashionable world. Something in him had collapsed when he heard the false news of 17th May. Or perhaps it had made him aware of the passive or slumbering depths of his real nature. He plunged with passionate devotion into the religious conflict that broke out over Germany. His selfless enthusiasm for the cause of Luther made him long to return to Nuremberg to uphold it, not with sword and lance, but with a spirit intently preoccupied with religious problems.

1512

THE DEAD BIRD. 1512.
ALBERTINA, VIENNA.

THE WINGED SPIRIT

Panic, initiated by some hallucinated shepherd or prophetic visionary, suddenly took possession of the country. In a few weeks the dreadful tidings had reached every road, town and village in

Germany. Pilgrims returning from miracle-working churches and sacred springs repeated the news with the utmost horror. The land, already suffering enough from genuine troubles, gave itself up unrestrainedly to lament, to self-scourging and to every excess that fanaticism or debauchery could suggest to pious or reckless minds.

A new Flood was being foretold. Such was the story whispered by the gossips, as they glanced anxiously about, apparently expecting to see the heavens open without more ado. The mentality of the Renaissance period, though it required logical explanations of natural phenomena from physics, retained a passion for presentiments and an astonishing quantity of superstitious beliefs. Magic still had a hold over the men of those days, in the sense that they continued to credit the intervention of supernatural power in history. When strange events occurred, they did not suppose the 'monster' to be a rare, accidental deviation from the laws of nature they were at such pains to codify in theory and application. On the contrary, they attributed a chicken with two heads or a five-legged sheep to the charitable intention of some divinity or other to warn mankind, by ridiculous symbols of this sort, that something extraordinary was about to happen.

The famous 'Sow of Landser', for instance, born in southern Germany in 1496, inspired Sebastian Brant to compose one of those broadsheets then distributed by pedlars, which contained sensational accounts of major and minor crimes, discoveries in distant lands and such monsters as the 'Sow'. In the circumstances of the time a humanist like Brant, capable of such witty mockery as that of the *Ship of Fools,* might easily in his turn commit the absurdity of commenting at length on the grotesque appearance of the Landser sow and deducing from it the advent of important changes in European politics. He described them, with the solemnity of an augur, to the emperor Maximilian, to whom the pamphlet was dedicated.

Brant's account of the sow is somewhat highly coloured. But Dürer, who had gone to see it at the little town of Landser, represented the monster faithfully in his well known engraving,

No. 95 in the Bartsch catalogue. Both men depict the town itself with equal accuracy. It had battlemented walls, a fortified gate with four towers and a drawbridge, and was situated near a lake and surrounded by forests and mountains. But Brant's description of the animal gives the impression of contrived extravagance, while Dürer copied it with as patient and meticulous an objectivity as he had applied to his paintings of a hare (p. 244) and of a rhinoceros. The engraving is in itself a very fine one, quite apart from its subject. The artist showed admirable skill in delineating the exceptional features of the beast, its four ears, the two feet projecting from its back, and its double hindquarters.

The most enlightened minds of those days shared the superstitions of the masses. In 1503 incredible rumours of a 'rain of crosses' spread through Germany. Dürer gravely records the fact, which he accepted as such on the evidence of an actual eyewitness, that one of Pirckheimer's maids had caught a cross in her apron. The sixteenth century was riddled with every variety of autosuggestion. Though it was an era of rationalism, discovery and scientific research, ordinary people seem to have resented the approach of a period of rigorous logical investigation and instinctively gone to the other extreme in their excessive cultivation of crude fantasies. They abandoned themselves to a positive orgy of weird suppositions. Man, disappointed by the dull monotony of his daily life, tried to escape by giving it the atmosphere of a wild fairy-tale in which mystery dominated every aspect of existence.

The political situation in Germany, however, would have been enough in itself to cause serious alarm. The religious dispute, tearing the country in two, encouraged the peasants to revolt. They had been suffering for centuries from the misery and humiliation of quasi-servitude. Following the example of the lords, who were rebelling against the emperor in the name of freedom of conscience, the labourers, on the same pretext, attacked their masters. The rancour, hatred and longing for vengeance, accumulated through generations, spurred them on. Luther protested in vain that those of them who were not thieves were murderers. Melanchthon's attemps to define liberty in reasonable terms were equally useless.

VIRGIN AND CHILD. 1512.

KUNSTHISTORISCHES MUSEUM, VIENNA.

Neither man could prevent the popular risings from deriving support through the new doctrines, which gave the revolutionaries a moral platform of the very kind to render them oblivious of all other considerations.

The Peasants' Revolt was a deluge very different from the prophets' natural catastrophe. The Archduke Ferdinand, like a wise statesman, saw what was coming and warned the Emperor not to disregard it. 'The masses are rising everywhere,' he wrote. 'They are athirst for freedom. They refuse to pay taxes. They demand their share from the possessors of all the goods of this world.' Armed bands assaulted the castles; then, finding them too strong, turned to sack the monasteries and abbeys, which were less well defended. For Luther, too, the rebels proclaimed, was hostile to the monks. Their wealth, in any case, made their destruction well worth while to the revolutionaries.

Dürer was disturbed by their successive conquests of the Duchy of Baden, Swabia, the Palatinate, Bavaria, Thuringia and Franconia. He was terrified when the savage hordes assailed the walls of Nuremberg itself, after carrying fire and sword through all the villages of the district. He knew that the furious mob would enjoy demolishing works of art, with the excuse that they were 'idolatrous', though the real motive would be the blind hatred of the populace for everything it neither possessed nor understood. He saw that the most precious productions of German art would be consigned to the flames like the churches and monasteries, while the leaders of society, plunged in fanaticism or self-interest, quarrelled among themselves over trifling questions of privilege and precedence or insoluble theological problems. When they at last realised their danger, they would make common cause against the peasants and inflict atrocities upon them as cruel as those perpetrated by the rebels themselves.

New commanders had arisen among the latter. Some were such unscrupulous adventurers as Hans Muller, who led the Black Forest bands. He wore garments of red, the colour of hell, on which bloodstains did not show. Others were warm-hearted and simple-minded idealists like pastor Thomas Munzer, who raised

THE NEGRESS KATHARINA. 1521.
UFFIZI, FLORENCE.

LUCAS VAN LEYDEN.
MUSÉE WICAR, LILLE.

Thuringia to take part in the 'Battle of the Lord'. The presence of pious and moderate theorists, Balthasar Hubmaier for instance, who tried to confine the movement to enforcing justifiable claims, could not stem the raging tide of revolution. They were swept from power by frantic extremists intent on sheer extermination. The rebels had chosen a shoe as their emblem. It was already trampling all Germany.

Some few nobles did at first favour the revolution, out of sympathy for the sufferings of the masses and in the belief that it might result in improved social justice. But its actual results were arson, murder and devastation. The peasants were now acting solely by instinct. They no longer listened to reasonable advice, but only to such of their leaders as used violent language and encouraged rapacity and thirst for blood. Luther himself condemned the outbreak. He called upon the German princes to unite for its suppression. 'I'd rather lose my head a dozen times than support this insurrection,' he wrote to Johann Ruhal. 'I believe the devil's behind it and, just to annoy him, I'm going to marry my Katie.' He was referring to Catherine Bora. But whether the marriage of a former Augustinian friar with an unfrocked nun eventually grieved or pleased the devil, it certainly had no effect whatever on the conduct of the rebels.

The revolt at last reached such proportions and brought about so many disasters that it became a matter of urgency to crush it. The repression equalled the rising in brutality, though it had not the excuse of passion and previous suffering. The cold-blooded massacres, executed with refined cruelty and arrogance, were as odious as the excesses which the peasants had perpetrated. If the prophesied deluge had not occurred as anticipated, a blood-bath, instead, inundated the whole country.

Dürer did not issue any engravings in connection with the Peasants' War. Some artists did so, though fewer than those who had illustrated pamphlets concerned with the religious controversy. But Dürer, unlike the Flemish and Dutch painters, had no knowledge of or sympathy with peasant life. Its obscure heroism, silent, suffering, simple pleasures, anguish and rage were a closed

ADORATION OF THE TRINITY. 1511.
KUNSTHISTORISCHES MUSEUM, VIENNA.

book to him. He did not even find rustics picturesque, as Pleyden-wurff and Wolgemut occasionally did. Such figures in Dürer's works are so rare as not to be worth mentioning.

But if they had in fact interested him to any extent he would have found them objectionable as soon as they rebelled. His view would have been Goethe's, who 'preferred injustice to disorder'. For Dürer knew disorder to be fatal to artistic productions and the creative spirit. Nor did his concern with morals, in all probability, go deep enough for him to realise that the mere existence of injustice is, in itself, the worst of disorders.

The misdeeds of the revolutionaries did not affect him in any material sense, nor does he seem to have felt any compassion for the wretched victims of either the peasants or the lords. He never asked himself who was in the right, as a matter of ethics. His mind did not take naturally to such problems. Even in the religious sphere Dürer, for all his warm devotion to Luther and despite the pressure of friends who were anxious for his active participation in the movement for Reform, made no practical efforts to support it. Such men as Johann von Staupitz, a leader of the Nuremberg intellectuals, Lazarus Spengler, Secretary to the Council and one of Luther's correspondents, and the Flemish painter Jan Scorel, one of Dürer's own pupils and an ardent adherent of the Reformer, made no more impression than appeals from outsiders or the promptings of his own heart. To the day of his death he believed, against all the evidence, that a settlement could be arranged, schism avoided and peace made with the Church.

And yet these religious and civil disturbances did affect him, in the sense that he did not escape the general anxiety, confusion, depression and actual terror he saw all around him. Nations are sometimes afflicted by epidemics of fear in which the individual conscience suffers from a moral uncertainty as dangerous as it is difficult to account for. Collective, unreasoning panic, one of the typical traits of the primitive mind, reappeared at the end of the Middle Ages and continued until the Baroque period began. Belief in a second Deluge was one of the manifestations of this psychosis. Dürer believed in the prophecy as firmly as **Luther** believed that demons interfered in all his actions. He made fun of, but secretly feared, the Devil. Mathias Grünewald and Hieronymus Bosch were also affected by this dread. For effective representation of the powers of hell is impossible without knowledge of them, which fear alone, the chief means by which they are perceived, can give.

The war of the 'peasant's clog' had aroused ruthless fury against the rebels, whose atrocities were eventually matched by those of their adversaries. But it is hard to forgive Dürer for joining in the public outcry to the extent of designing a monument to commemorate the defeat of the revolutionaries. It is true that he did not intend thereby to glorify their conquerors. Yet, in view of the torrents of blood which flowed during the war, it is sad to find that Dürer could see nothing at the end of it but a column bearing the crouching figure of a peasant struck down by fate, grasping the great sword that could not save him and perched on a pile of objects associated with agriculture. There are other illustrations of triumphal columns, of classical type, in the artist's book *On Measurements*. But that which he conceived to record the defeat of the 'clog' rebels substitutes for weapons a collection of common household utensils, kneading-troughs, saucepans, mugs and chicken-coops, all precariously balanced in a heap, as though in mockery, to uphold the desolate and hopeless form of a labourer who fell in the attempt to improve his lot, to increase the sum of justice and charity in this harsh world.

In Dürer's written comments on the political and social turmoil that marked the opening of the sixteenth century he shows himself indifferent to human misery, coldly arrogant and heedlessly cruel. In his lack of understanding of the situation, cut off and enclosed in the selfish pride of a famous artist and prosperous citizen, he seems incapable of pity or sympathy. There is no trace in his attitude of Rembrandt's warm affection for suffering humanity, evident in the slightest sketch by the Dutchman. Perhaps the habits, first of working in metal and then of engraving, had some effect in hardening Dürer's character to this degree.

Obsession with the macabre was typical of the age and may be regarded as carrying well into the sixteenth century the late

ADORATION OF THE TRINITY. Detail.

THE KNIGHT, DEATH AND THE DEVIL. 1513.

medieval 'epidemics of fear'. The greatest of the German artists lived, literally, in the presence of symbols of mortality. The 'Dances of Death' by Aldgrever and Holbein, to cite only the most familiar examples, introduced grinning skeletons into everyday scenes. In Baldung's pictures these bony intruders, behind a handsome female nude, plant kisses on the nape of her neck. The sculptors of tombs often carved a worm-eaten skeleton below the reclining figure in armour. The remarkable Swiss painters known as *Lansquenets* (infantrymen), who divided their time between the battlefields of Italy and their studios at Berne, derived from their constant encounters with the reality the ability to evoke sensational images of death in all the sumptuous trappings of its most terrifying and funereal aspects.

In Dürer's work this 'death constant', like that of 'fear', is also present. The latter appears in the fine engravings, the *Unicorn* (p. 268) and the *Sea Monster* (p. 273), on the theme of rape. In the *Unicorn* a wild, menacing landscape, shaped like a beast's muzzle, seems about to fall upon the nude couple riding the horned steed. In the other case the expression of fear is more restrained, more 'classical', as compared with the direct impact and enigmatic, nightmarish energy of the *Unicorn* vision. It was also in 1516, the date of this last engraving on iron, that Dürer produced the puzzling composition which has been called *Despair* (p. 283).

Though this print is not so rich in magical symbols as the *Melencolia,* it is nevertheless one of the most mysterious and characteristic of the artist's works in his evasive and mystic mood, when he was open to every assault of the powers of darkness and filled with transfiguring revelations of the supernatural. The implication of the group represented is obscure. One of these ambiguous figures is supposed to be a portrait of Michelangelo. The picture has therefore been entitled 'Homage' to that sculptor. But the persons depicted bear no apparent relation either to those of Michelangelo or to one another. The composition may be a 'Caprice', like one of Goya's, purely imaginative, or an allegory no longer intelligible. The writhing apparition tearing its hair might be seen in a bad dream, while the frontally presented face above it has the disturbing character of such phantoms as haunt the threshold of sleep.

But whether this engraving is regarded as a record of deceptive dream-images or has a metaphorical sense to which the key has been lost, it marks an important stage in the flight of that 'winged spirit' which Dürer himself described as the 'charger of fancy'. Apart from its possible anecdotal significance, it illustrates the primeval terrors which were Dürer's constant, rather than occasional, companions. His familiarity with the superhuman is proved again and again in his works, especially in the prints and drawings, where his 'winged spirit' seems to move with more freedom than in his painting. He never achieved, in that field, the imaginative range of Grünewald's Isenheim altarpiece. The act of painting, in Dürer's case, might almost be thought a species of exorcism. His colour is rarely so eccentric as that of Grünewald. It is never, as with Baldung, the origin or the working out of a pictorial idea. Dürer's visions are inscribed in black and white. They assume, through the varied interaction of light and shade, a vehemence, which is often hallucinatory in effect.

A considerable proportion of Dürer's work is the direct outcome, in this way, of his actual or waking dreams. It is important for the light it sheds on his unconscious life, repressions, anxieties, involuntary admissions and urgent problems. Even his landscapes in wash or water-colour occasionally suggest, in their obscure depth of feeling, the literal depiction of some such fragmentary vision. It is as though the painter were trying to express in the material form of a landscape a state of mind, conscious or unconscious, which he could not otherwise define. The iridescent delicacy of the 1495 *Sunset,* for instance, is somewhat surrealist in manner. An existent scene may well have provided the starting-point of this 'meditation'. But the artist's imagination gave its own truth to the data, design and character of the natural features, thus revealing to the full their underlying significance. The mystery of the pool that reflects the changing hues of passing clouds, the twilight already deepening among the firs and the strange group of dead trees, pathetic and desolate as a burned out planet, were

Kidnapping of a Young Woman ('The Unicorn'). 1516.

not seen with the physical eye. This normally realistic painter transformed such landscapes into the supernatural images of those he beheld inwardly. It was his essential self, rather than a passing mood, that he sought to express by these enigmatic disclosures of his fantasy.

He did once, however, on waking from slumbers disturbed by foreboding apparitions, make an immediate record of one such visitation. This pencil drawing (p. 282), extraordinarily moving and beautiful, represents an apocalyptic landscape. It dates from 1525, when the terrible Peasants' War, descending upon Germany like a new Deluge, to sweep away the follies and wickedness of mankind, threw the population into a panic, affecting all classes, the most sophisticated as well as the most simple-minded. Dürer shared the general dread. He dreamed one night of the Flood of which everyone was talking. The nightmare was so vivid and striking that he made a rapid sketch of his recollection of it as he woke. So far as I know this was the only time Dürer ever set down, in a drawing accompanied by words, one of the visions to which he was subject. His other revelations of the supernatural can only be experienced by reading them into his objective works. It would not be difficult to reconstitute his darker, more morbid side from a close study of many of his engravings. But such vague suggestions lack the tragic eloquence of the 1525 drawing, the direct result of a mysterious dream-image.

He notes:

'In the year 1525, on the night between the Wednesday and Thursday after Whitsun, I dreamed that I saw four great columns of water descending from heaven. The first fell most furiously, with a dreadful noise, about four miles away from me, and flooded all the countryside. I was so terrified by it that I woke. Then the others fell. They were very great. Sometimes they fell far off, sometimes near. And they descended from such a height that they seemed to fall slowly. The falls were accompanied by so much wind and flying spray that when I awakened my whole body still shook with fear. It was long before I regained my equanimity. On rising in the morning I painted what I had seen. May God mend all.'

The distress with which a nightmare is recalled on waking appears clearly in the drawing. The vast columns of water mentioned by the artist are shown descending from the sky in parallel masses, like vertical clouds or irregularly shaped pillars, darker or lighter in tone according to their density. The hugest and darkest crashes to the ground, where it spreads with terrifying effect, flinging aloft wide curtains of spray, as Dürer states. An impression of extraordinary weight is conveyed by this fall. The artist's vision of the flood is essentially plastic, having nothing in common with either the popular or the traditional idea of the Deluge, generally represented as merely a prolonged downpour. Dürer thought of it as an unprecedented natural catastrophe. His columns of water are scarcely even liquid. They are more like thick mud, descending in streams of slime, in such quantities as to choke all mankind to death.

Plastically alone, the drawing is of outstanding beauty. The simplicity of the treatment, the flow of the washes, the brief touches defining contour, the groups of trees, the roads which show no sign of dwellings or living beings and the thick, heavy, stabbing shafts of rain falling with a steady, remorseless and savage malignity are as strikingly expressive in handling as the best works of Friedrich. But the latter, imaginative as he was, could never have depicted the sheer, penetrating horror, the density, of Dürer's Flood. The artist's own feeling of panic affects any spectator who closely examines a rendering so full of mystery and terror. Its unveiling of naked fear is so dramatic as far to surpass that conveyed by the text rapidly scribbled below the drawing.

This text is, however, important and worth analysing. It makes a useful addition to the work itself. For it may be supposed that Dürer began by merely wishing to record the dream that had so shaken him and then remembered that it had come in stages, which ought to be indicated in order to enhance the importance and meaning of the vision. A study of the text in fact shows that the phenomenon was a double one, being both dream and vision. The artist makes the fact quite clear. He states that he was awakened by the noise of the first column of water, apparently about four miles away. It was only after waking that the three others were revealed to him. The deluge therefore came in four successive manifestations, first in the actual dream from which he woke in a fright and thereafter in a waking vision which continued scenes whose beginning had been presented to him in sleep.

Considered as a spiritual phenomenon, therefore, Dürer's Flood seems to have been successively dream and apparition or, if the term is preferred, hallucination. People often dream that they awake when a new dream develops. But no such mistake could have been made in the present case. Tremors and distress marked the artist's passage from dream to vision. He was perfectly conscious of waking and it was only after doing so that he perceived the three other waterfalls. The inscription leaves no doubt that the second presentation must be regarded as part of the dream proper, but as a secondary or 'visionary' state of it and therefore certainly a 'vision', with a prophetic character in his own view. He underlines this quality in the last phrase of his note: 'May God mend all.'

FACE TO FACE WITH GOD

On 6th March 1522 Martin Luther, after leaving the castle of Wartburg and resuming his real name, returned to Wittenberg. For the Reformation was entering a new phase. As the friar had not succeeded in persuading the Pope to act against the abuses rife in the Church, he was determined to attack ecclesiastical organisation itself. His object was now less to reform than to demolish and reconstruct. Hitherto he had continued to wear the habit of his Order, but on 9th October 1524 he ceased to do so. It was a symbolic gesture, intended to indicate his separation from the Church and rejection of its authority. This step amounted to a declaration of war.

Events then moved fast. A few months later Luther, in order to show that his decision to break with the Church was definite and irrevocable, married Catherine Bora, in the very monastery where he had originally taken vows. In the same year, 1525, the support of reform by such rulers as the Elector of Saxony and the Grand Duke of Hesse suddenly transformed a mere theological problem into a political movement the extent of which had not been anticipated. The whole country excitedly took sides and both parties prepared for war. Those who remained orthodox were led by the Pope, the clergy and the Emperor. The rebels were backed by the majority of the learned and by a few princes who foresaw in future disorders opportunities to increase their own power at the expense of the Emperor's. As for the masses of the people, any revolutionary agitation, whatever its character and origin, offered the prospect of some alleviation of their grievances and apprehensions.

The conflict of opinion also affected Nuremberg. Luther's partisans gained ground daily among the citizens. The Emperor had condemned his theses and threatened all who dared to defend them. His representative, the Grand Duke Ferdinand, took steps to repress popular rioting and managed, by intimidation, to prevent the municipal councillors from adopting the heretical doctrines. Yet even so they made headway among the monks themselves. Luther's Augustinian Order became a centre of propagation for the new teaching. The Prior Volprecht invited his flock, during the Holy Week of 1524, to communicate under either system while he himself officiated. At the same service the Epistle and Gospel were read in German, a proceeding which had formerly only taken place at Wittenberg. The bold Father was summoned before the Bishop of Bamberg to be reprimanded. But he rejected the episcopal authority in such haughty and provocative language that the joint thunders of Rome and of the Emperor were loosed against him. 'This is no matter for papal or political settlement,' he had exclaimed. 'It concerns the citizens of Nuremberg only. If they are satisfied with the position, no one can take it amiss.'

The magistrates, who in theory at any rate represented the population of the city, avoided committing themselves as long as possible in a dispute which they greatly feared would end in civil war. They made every effort to keep the peace, at least outwardly, between the mutually hostile factions. They stopped the papists from interfering with the reformers, while they forbade the latter to be

The Sea-Monster. About 1500.

too fiercely zealous in their proselytising activities. The citizens as a whole favoured Luther's views. Melancthon, on a visit to Nuremberg to reorganise its School, lent powerful support to the cause of reform in his lectures. The aldermen were careful to maintain their independent status and impartial attitude. They did their best to uphold true liberty of conscience by opposing every attempt by fanatics on either side to enforce their beliefs. As invariably happens in such cases the prudence of the councillors antagonised both parties. Each accused the municipality of conspiring with the other.

The local authorities in fact, without favouring the new ideas openly and officially, took certain steps indicating their sympathetic attitude. The Passion and Mystery play were abolished on the ground that they brought religion into contempt. The traditional processions were retained for the time being, but organised in such a way as to substitute a rigid austerity for the innocent exuberance of former days. Canopies and showers of roses were no longer permitted. Representations by students of the entry of Christ into Jerusalem on Palm Sunday were broken up and forbidden. In order to avoid even the faintest suggestion of idolatry, the solemn ceremony of escorting the reliquary of St Sebald through the streets was discontinued. The annual display of the Emperor's crown jewels was allowed as usual in 1524, but only because the pilgrims who entered Nuremberg from all over Germany to attend the exhibition threatened on this occasion to plunder the town if they were not given the customary opportunity to inspect the treasures.

The municipal officers were faced with even greater difficulties in the matter of press censorship, for the local printers issued all sorts of pamphlets and caricatures in which adherents of the rival factions indulged their zeal and imagination with varying degrees of freedom. The satirical poets, draughtsmen and engravers on both sides fought a 'battle of the books' which exercised a powerful influence on the controversy. Luther's popularity was enormously increased when the Mastersinger Hans Sachs rallied to his cause. The versifying shoemaker's gibes at the Cardinals and his ecstatic praises of the 'Wittenberg nightingale' probably had even more effect than Melancthon's lectures. The aldermen had their work cut out to prevent this literary conflict from becoming too embittered, especially when the behaviour of foreign rulers was called in question. Determined attempts were made to suppress excessively scurrilous publications. But banned editions were sold 'under the counter'. At last the magistrates, overwhelmed by the flood of pamphlets, ballads and grotesque pictures, gave up trying to enforce respect for individual dignity and liberty of conscience.

Engravings, as instruments of propaganda, education or edification, played a leading part in the struggle. Both parties realised the efficacy of illustration, amusing or thrilling, in direct appeals to the unsophisticated mind. Consequently, satirical woodcuts aimed at either Luther or the Pope appeared everywhere. Every device, from the crudest to the most subtle, was used to attract and convert the populace. Methods varied between obscene mockery and the most refined irony. The former style proved the most persuasive in dealing with the peasants: slander, whether in foul or delicate terms, always wounds. It was found that the best way of stirring up hostility to the Pope or Luther was to show them boisterously carousing over their wine. Such scenes would be sure to arouse the rage and envy of a starving rustic. The draughtsmen and 'librettists' were not asked for any specimens of fastidious talent. On the contrary, the more gross their efforts were, the greater would be their success.

In order to reach a more cultivated public the erudition and elevated language of the humanists were employed. Famous artists were called upon, in the belief that prints by the best engravers would be prized by interested persons on aesthetic grounds, quite apart from their value as propaganda. Lucas Cranach and his pupils, for instance, were enlisted by the Reformers to put their gifts of insight and wit at Luther's disposal by illustrating the literature issued on his behalf.

Dürer was undoubtedly canvassed by both sides, but he refused to serve either. Though far from indifferent to the quarrel, his piety was deeper and more sincere than that of the artists who dashed off caricatures to amuse or enrage the populace. He was actually too religious by nature to take any active part in a dispute between the Church, to which he always remained loyally attached, and Luther, who commanded all his sympathy as a man. He respected religion too

VIVENTIS·POTVIT·DVRERIVS·ORA·PHILIPPI
MENTEM·NON·POTVIT·PINGERE·DOCTA
MANVS
1526

BILIBALDI·PIRKEYMHERI·EFFIGIES
·AETATIS·SVAE·ANNO·L·III·
VIVITVR·INGENIO·CAETERA·MORTIS·
·ERVNT·
·M·D·XX·IV·

PHILIPP MELANCHTHON. 1526.   WILLIBALD PIRCKHEIMER. 1524.

highly to make use of it, for good or ill, in truckling to base emotions. In his view the cause of reform had overshot its mark when it began to appeal to mass sentiment. By this time too many persons had entered the struggle who were not in the least concerned with theological and ecclesiastical questions that had initiated it. Luther had been obliged, for the sake of ultimate success, to seek out allies who were now going to make him pay dearly for their help. The pride and greed of the princes, the resentment of their subjects and the vengeful temper of the peasants saw, in the religious controversy that divided the country, a wonderful opportunity of increasing a disorder from which they confidently expected to draw profit. Luther could no longer control the tide he had set in motion. Swollen by the coarsest of appetites as well as by the noblest of ideals, it was bearing him helplessly on. Rascal elbowed visionary in the ranks of his army, where fanaticism sometimes cloaked the most dangerous impulses. Erasmus understood the position. He took care, accordingly, having

COLUMBINE. About 1502.
ALBERTINA, VIENNA.

only intellectual interests, not to commit himself directly to a quarrel which might compromise both his independence of judgment and his personal dignity. It was in vain that Luther flattered and eulogised him at first, later tried to spur him into action by sarcasm and insult. Erasmus, with a quiet smile, declined to be drawn, in discussing the matter, from the context of logical debate into that of political tumult.

Dürer himself, on his return to Nuremberg, was still of the mind which had thrown him into such despair when he heard, at Antwerp, the baseless rumour that Luther had been arrested. He, too, had listened with sober satisfaction to the song of the 'Wittenberg nightingale.' He wholeheartedly admired the man's personality, more perhaps than he subcribed to his ideas. But the growing violence of the religous dispute in the city disturbed him. He feared its impact upon all that concerned art and the artist's liberty and self-respect. He foresaw the destruction of works of art in popular risings and the loss of his colleagues' independence and even honour in blind partisanship.

It is a curious fact that Dürer and Luther never met. The two greatest Germans of the sixteenth century never exchanged a word. Dürer left any possible encounter to chance. Great traveller as he was, he never made the slightest effort to see the Reformer. He was content to hope for a meeting without attempting to bring it about. 'If by the grace of God,' he wrote to Georg Spalatin, 'I ever come across Martin Luther, I'll engrave a portrait of him on copper, for he has saved me from those terrible fits of depression.'

The letter is dated 1520. At that time Dürer had found a solution of his spiritual problems in Luther's thought. He could not have anticipated that, as the Reformation developed, his conscience would be subjected to even severer trials, when the question of loyalty to the Church itself would arise.

Luther, for his part, admired Dürer. He knew his engravings, but had no idea of his real stature as an artist. The letter he wrote to Eobanus Hesse after Dürer's death, in reply to the elegy composed by the humanist, is highly charateristic. 'As for Dürer, we may well mourn him as the most pious of men. Yet you may hold him happy in having been protected and removed by Christ in time to escape the troubles of this age, and more to come. Thus he, who deserved never to see anything but good, was not obliged to see the worst. May he rest in peace with his fathers. Amen.'

This obituary comment does not mention the artist's genius. The visual arts did not appeal to Luther. He cared only for music, primarily for its own sake and secondarily for its stirring and edifying effects upon pious listeners. Though suspicious of or indifferent to painting, he realised the value of the portrait as a ready means of rendering a well known man's features familiar. He therefore made considerable use of it. He also successfully employed a still more profitable weapon, engraving, which had a wider field of distribution. He may have borne Dürer a grudge for not having served the cause of Reform professionally. Or he may simple have thought painting a frivolous occupation or, since it might lead to idolatry, a sinful one. Dürer had given Luther many engravings. But the latter forgets this fact in his posthumous eulogy of the artist, finding his piety the only virtue worth a reference.

On Dürer's return to Nuremberg after his sojourn in the Netherlands he began one of his most important works, a companion piece, in his own view, to the Apocalypse series executed nearly thirty years earlier. The new undertaking, like its predecessor, was a labour of love. No one had commissioned it. Dürer's productions may in fact be divided into two classes, those due to the requests of others and his self-inspired creations. These last are clearly the result of spiritual compulsion and personal enthusiasm. They were 'dictated by heaven' and the basic needs of his moral nature. Such had been the *Apocalypse* of 1498. The *Four Apostles* of 1526 (p. 288), more than twenty-five years later, may be regarded as the final statement of his religious and also of his aesthetic opinions.

He did not sell this new series, feeling, perhaps, that to do so would invalidate its sacred character. He presented the work to his native city as a token of gratitude. The councillors had not always been generous to him. It was not so long since they had disputed his legal right to his pension. But the new emperor's patronage of Dürer and the growing fame of their fellow-citizen had

279

THE VIRGIN PRAYING. 1518.
DAHLEM MUSEUM, BERLIN.

ultimately persuaded the municipality to offer some reward to an artist who had conferred such honour on his birthplace. His renown being general and uncontested, they ran no such risk as the philistine always fears in showing their appreciation of his work by a commission. While he was absent in the Netherlands, the aldermen had decided to renovate and adorn with due splendour their Town Hall. When Dürer returned, they felt it would be proper to invite him to decorate the building.

He would have been flattered by such an offer in the past; now it embarrassed him. For he was by this time more interested in psychological problems, to say nothing of his 'mathematical constant', than in ordinary decorative labours. He set to work, however, rapidly sketching out, with the aid of his pupils, the compositions required. In order to meet the public demand for that mingling of realism and grandeur which always appeals to the masses, he produced allegories, copies of the *Triumphal Procession* of Maximilian and scenes of common life. He then turned to a more congenial type of art, painting portraits and the *Four Apostles* series which was to be in some degree a profession of artistic faith and his last assertion of moral beliefs.

Portraiture, as it happened, had gained a new lease of life from Reformation thought. Most of the old themes were forbidden to artists owing to the new distaste for 'images'. Mythological subjects were considered licentious and frivolous. Illustrations of sacred history also fell under suspicion as possibly conducive to idolatry.

Accordingly, even those who had specialised in religious art were obliged to resort to historical painting and portraiture. Portraits, fortunately for such artists, had recently become fashionable, for the moral revolution involved a new respect for the individual. Attention to physical and psychological detail had always been an essential virtue of the portrait painter, even when his only task was to depict the donor of a sacred picture as one of its figures. But the unprecedented metaphysical primacy now accorded by the Reformers to the individual was accompanied, it may be affirmed, by a change in the aesthetic attitude to such a subject. In this connection it is interesting to compare portraits by Dürer prior to 1524 with those dating

281

DÜRER'S VISION. 1525.
KUNSTHISTORISCHES MUSEUM, VIENNA.

from the last years of his life.

In the first period portraiture was subordinate to his other activities and perhaps the most exclusively utilitarian in purpose. He was more seriously concerned with religious painting and its subsidiary partner, engraving, on the one hand, and with mythological or purely imaginative themes, on the other, than with the mere reproduction of a human face. But it was always character he sought in the lineaments of his sitters, the expression of a dynamic, Faustian urgency, rather than ordinary physical or social attributes. In generalised works he aimed at the ideal of beauty which he hoped mathematics would reveal to him. But in portraits he stressed the vitality more

Despair. About 1516.

than the formal beauty of the model. He preferred strongly marked features, indicating vigour and originality of mind, to mere grace. He longed subconsciously to discover some sort of heroic energy in the persons he portrayed. A man, he considered, should be 'captain of his soul'. He rated such interior force more highly than an attractive face or figure.

When he had the choice of a model, he looked for a brisk, resolute expression and a countenance moulded on emphatic lines. In thus accentuating psychology he upheld the tradition of German portraiture, repudiating the Italian principle of the sovereignty of beauty, even that of the positive type, known as *virtù,* entirely distinct from the aesthetic or moral variety.

These two elements are combined in Dürer's portraits. He associates, so to speak, *St Jerome* with the *Knight,* adding, perhaps, a contribution from *Melancholy.* He assembles such superficially incompatible components, not to create an ideal figure, but to unveil the fundamental truth about the sitter. A trinity of characters comes out in every portrait he painted. One or another generally appears predominant: only occasionally is one of the three lacking.

It was not, in my view, pure psychological insight that enabled Dürer to detect in his models the inner being masked by the trivialities of habitual behaviour or even by the version of himself which everyone cherishes. Nor do I believe that the artist idealised his sitters to any considerable extent. He painted only men of genius or unusual force of personality. Many were substantial citizens of Nuremberg. But the painter's own genius enabled him to extract the secret that really gave them life and to strip everything that did not matter from the essential aspect of he individual. In thus sublimating his subject's bourgeois features – for some of the men may only have been small shopkeepers – and bestowing upon them a moral and spiritual nobility, a kingly air, Dürer was simply bringing to light the inviolate mystery in every human being, revealing the unknown dweller in the shadowy regions of the subconscious. He struck from such people as Kleberger (p. 295), Muffel Imhoff, Starck and Holzschuher (p. 292) the precious, heavenly spark, the sudden flash that illuminates a face with a spiritual beauty, that of the soul itself. In

PORTRAIT OF AN UNKNOWN MAN. 1524.
PRADO, MADRID.

such conditions an unpleasing or commonplace physiognomy makes hardly any difference. The mere assertion of character confers a kind of beauty on the harshest features. The assertion of the 'man within' consequently has a still more ennobling effect. The individual then assumes a sort of sanctity, simultaneously transcending and constituting an essential part of his actual personality. Dürer's religious feeling was not only heartfelt and orthodox. It was even more conspicuous in his longing to discover something of the divine in all men.

During his last years in particular he was trying, through his statements of individual character, to ascertain the nature of God. He seems to have attempted some degree of integration of the sacred with the profane, not by painting religious pictures, but by infusing religious sentiment into his portraits. It was no longer in subjects drawn from the Old or New Testaments that he sought to express the heavenly gleam. He showed it in the eyes of his sitters. For he was determined to prove each individual a mouthpiece of the Creator.

Dürer had not learnt from the Reformers to approximate the human so closely to the divine. In my opinion he had himself discovered, at the same time as Luther, the principles of personal independence affirmed by the latter, whose moral development in the metaphysical and theological fields had been parallel to his own. As soon as Dürer's portraits began to assume their profoundly spiritual character, without losing a trace of their individuality, in fact asserting it the more emphatically for that very reason, he undertook, by painting the *Four Apostles* (p. 288), the inverse operation, integrating the profane, to its full extent, with the sacred. This series, issued just before the final period, in which he produced very little, represents the artist's spiritual testament, both his confession and his profession of faith.

The fact that these works were not executed for any reward stresses what they meant for him. They were private in the same sense as is a prayer offered up when the conscience is wholly at peace, in undisturbed contemplation. No patron had commissioned them: the panels were to be presented, on completion, to his native city. One dare not take money for a confession, even for one of such supreme eloquence.

The two pictures are altarpiece wings, without a central panel. The practice hitherto had been for the wings to depict saints, apostles, evangelists and donors, while the centrepiece was reserved for a scene from the life of Christ or the Virgin. The figures on the wings were thus supporters of the main composition, witnesses to or spectators of its action, or supernumeraries. But in this case the centrepiece is absent, not because it has been lost, but because the artist did not wish to have one. The focus of interest is not the illustration of some event, but the four personages themselves. They do not appear on this occasion as accessories to an act; they constitute the very essence of the production. No proceedings from sacred history are represented. The figures take the place of such a scene, and they express directly, as men, the divine element. These wings, for once without a central panel, afford a clear exposition of Dürer's religious outlook in the year 1526. In his judgment at that date the individual was of the greatest importance to the consideration of matters of faith.

Man is here represented as alone in a world without landscape or other background. But he is so pervaded by spiritual, sacred and divine elements that the whole energy of creation is concentrated within him. He is the mouthpiece and voice of God, the vehicle of His word. To ensure that the meaning of these works could not be mistaken, the artist arranged for an explanatory text to accompany each of the four figures on the panels. The words were inscribed by the Franconian calligrapher Neudörfer in Dürer's own studio. They do not, therefore, provide a later interpretation or any subsequent attempt by the Reformers to lay claim to Dürer's thought; these are his own ideas expressed as precisely and forcibly by the images as by the texts. The figures might indeed well have dispensed, in my view, with literary aid. They are no less explicit for being dumb. But as these works were to be hung in the Council Chamber at the Town Hall, for the edification of all the citizens, it was necessary for everyone to understand what was meant.

I myself find the inscriptions otiose and even distracting. The

THE FOUR APOSTLES. 1526.
ALTE PINAKOTHEK, MUNICH.

majesty and truly venerable grandeur of the figures seem to me more eloquent than Master Neudörfer's letters. They quote in the case of each Apostle, the passage in his Gospel which best suits the character of the Reformation and in Dürer's opinion most adequately summarised the saint's message. But it appears pointless thus to restrict the superhuman range of the Gospels and Epistles to partisanship in a dispute about doctrine. In whatever sense the Apostles may personify the Reformation, they stand to a far greater extent for Christianity as a whole, the spirit of which takes no account of the personal sentiments represented by the various Churches and extends its proclamation beyond temporal and national frontiers to the infinite, uncontaminated atmosphere of Divine revelation.

A work of art, however, should not be overburdened by interpretations bound to distort its essential significance. Dürer, as well as putting the core of his religious thought into these pictures, filled them also with his gifts as a colourist and his sense of form. The *Four Apostles* represent not only the culmination of his pious meditations but even more the results of his long professional experience and the perfect expression of his fully matured genius. They are imaginary, idealised portraits of his conceptions of St John, St Peter, St Paul and St Mark, drawn partly from their writings, but to a still greater extent from the kind of energy they displayed as men.

He regarded their imposing personalities as the four pillars of Christendom. In these two panels they resemble heavenly, in a sense apocalyptic, apparitions, men filled with the Word of God, which almost transfigures them, and pervades to the limits of their self-expression. Their individuality is not lost in their message to mankind, but rather, on the contrary, intensified by it. Their transmission of the Word of God to humanity renders them more fully themselves. Their sacred function does not annul their personal characteristics, but develops their singular capacities to the highest degree. Their general humanity and its particular quality in each of them are brought to perfection by their possession of the Word in all its implications. They are not visionaries, or transformed. The fact is simply that all their faculties have been raised to the maximum of efficiency and definition. Their heavenly mission is not indicated by any halo or setting of mysterious illumination. Yet they stand in light, a light which comes, not from without, but from their own persons, as if it were the sublime emanation of a humanity dedicated to the service of the Divine.

The faces are not idealised. They retain in each case the character assigned to the Apostle by history and legend. The traditional symbols of Christian iconography, the Keys of St Peter and the Sword of St Paul, are shown. These emblems are often the only means by which the apostles can be distinguished from one another in art. But Dürer seems to have introduced such tokens merely as plastic modifications. For the figures display such decided individuality that no separate object is required to identify each one.

It was by daily reading of the works of the Apostles and still more by intent study of their personalities that Dürer was enabled to recreate them in a fashion which seems almost magical. There is no trace whatever of fantasy in it. And yet the figures give the impression of being charged with a tremendous force of superhuman vitality. The massive, vigorous objectivity of the style dispenses with all fanciful detail, imparting by its own power a feeling of the supernatural. The towering, stationary images are practically bodiless. Of St Peter and St Mark only the faces are visible. St John and St Paul are clad in sweeping draperies, which absorb their bodies in a mass of fierce colour. This monumental effect is produced solely by the pictorial expression of inner animation, meditative and contemplative moods, St Peter and St John personifying prayer and the gleaming eyes of St Mark and St Paul an effervescent, more than human, zeal for action.

The sense of form has reached a stage halfway between disembodied medieval spirituality and the dramatic vehemence of the Baroque period. The personages have flesh and blood. They are seen as realistically and dispassionately, in their earthly guise, as any of Dürer's living sitters. There is no substantial difference between them and a Holzschuher or a Muffel. The difference is only apparent in the degree of intensity of the artist's vision of ordinary Franconian citizens and of superhuman actors in the drama of the Redemption. In both cases a similar will to power is evident. But

290

its direction and force vary in accordance with its manifestation in common man and saint. Thus the distinction between a mere portrait and the creation of the Four Apostles lies only in the measure of saturation, the 'load' of intensity, which characterises each work, leaving one on the plane of this world and elevating the other beyond it.

The exaltation to such a level of these extraordinary pictures, in which Dürer's art both culminated and exhausted itself, was due to the profound humanity of his Christian sentiment as a whole, by no means only to his adoption of Reformation individualism. He produced no more paintings, though his brain remained active despite the steady encroachments of his painful malady. He retained enough strength to devote himself to literary work and the propounding of theories, labours which cost him just as much effort as his former productions. The unhappy circumstances of the time overshadowed both his thought and his feelings. Yet his discouragement did not depress him to the point of inertia. He had never been so interested in novelties. It may well be deduced that Dürer, after completing the *Four Apostles*, believed that he had realised to perfection all his moral and artistic aspirations.

In this masterpiece he had reached the final stage of both technical and aesthetic development. The problems of form, colour and space had been solved. He had nothing more to learn. He was the equal of the greatest German and Italian painters. Michelangelo, whom he admired, had never designed more monumental, majestic figures. Raphael had never surpassed the static, concentrated simplicity with which their living forms were treated. He knew that when he gave the eyes of St Mark their restless, visionary glitter and clothed the noble features of St John in the radiance of heavenly love, he was putting the finishing touches to his life's work. He wished for nothing more. The Sixth Day of creation was ending. Man lived, in full enjoyment of his faculties. The object represented had received a soul that burst the envelope of fleʒh in every direction and shone with an unearthly light. The miracle of art could go no further. Its creator had conjured his figures from the void and given them life. It was time for him to rest.

JEROME HOLZSCHUHER. 1526.
DAHLEM MUSEUM, BERLIN.

292

IN QUEST OF ETERNAL TRUTH

The two panels of the *Four Apostles* were solemnly installed in the Council Chamber. The aldermen made long speeches praising the genius of their fellow-citizen Albrecht Dürer and declaring the pride of the city in the most illustrious of her sons. Entertainments, processions and banquets were organised, though only to the extent permitted by the austerity of the new religion, to which the Councillors had been officially converted, and by the severity of the times. For burning castles and villages could still be seen on the horizon and the country roads still shook to the tramping of the symbolic Peasant's Clog.

Dürer, at home once more, knew that he had painted his masterpiece, not the 'master's piece' required by the Guilds for the bestowal of that title, but the masterpiece of which every true artist dreams, the debt he owes, so long as the work remains undone, to himself and to God. Now that the *Apostles* panels were completed, there seemed no point in continuing to paint. He could go no further. He had given the best of himself and his art. He had scaled the peak, could lay down his burden and wait patiently for death to release him from a life grown aimless. It was impossible for him to surpass the degree of excellence attained in this last stage of his career. His work was over, he had seen that it was good. Now he might rest. He hoped for nothing more, since he knew that he was the greatest of German painters, combining within himself all the elements, even those most mutually contradictory, of the national genius. Without having renounced any of his most distinctive peculiarities he had become a great classic artist, the first to appear in his country and one destined to remain unrivalled for more than two centuries, till the advent of Goethe.

The new tendencies of Italian painting and the eccentric innovations of such German contemporaries as Grünewald, Baldung and Altdorfer did not trouble him. He had traced out the cycle of his own life to its close in a pattern as unmistakable in its complexity as the interlacing designs he had drawn in emulation of Leonardo's. He was content for others to provide what he himself could not or

293

EOBANUS HESSE. 1526.
BRITISH MUSEUM, LONDON.

JOHANN KLEBERGER. 1526.
KUNSTHISTORISCHES MUSEUM, VIENNA.

did not wish to contribute. He had guided his own genius successfully to its goal. His rivals could go where they wished, wherever their talents led them. He was not conceited or charlatan enough

295

to proclaim that he knew all that could be learnt. But he was well aware that he had done well the work he was born to do and which no one else could have done. Yet he had one more task to accomplish, the most difficult of all, perhaps. He intended to devote to it the rest of his life and the last of his strength.

His long-standing malady was attacking him more and more fiercely. Ever since the fever he had caught off Zeeland, during that absurd and unprofitable expedition in mid-winter to examine a stranded whale which the tide had in fact already carried away, he had been growing weaker every day. The robust frame he had often enjoyed drawing, without the slightest self-consciousness, from its reflection in a mirror, was getting thin and bony. Neither he nor his doctors could identify his disease. When consulting famous physicians abroad he would send them sketches indicating the organ in which he felt pain. But with advancing age inflammation or atrophy seized one organ after another. Obstinate fevers frequently prevented him from working. They must have been serious to enforce repose upon so indefatigable a toiler. He was tormented by headaches and nausea. The least effort exhausted him. He became so emaciated that the worthy Pirckheimer compared him with a truss of straw.

His character, too, had changed. The once gay and sociable reveller in boisterous company, who ate and drank so heartily, now lived secluded in his big house, where no child ever laughed. A childless and ageing man who, as a child himself, had played with seventeen brothers and sisters, may well have been so depressed by his loneliness as to turn hypochondriac and misanthrope. His pupils were his only 'children'. And they, no doubt, like all disciples, regularly tried to rob or betray him. He was not yet sixty, but under the crushing burden of his afflictions he had gone to earth like a sick animal, to suffer and die in silence, far from prying eyes.

He had lost, since his dream in 1525, the zest for life which had previously sustained him. He may not have realised himself the extent to which his vitality had been sapped by that vision. Fear of the new Deluge had not driven him, like some of the most sedate of his fellow-citizens, to take such ridiculous steps as going to live

HEAD OF AN OLD MAN. STUDY FOR THE 'ST JEROME'. 1521
ALBERTINA, VIENNA.

297

on top floors or the summits of mountains. But the poisoned arrow of anxiety had sunk into his soul. His friend Melancthon refers to the *melancholia generosissima Dureri*. That melancholy was in essence a deep disillusion, an irremediable weariness of body and mind. However 'generous' it may have been, it had lost the energy and ardent curiosity which had once inspired the figure of a giantess with eagle's wings. His present melancholy would have been no more than a sterile quietism if, after he had ceased to paint, there had not survived in him other types of eager enquiry, to be pursued in fields other than that of painting and for different ends.

Dürer had practised art for forty years. Now he wished to teach it. He had long been instructing pupils in his own technique and aesthetic principles. He had already trained or was still training painters who eventually did him honour. Such men as Schaufelein, Kulmbach, Georg Pencz, Hans Sebald Behaim and his brother Barthel, together with Altdorfer, the greatest of them all, owed the best of what they knew to Dürer. Jan Scorel, after bringing his Flemish style to perfection in the Nuremberg studio, was to take back with him to Utrecht and teach in his turn the valuable lessons he had learned from Dürer. But the latter was not content with having educated apprentices to become masters. He wanted still more pupils, more than his studio could ever contain, more than personal contact could enlighten. He wished to speak to the whole world, not only to Germany, and to posterity as well as to his contemporaries.

'My remarks are addressed only to German youth,' he writes, 'for those young people who love art more than gold and silver.' Nevertheless, he was writing for all Europe, and for the generations as yet unborn. He would have been very proud to know that his books were to be translated into so many languages. His pride would not be the vanity of 'success' but the happiness of knowing that his lessons were reaching age after age and country after country. He would not have understood the disappointment of his modern admirers at the mediocrity and dubious value of the books he wrote instead of painting pictures. He considered it his chief task to teach, to pass on the truths he had discovered or learned from others, to be a pedagogue in the noblest sense of the term as it was current in his own day, such a mixture of strictness and affability as in fact appears in his publications.

Though so essentially a painter, and one of the greatest in the history of European art, he probably thought more highly of his mathematical researches than of his *Festival of Rose Garlands* or *Trinity*. He doubtless, like his contemporary Leonardo, rated his pictorial masterpieces lower than the scientific data he had acquired, so likely to be found wanting or commonplace by later ages. He wanted to be more than a painter, and was never satisfied with concrete artistic accomplishment unless he could explain the technical methods contributing to it. The creative impulse is always backed or restrained, in his case, by critical control. He rarely let himself go. He is perpetually preoccupied by the precepts of Fra Lucas Pacioli, the diagrams of Piero della Francesca, the abstract designs of Paolo Uccello, the problems set by Leonardo and the secrets of Jacopo de Barbari. He was not sure of having fully mastered the 'eternal truths' he had sought throughout his life. But such knowledge of them as he had he meant to transmit to posterity, as a positive duty. For the born schoolmaster always considers himself morally bound to teach.

It was for this reason that Dürer left his palette and brushes to shut himself up in his room and scribble his abstruse jargon, while his pupils toiled at the unfinished panels in his studio. He had an insatiable thirst for all knowledge. Like Faust, he believed that a scientist must study the entire universe. He considered that mathematics, geometry and such astronomy and natural science as were then available should be part of a fully qualified painter's equipment. He had himself learnt a good deal from such friends as Celtis and Johann Stabius, who had instructed him in the motions of the stars. He had designed a planisphere and a chart of the heavens for the astronomer Heinfagel. He remembered visiting in his childhood the observatory of Regiomontanus, close to the elder Dürer's workshop, and studying the night sky there, hour after hour, with intense pleasure. He had become familiar with Ptolemy's theories in Pirckheimer's translation and been sometimes enlightened, sometimes baffled, by the works of Kratzer and Nicolas de Cues.

Dürer was also interested in metals, with which he had dealt as a craftsman in his youth. He had never actually gone down a mine. But he was fascinated, like Novalis at a later date, and so many other German poets and artists, by the mysterious element of 'lyricism' in the behaviour of minerals. Practice and direct contact were always, for him, the road to those 'lasting thoughts', immutable certitudes, that opened the door to universal knowledge. Though he had not read Plato in Greek, nor perhaps even in German, he had heard the *Dialogues* discussed often enough to understand what the philosopher meant by his Ideas. Like the Greek, he wished to grasp the reality behind appearances, set it down in writing and hand it on for the benefit of the innumerable disciples he hoped to attract.

Food for the Painter's Apprentice was the title he chose for the great work over which he spent so much time that he never finished it. To modern eyes it seems a curious miscellany of technical advice, rules for respectable social conduct, valuable professional prescriptions and moral platitudes, no more exempt than Goethe's work from a certain prosaic tinge. It treats of every aspect of an apprentice's life and duties, from his physical bearing and grooming to the need for thrift, religious faith and the Latin language. The subjects are elaborated down to the smallest detail, with meticulous pedantry.

Yet this book – in German, *Die Speise der Malerknaben* – should not be regarded as merely a manual of dubious practicality. There is an admirable magnanimity in even the slightest of its recommendations for the moral and material welfare of the young artist. Nor should the element of altruism in Dürer's composition of these pages be forgotten. He might have gone on happily painting. But he gave up his failing strength and days wholly to what he considered his duty, the education of others.

The work remained unfinished, probably because the author could never resist adding another chapter. On the other hand his treatise on perspective was completed in 1525, printed by Koburger and dedicated to Pirckheimer. The emphasis in this case was on practice. Painters must have found the book useful, for a large number of

Bernhard von Resten (?). 1521.
Dresden Museum.

copies were issued. Perspective, or the control of space, the domination by man of a dimension he needs to establish his own position in the universe, had been intensively studied throughout the fifteenth century, notably by that ardent investigator Leonardo, who considered the problem highly important. The Italian masters who influenced Dürer unquestionably knew more about the matter than his fellow-countrymen did. But the former guarded their secrets jealously. Jacopo de Barbari replied only in the vaguest terms to Dürer's urgent letters to him on this subject. Research on perspective proceeded in an atmosphere of mystery. The precious manuscript by Jakob Walch, which Dürer coveted so keenly, was given by the Archduchess Margaret to Barend van Orley instead of to him. In these circumstances Dürer was obliged to seek out the laws of such composition in books, old and new, and by personal experiment. It was only gradually, with much effort, that he came to understand them.

The *Unterweisung in der Messung mit Zirkel und Richtscheit* ('Measurement by Compass and Ruler') describes the result of his labours. The book can be read with sympathy, despite its dry technicality, on account of the years of arduous toil that went to its preparation and the importance attached by the author to principles now taken for granted. He may have taken more pride and delight in the invention of his 'drawing-machine' than in his Paumgärtner altarpiece or *Virgin with the Canary*. In post-Renaissance painting perspective became a simple matter of mechanical routine in the application of a few easy formulae. This conventional pattern was only broken and true spatial relations ascertained in the days of Cézanne, Gauguin and Van Gogh. But in the sixteenth century perspective was still a mysterious science, with data depending on the totality of postulates concerning the structure of the universe. It was not so much the exact relative positions in recession of objects or parts of an object that the artist wished to represent. His aim was to define space in both physical and metaphysical terms and ascertain his own place in the universe both as a 'breathing' and as a moral entity.

Dürer realised the value of the information he was imparting in this book. He knew how useful it would be to artists, who would thus be spared the arduous investigations he had himself been obliged to make in gaining the knowledge which he now generously transmitted to his contemporaries and to posterity. He felt morally bound to reveal the precious truths he had discovered to those still unaware of them.

The *Unterweisung,* accordingly, is the work of an author both zealous and conscientious. The text is based partly on Dürer's own practical experience and partly on the theoretical knowledge he had amassed by studying both ancient and later literature and questioning scholars and artists. Pirckheimer's bookplate, engraved by Dürer himself, states that the former's library had been assembled for the benefit of his friends as well as himself. Consequently, Dürer is certain to have used it. He is unlikely to have known much Latin, since he left school so early. But his old friend, much more learned than himself, could give him all the information he needed, which was doubtless a good deal.

It was Dürer's anatomical researches which led him to formulate a theory of proportion distinct from that of Vitruvius, who was considered an infallible authority on the subject at that time. The fact that Dürer found the results of his own experience better guides than the precepts of Vitruvius proves the strong and genuine scientific, as well as artistic, cast of his mind. He pursued his investigations in the spirit of a naturalist, not on aesthetic principles. He regarded no theory as valid unless it could be incessantly verified by practice. He knew enough philosophy to participate in the talk of scholars, a fact which surprised Erasmus when they met, the great humanist having apparently supposed all painters to be illiterate. But Dürer did not rely on philosophy to substantiate his written work, which was founded on empirical tests. Nevertheless, he did not think philosophy superfluous, for he actually claims, after referring to Plato's 'internal ideas', that an understanding of them is essential to the representation in art of 'internal fullness' in a figure.

Dürer's character shows both the virtues and the failings of self-education. He was modest enough, however, to submit his

MDXXVI

ERASMUS OF ROTTERDAM. 1526.

KUPFERSTICHKABINETT, BERLIN.

works to learned friends and 'specialists' before publication. The fact proves that he distrusted his own scholarship, welcomed criticism and believed that theory and practice should always go hand in hand. He owed much to German and Italian humanists like Reuchlin and Ficino. He seems to have seriously studied Kratzer, Pomponius Gauricus and the De Artificiali Perspectiva of Jean Viator, to have understood their proofs and digested their conclusions. His renunciation of painting to devote himself entirely to science shows clearly enough the great attraction exercised by this new interest upon both his intellect and his feelings.

Predominantly practical by nature, he had been led to the consideration of scientific theory by the need to confirm in this way what he had learnt by experience. Aesthetics only engaged his attention incidentally. There are far more concrete prescriptions than dogmatic assertions in his books. In his insatiable, restless thirst for truth he still thought of the ideal beauty he longed to codify as an objective reality, not a mere concept of the mind. His attachment to theory does not seem to have divorced him from nature but rather drawn him closer to it. For by lending it a philosophical basis he was enabled to penetrate its essence more deeply. He is never ashamed to confess ignorance. As he felt that he could never understand Euclid in Latin, he asked Niklas Kratzer to write out a German translation for him. He laid all his friends under contribution, from Konrad Peutinger of Augsburg, the humanist and business man so strikingly portrayed in the Rose Garlands, to Eobanus Hesse, Conrad Celtis and Johann Stabius.

He would also have been glad to make use of the great erudition of Erasmus. But the latter's ironical attitude intimidated him. The two men were so different that they could neither like nor even understand each other. Dürer showed as little comprehension of the reaction of Erasmus to the religious controversy, as Erasmus showed of the portraits Dürer painted of him (pp. 246, 304). These had been asked for by the humanist through Pirckheimer, a willing intermediary between the two men of genius. But Erasmus did not care for the result, declaring the likeness a poor one. Consequently Dürer, so ingenuously free, as a rule, with his questioning of

305

scholars, always felt shy and even resentful in the presence of Erasmus, whom he came to admire less than formerly as a philosopher.

He could not forgive the other for not being a man of action like himself. For such Dürer never ceased to be, even when he substituted the pen for the brush and gave up all his time to theory. Every book he wrote remained an act. The character and significance of these works cannot be comprehended in any other light. His verses, whether occasional poems, light humorous pieces, satires or prayers, are always somewhat didactic, edifying or polemical in tone, in other words undertaken for a purpose. The *Food for Apprentices,* too, and the treatises on perspective and proportion, have the dynamic quality which Dürer's verbal teaching would have assumed if he had occupied a university Chair instead of being content with the silence and solitude of his desk. The treatise on fortification, which he composed at the same time as his notes on anatomy, also has this 'active' stamp, typical of an author, infatuated by 'everything that could be known'.

He had been interested in the art of war ever since his childhood. As a boy he had enjoyed visiting cannon-foundries and watching military processions, noting the weapons and elaborate equipment of the soldiers. The Irish mercenaries, with their bare feet, shaggy tunics and huge battle-axes, particularly intrigued him. Professional fighting men were favourite models for the artists of the day, both on account of their grotesque and gaudy uniforms and because they were always available. Even at Nuremberg the city's standing army of forty horse and 250 foot were almost constantly in action. Dürer himself, as a lad, may have served in the militia recruited from the labouring and trading population of the town to assist the paid troops in emergencies. Pirckheimer, at any rate, had been on the staff of Ulmann Stromer when the latter defeated Götz of the Iron Hand.

In 1500 the painter and his martially minded humanist friend collaborated in a book on fencing, which the former illustrated. At a later date Dürer gave full rein to his love of armour and tournaments in the extraordinary *Freydal,* a work issued to commemorate

306

the feats of Maximilian. For a romantic attachment to medieval chivalry had always been characteristic of the artist. Its ideals as well as its picturesque splendour appealed to him. He loved its sentiments and its settings, its heroic aims and its material extravagance. Some of the most famous of Dürer's contemporaries, Charles the Bold for example, Francis I and Maximilian, were inspired by knightly legend. Art, too, showed at that time many traces of a nostalgia for the 'tremendous and exquisite' life of the Middle Ages, represented in its purest, most fundamental and complete form in the chivalric convention.

In addition to Dürer's delight in magnificent and fantastic armour he also recognised the importance of the new military apparatus of artillery and foresaw its future functions. As artist and technician he was attracted both by the decoration of cannon and the process of casting them. But he was even more drawn to a study of the changes they were bound to introduce in architecture. He was inclined, too, to attribute individuality to them, that of all sorts of strange beasts, with lives of their own, as can be noticed in his 'portrait' of various types of cannon. It was a habit of the period, proving the way in which these weapons were subconsciously regarded, to give them names. Peutinger, for instance, called Maximilian's pieces of artillery after well known female figures in mythology and ancient history.

Siege tactics were revolutionised by the introduction of ordnance. Dürer was led to study the new systems less by the desire to rival such great Italians as Michelangelo, Francesco di Giorgio and Leonardo, or out of mere curiosity, than to contribute to the defence of his native city against the remote menace of the Turks or the nearer dangers of the Peasants' War. In this case, too, he based his researches on experience, for he had been with Frundsberg at the siege of Hohenasperg in 1519 and examined the results of artillery and fortification respectively in that operation. The drawing he then made has considerable documentary value. The plan of Frundsberg's camp and the disposition of his batteries, together with notes of the effects of their fire, prove that in this connection as in so many others Dürer had become an expert, almost a specialist. His practical knowledge, as well as the theories he had worked out in other studies, enabled him to invent, in the book on fortification he dedicated to the Emperor, some very remarkable examples of it, impressively beautiful, in a monumental style, to modern eyes. But their chief merit in Dürer's own view was their efficiency, which he had calculated with meticulous care. There is nothing amateurish about his treatise. As he never embarked upon any problem, whether military, religious or artistic, without the fullest consideration of it, this production is also one of faith and love. He was undoubtedly as accurate and scrupulous in preparing it as was Goethe in his collection of data for the exploitation of the Grand Duke's mines. Those who aim at coordinating all knowledge never think anything superfluous, negligible or insignificant.

The treatise had the further useful effect of causing Dürer to conceive an ideal city. He felt that it would not be enough to surround the place with strong walls if disorder prevailed within. Dürer shared with Goethe, sometimes to a slightly irritating degree, a passion for order, precision, detail, convenience and practical utility. It is as though the two greatest of Germans did not disdain, for all their genius, to be on occasion pedantically fussy. Consequently, Dürer's ideal city, as rigidly laid out as a Roman camp, has no room for the picturesque. The imaginative originality that Claude Nicolas Ledoux was to show in his plans for Chaux is quite absent from Dürer's sketch. The classicism of the Besançon theatre appears wildly romantic in comparison with the German artist's dry, almost abstract, geometry. A somewhat plodding taste for codification, a clearer recognition of utility than of beauty, make an unexpected impression in Dürer's last work. Perhaps his ultimate project was not the composition of some great painting, brilliant in colour and design, but the execution of a practical town-planner's unemotional blueprint.

Death, meanwhile, was approaching him. It may have been Dürer's reluctance to catch sight of that ominous rider at the corner of the street, to hear the tinkling bell slung at the neck of the lean horse, which buried him, at that moment, so completely in his books. Worn out by unremitting, selfless labour, indifferent to the shrivelling flesh that was reducing him to a skeleton, he toiled on still, if only to forget the touch upon his shoulder that must soon come.

The most tragic of all Dürer's representations of death is his drawing of 1505, inscribed in large letters MEMENTO MEI. There Death does not appear in the uncouth guise of an incubus nor as the phantasmal apparition which unseats a horseman, nor as the terrible, insinuating skeleton of the *danses macabres*. The 'King Death' of 1505 is both fantastic and tragically real. Wearing a sharp-pointed crown and wielding his scythe as if it were a hunting-crop, Death urges on a lank nag, the beast's reeling pace and tremulous head sounding the funeral-bell.

That was how Dürer had seen death twenty-three years before. The self-portraits he produced subsequently, even when they show a robust figure, convey, through the eyes, his ever present dread of the 'beyond'. It was perhaps in order to overcome this fear that he worked so furiously during his last years. He, too, could have written, like Michelangelo, that death was forever in his thoughts. Nor were the periods in which he portrayed no images of death any the less dominated by the idea.

Inevitably, the reality triumphed. The Lemurs appeared to carry Faust's body to the grave. 'Come what may, life has been fair!' The burden of his weariness grew daily heavier. His body seemed to shrivel up even before he died. Like a truss of straw, as Pirckheimer had said. On 6th April 1528 the bell at the neck of King Death's horse rang for the last time in the ear of Albrecht Dürer, seeker of eternal truths that were now to be made manifest.

LIST OF ILLUSTRATIONS

312

315

316

INDEX OF NAMES

317